Managing and Marketing Services in the 1990s

Other books of interest from Cassell

The Management Services Handbook – ed. Bentley (1984)
Computer Systems in the Hotel and Catering Industry – Braham (1989)
Marketing for the Small Firm – Brown (1985)
Hotel and Food Service Marketing – Buttle (1986)
Basic Marketing, 3rd edition – Cannon (1990)
Changing Consumer Behaviour – East (1990)
Service Operations Management – Harris (1989)
Food Service Operations, 2nd edition – Jones (1988)
The Management of Hotel Operations – Jones and Lockwood (1989)
The International Handbook of Production and Operations Management – ed. Wild (1989)
Production and Operations Management, 4th edition – Wild (1989)

Managing and Marketing Services in the 1990s

Edited by
Richard Teare
Dorset Institute

with
Luiz Moutinho
Cardiff Business School

and
Neil Morgan
Cardiff Business School

First published 1990 by *Cassell Educational Limited*
Villiers House, 41/47 Strand, London WC2N 5JE, England

© Cassell Educational Limited, 1990

British Library Cataloguing in Publication Data

Managing and marketing services in the 1990s.
  1. Service industries. Management
  I. Teare, Richard II. Moutinho, Luiz III. Morgan, Neil
  338.4

  ISBN 0-304-31816-7

Printed and bound in Great Britain by Dotesios Printers Ltd, Trowbridge

Contents

Contributors

Edited by:
Richard Teare BSc, Ph.D., MHCIMA, Cert.Ed.
Reader in Hospitality Management, Department of Food and Hospitality Management, Dorset Institute
with:
Luiz Moutinho BA, MA, Ph.D., MCIM
Professor of Marketing, Cardiff Business School, The University of Wales College of Cardiff

Neil Morgan BA, MBA
Lecturer in Marketing and Strategy, Cardiff Business School, The University of Wales College of Cardiff

Biographies
Richard Teare is Reader in Hospitality Management at the Dorset Institute and Editor of the *International Journal of Contemporary Hospitality Management*. A graduate of the University of Surrey, he has held management positions with both national and international hotel companies. He gained his Ph.D. in Business Administration from the City University Business School, London, and has undertaken a variety of research and consultancy projects for hospitality firms.

Luiz Moutinho is Professor of Marketing at the Cardiff Business School, and has held academic posts at Northern Arizona University; California State University, Long Beach; Cleveland State University; and Glasgow Business School, University of Glasgow. He is a former director of the doctoral programme of the confederation of Scottish Business Schools.

Neil Morgan holds a BA from the London School of Economics and an MBA from the University of Wales. He is currently Lecturer in Marketing and Strategy at the Cardiff Business School. He has published a number of articles in professional and international academic journals on the marketing of services.

Other Contributors

Colin Armistead, Senior Lecturer, Cranfield School of Management

Peter Daniels, Professor and Head of the Department of Geography, Portsmouth Polytechnic

Christine Ennew, Lecturer in Marketing, University of Nottingham

Lin Fitzgerald, Lecturer, Warwick Business School, University of Warwick

Evert Gummesson, Director, Cicero Management AB; Professor, Services Research Centre, University of Karlstad, Sweden

Barry Howcroft, Deputy Director, Banking Centre, Loughborough University

Robert Johnston, Lecturer, Warwick Business School, University of Warwick

David Litteljohn, Senior Lecturer, Department of Hotel and Catering Studies, Napier Polytechnic of Edinburgh

Ian Miles, Senior Lecturer, Science Policy Unit, University of Sussex

Nigel Piercy, Professor and Head of Marketing and Strategy, Cardiff Business School, The University of Wales College of Cardiff

Julia Schauerman, Researcher, Cardiff Business School, The University of Wales College of Cardiff

Rhian Sylvestro, Lecturer, Warwick Business School, University of Warwick

Christopher Voss, Professor of Manufacturing Policy and Strategy, Warwick Business School, University of Warwick

Stephen Wanhill, Professor of Tourism Management, Department of Management Studies for Tourism and Hotel Industries, University of Surrey

Trevor Watkins, Professor and Head of the School of Business, Oxford Polytechnic

Stephen Witt, Professor of Tourism Studies, Department of Management Science and Statistics, University College of Swansea

Peter Wood, Senior Lecturer, Department of Geography, University College, London

Mike Wright, Reader in Financial Services, Department of Industrial Economics, Accountancy and Insurance, University of Nottingham

Preface

As the contribution of the service sector in the modern economy continues to grow, it is vital to assess the implications for managing and marketing services into the next decade. To compete effectively in an era of rapid change, service firms will need to be more innovative and responsive, organizing their resources and delivering their products with greater flexibility and customer awareness. In addressing these issues, this book brings together research evidence relating to current trends, developments and practices in the service sector.

The book is divided into four parts. It begins with a broad analysis of the market for services by considering their role in the economy and aspects of their geographical expansion. Part 2 considers some of the strategic issues which will influence the development of services in the 1990s. Topics include marketing organization, the role of information technology, service quality and productivity, and the measurement of service performance. Parts 3 and 4 focus on two service industries which exemplify the patterns of change, innovation and growth which are occurring in the service sector. Part 3 is concerned with financial services and includes chapters on marketing policy and practice, recent developments in personal financial services, the evolution of retail branch banking in the UK and a new method of segmentation for the corporate banking market. Part 4 examines the role of statistics and forecasting in tourism, and research paradigms for hospitality services emerging from research classification and research in consumer behaviour. The book concludes by identifying some of the general themes emerging, and their implications for the development of the service sector into the 1990s.

Each chapter begins with an overview which introduces the topic area and summarizes current thinking and practice. Emerging issues for services in the 1990s are discussed in relation to new perspectives, and methods which might be applied to resolve problems and maximize development potential are suggested. In this way, the book integrates theory and practice, making it relevant to the needs and interests of students, researchers and practitioners.

The idea for the book developed from a conference on services research held at the Dorset Institute in November 1988. I believe that the contents of the book have benefited greatly from the opportunity for prior discussion and debate, and I would like to thank all the contributors for participating so enthusiastically in this process. I am especially grateful to Luiz Moutinho and Neil Morgan who assisted me in compiling the text, to Chris Bessant who did the copy-editing and to Diana Russell at Cassell for her support and encouragement.

Richard Teare
June 1989

Part 1

Services Market Analysis

Introduction

Richard Teare

The Western industrialized nations have been transformed by the growth of services during the 1980s, to the extent that their economies are now reliant on services. Gross national product (GNP) statistics for the USA and Western Europe indicate that the contribution from the service sector now exceeds 50 per cent of total GNP, reflecting the trend towards a more service-orientated society.

The transition from a manufacturing-based economy has to some extent been confused by aritifical distinctions between goods and services. Manufacturing skills have traditionally been associated with the technical aspects of production, whereas service skills are primarily represented by the employee resources of a firm. Historically, the manufacturers of goods operated in a seller's market where the technical merit of the goods themselves was thought to be sufficient for the buyer. The manufacturing sector provided little by way of support to their customers and, because the market-place was less crowded, product differentiation was relatively unimportant. The post-war rise of Japan as an industrial nation, and the declining competitiveness of manufacturing output in Europe and the USA, has challenged this traditional thinking and practice. In order to survive, manufacturing firms are having to embrace the ethos of a service economy by integrating goods and customer services.

The strategic management process begins with the acquisition, analysis and interpretation of information about the market-place and business environment. It is therefore appropriate that Part 1 should be concerned with service market analysis in order to provide an overview of the environment in which service firms operate. In doing so, the conventional parameters defining the nature of service activity are challenged, and an integrated view of the role of services in all economic activity is encouraged. It is argued that services are intimately involved in material processing, and so they are of fundamental importance to the market orientation of manufacturing firms. Recent interest in producer (or intermediate) services exemplifies this approach, as they are marketed to firms and public institutions rather than to the customer.

Chapter 1

An integrated view of the role of services

Peter Wood

Services are embodied in all products of an economy, whether these provide for the needs of producers or, as they ultimately must, of consumers. The fundamental nature of this view of the economic role of services is the basis of this chapter. Service activities are implicated in every process of economic change, whether of restructuring, growth or decline, at local, regional, national and international levels. The quality of services has always been critical to economic development, perhaps even more than to the employment they provide. This is increasingly true, however, as production processes become more complex, large organizations more dominant, technology more rapidly changing, expertise more significant, consumer demands more diverse and the influence of public agencies more pervasive.

To a geographer such as this author, concerned initially with sub-national scales of change, the significance of modern developments in the organization of services is that they support increasingly specialized patterns of regional economic development. The growing dominance of large organizations has released the geography even of consumer or public service supply from dependence only on local demand. Spatial divisions in the quality of service provision, and the employment it supports, have therefore become more marked. Corporate developments in the production-related and financial services, alongside tourism, have extended this process to the international scale. It is no coincidence that the most marked inter-regional differences within the UK are found in the very financial, trading and producer services that are most prominent in international economic comparisons and trade negotiations.

This chapter will explore the implications of these perspectives. First, some fundamental characteristics of all services will be outlined. Then the complex, and sometimes contradictory, processes by which they may contribute to economic growth will be reviewed. Finally, a framework emphasizing not individual service functions, but the interactions between them and all other economic functions, within broad 'arenas' of economic change, will be suggested and explored, including its implications for the operation of the service industries themselves.

Key characteristics of the modern service economy

What is the distinctive economic role of services as a class of activities? Is the only characteristic that services share a negative one: that they are *not* engaged in the extractive or manufacturing transformation of materials? This assumption certainly seems to be embodied in process-based 'industrial' classifications (Marshall, 1988, Ch. 2; Ochel and Wegner, 1987, 10). Services are treated as residual, at best analogous to the 'non-production' functions of extractive and manufacturing firms themselves. Even in its own terms, such a view of services is misleading. Recent interest in 'producer' or, better, 'production-related' services has confirmed that many services are, in fact, intimately involved with material processing, and that their quality exerts an increasingly significant impact on the efficiency and competitiveness of production (Marshall, 1988; Wood, 1986).

If only for these reasons, therefore, such a negative definition of the economic role of services can no longer be accepted. It also, however, evades the main challenge that faces service studies: the development of a conceptual framework for the practical analysis of service functions that builds upon their most important common features (Daniels, 1985, 14–16). Such a framework must have theoretical justification, although it may not itself be a 'theory' of service development (Walker, 1985, outlines wider theoretical issues; see also the literature on the emergence of the 'post-industrial' economy, e.g. Kumar, 1978; Piore and Sabel, 1984; Lash and Urry, 1987). It must illuminate the economic role of all services, whether they are producer or consumer orientated, in the private or public sector, or concerned with handling information or materials. The framework must enable the net wealth-creating capabilities of service functions to be evaluated, as well as their distributional and welfare effects. In practical terms, it should also suggest critical avenues of research and allow the wider economic significance of individual activities to be assessed. In sketching such a framework here, some basic propositions may be outlined, in the light of growing research interest in services during the 1980s.

Although, no doubt, there are other common characteristics of services, four seem to be paramount. The first of these reflects their fundamental economic purpose. What all services have in common is that they offer the *expertise* – 'structured information and technical knowledge, relating to the manipulation of either information or materials' – required to support other economic activities. Such expertise, whose value is dependent upon the wider division of labour into specialist tasks (Walker, 1985), may take the form, for example, of knowledge and experience of financial markets, technical or managerial support to production, transportation and distributional skills, maintenance and repair services, provision for leisure, or support for health and educational needs. This characterization of services is demand orientated, and evaluative, emphasizing the worth of information or materials handling services to other production or consumption activities (Marshall, Damesick and Wood, 1987).

Secondly, this fundamental orientation of services to particular market needs means that their economic contribution, at any stage of production, can be measured only in relation to the benefits they bestow, directly and indirectly, on these other activities. Such benefits are not accurately reflected in conventional productivity measures, as applied to industrial processes, which compare the value of service activities' inputs and outputs in isolation. One evident reason for this, of course, is the 'non-market' conditions under which some services are supplied. More generally, however, the value to their customers of service purchases depends on how these are combined with other inputs. The use of business services in manufacturing, for example, reflects their contribution to the overall production process, rather than the technology of service production itself. The worth of certain financial services relates to the specialized form of knowledge involved and the scale of profits that may result. In turn, however, it also depends upon the operation of a world network of *other* service functions. The tourism 'industry' is a complex of interdependent financial, transportation, catering, accommodation and recreational functions, operating under the impact of major manufacturing innovations, including mass air transportation and computerized booking networks. None of these activities can be evaluated without regard to the activities of the others in their market 'arenas'.

Such evaluation requires, at the very least, a 'total factor productivity' approach to assessing the economic contribution of services to other sectors (Wood, 1987, 1988a; Postner and Wesa, 1984). Employing input–output tables and data on labour and capital inputs, this estimates the contribution to the efficiency with which final demand is served of productivity improvements in all the direct and indirect supply sectors involved, including services. Thus, the wider efficiency contribution of apparently 'high-productivity' sectors is shown, in some cases, to be held back by the low productivity of their service and other inputs. Elsewhere, efficiency improvements in some services, such as transport and distribution, have had widespread beneficial effects on the productivity contribution of other sectors. In this light, of course, the whole notion of a distinct 'service sector' is fundamentally misleading, as consequently is that of a discrete 'primary' or 'manufacturing' sector. In reality, all products of an economy, whether mined or manufactured used to serve producers or consumers, depend upon inputs from primary, manufacturing *and* service enterprises. Any understanding of services must be based on this simple fact of economic interdependence, even while acknowledging its complex reality. For this reason, the proper conceptualization of service functions has critical implications for our appreciation of how the whole economy operates.

Thirdly, control over patterns of both private and public service activities is increasingly dominated by large, multi-estalishment, and sometimes multinational, organizations (Howells and Green, 1988, Ch. 6). This defies the common proposition that services are primarily competitive, 'small-firm' activities. While there are many small service firms, of course, and trends towards franchising and the 'externalization' of service functions have been widely noted, their realm of activity is, more than ever, dominated by the strategies of large private and public organizations. The dynamics of service change, whether in the products or employment offered, depend on corporate developments which increasingly link diverse sectors of economic activity. The emergence of conglomerate control, for example in the financial, leisure or media services, crossing many conventional sectoral barriers including those between 'manufacturing' and 'service' functions, reinforces the need to examine the interdependencies between activities, rather than studying them in isolation from each other.

Finally, the most significant outcomes of the strategies pursued by large and small service organizations are not to be found simply in quantitative change. Rapid changes in the quality of both products and employment are inherent to service sector development. For products, the competitive nature of modern service markets means that, in general, they need continually to adjust to changing demand. In employment terms, competition also sustains the persistent pressure to improve labour productivity and reduce job numbers. The modern growth of employment in some services reflects, in part, the development of new products. More generally, however, it arises from qualitative shifts, on the one hand towards more highly differentiated specialist expertise, and on the other towards low-cost, routine jobs (Massey, 1984). This polarization trend has also encouraged a new flexibility in the role of large and small firms (Lewis, 1988). Thus, the search for specific qualities of workers in the service sector is now much more significant for contemporary social and spatial change than are labour changes within materials production alone.

Services as 'engines of growth'

Production and Producer Services

This view of services as an interdependent rather than a dependent sector, whose economic value to the wider production process is underestimated because it is difficult to measure, and whose national and regional employment patterns, increasingly dominated by large organizations, are subject to a marked differentiation in both the amount and the quality of work on offer, has revolutionized thinking about their economic and geographical significance in recent years.

An important casualty of this reappraisal has been the assumption that services cannot drive the process of economic change, or create growth or decline, as do materials processing activities. This shift of view has been of particular interest in the study of regional economic growth since, in many cases, including financial and production-related services, tourism and even some public services, major market and organizational developments have extended provision far beyond the needs of local demand. Even at the national level, in the UK, the shift has attracted attention as 'invisible' earnings, especially from financial services and tourism, have apparently filled part of the trade gap left by the decline of manufacturing (Key, 1985).

We have already noted that a significant step in this rethinking has been recognition of the role of 'production-related services': functions, such as technical and business consultancy, financial and legal advice, maintenance and transportation services, or marketing and advertising, whose contribution may be as critical to production and sales effectiveness as the quality of materials processing itself. As outside services they are, in fact, often interchangeable with primary producers' and manufacturers' own 'in-house' expertise (Wood, 1986, 1988b). Even without the employment they provide, the supportive economic role of such services is a powerful argument for regarding them as an integral part of the 'engine of growth' for a regional or even a national economy. They form part of the whole network of activities that make up the 'arena' of production.

While the obvious dependence of materials production on support services may make it difficult to understand why they have been so neglected in the past, the paradox nevertheless remains that production-related services have attracted new attention at the very time that manufacturing decline in the UK has markedly reduced the level of such service employment (Marshall, 1988, Ch. 3). This decline, both of in-house and independent provision, has probably been at a slower rate than direct production work, but these activities still cannot escape the consequences of their close dependence upon the extractive and manufacturing sectors.

The availability and quality of the production-related services is no doubt more critical to the success of UK manufacturing than ever before. However, the recent growth of service employment in the UK and elsewhere is not associated directly with changes in primary or manufacturing activity. The main sources of service growth have to be sought in other arenas of interdependent activity to which individual services contribute, and the division of labour between and within them. In exploring these, it is clear that *any* of the interconnected service elements of the modern economy may make, in conventional terms, a 'basic' contribution to economic change, especially at the regional level. In analysing further the economic role of services, therefore, we must examine the ways in which this may be done.

The contribution of services to economic growth

The operations of any economic function may lead regional or national economic change by a variety of direct and indirect means (Howells and Green, 1988). Individually or, more commonly, in groupings of functions linked to particular production, service or consumer markets, services may do so as a result of the degree to which they:

(1) offer directly exportable expertise;
(2) combine with other activities to export 'indirectly', so that an improvement in the *quality* even of apparently home-market services enhances export competitiveness;
(3) offer expertise that is currently imported.

These mechanisms are no different, of course, from those by which material commodities create income. Services are, however, distinctive in the relative significance of (2) over the more conventional 'export-led' (1) or 'import substitution' (3) mechanisms.

Also more distinctly for services, these effects must be assessed in *net* terms. A developed service economy makes it easier for *outside* manufacturing or service activities to penetrate a regional or national market. A comparative advantage in the quality of some services may operate at the cost of exposing other local economic activities to more direct competition. At the regional scale, the example of tourist development is the most obvious: local hotel and catering, transportation and retailing services will be affected by new exposure to outside competition. Even regions that acquire the headquarter functions of large firms may find this a mixed blessing if most of the services they employ are brought in from outside (Marshall, 1979, 1985). An efficient retailing sector also makes it easier for national or international commodities to compete with local products. Perhaps only investment in public services is without such potentially adverse consequences, although they may still be felt at the local, sub-regional level as a consequences of public sector reorganization. The net economic value of service quality may therefore depend on the response of other regional activities to any resulting increase in competition.

Arenas of change

The conceptual framework for evaluating the economic role of services described so far has proposed four fundamental characteristics of service functions. As a result of their operational and increasingly corporate interdependence with other economic functions, it has been suggested that changes in services may affect wider economic prosperity as much as may any others, including those in production. The mechanisms by which this occurs are, however, complex and sometimes indirect. The overall benefit upon an economy is also refracted through the responses of other activities to the changes brought about by service innovation.

Service studies therefore need to explore not simply trends in the supply of individual services, whether producer or consumer, public or private, or based on the handling of information or materials. More significant for their understanding is how individual functions (e.g. advertising, the provision of accommodation, preventative medicine) operate together with others in broad market sectors (e.g. retailing, tourism, health care). At the broadest level, the operations of the dominant *arenas of change* in service activity should encompass the complete range of relationships that govern changing demand and supply. As well as the production arena already discussed, three others can be identified. The four arenas, summarized in Figure 1.1, are:

(1) financial or *capital circulation* functions;
(2) *production-related* services;
(3) functions primarily serving *domestic consumption* needs;
(4) *public service* activities.

The market interrelationships that bind functions together within these various arenas of service activity, and also govern their wider economic contribution, are highly complex, dynamic, operate at various levels and are sometimes ambiguous in their economic effects, especially at the regional scale. The arenas

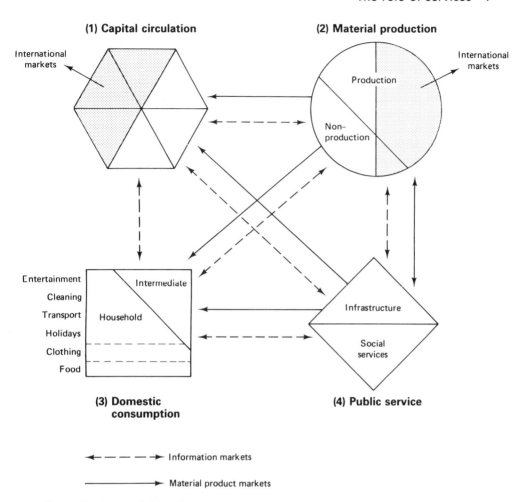

(1) Capital circulation

(2) Material production

International markets

International markets

Production

Non-production

Entertainment

Cleaning

Transport

Holidays

Clothing

Food

Intermediate

Household

Infrastructure

Social services

(3) Domestic consumption

(4) Public service

←— — — —→ Information markets

————————→ Material product markets

Figure 1.1   Arenas of change for service functions

also exhibit important but often neglected interdependencies *between* them. Exploration is needed of these interdependent relationships, their efficiency and how they adjust to change. The part played in driving change by a large organizations, often with wide service sector interests, is a critical issue. Corporate strategies within particular arenas, and increasingly across diverse types of market, including the public sector, underlie service trends, including their employment effects.

What follows simply indicates some of the distinctive relationships that underpin the various arenas. For the production-related services, the implications for the efficiency of production, and for employment, of the interdependencies between in-house and outside service functions have already been outlined. These relationships govern the structures of service provision within the production arena. In a similar vein, some of the more significant relationships that characterize the other three arenas can be sketched, governing their contribution to the successful operation of other sectors of the economy.

The capital circulation services

The 'circulation services' are those activities, including significant elements of banking and insurance, whose success depends on the exchange and manipulation of finance capital. They have been the most rapidly expanding service activities in recent years, but their geographical distribution has also made a major contribution to increasing regional inequality in the UK (Marshall, 1988, Ch. 9).

Much discussion of producer services has failed to distinguish adequately between circulation services, whose key expertise relates to deriving profit from the circulation of capital, and the more directly 'production-related' services, described above (Allen, 1988). Their economic functions are nevertheless fundamentally different. For example, 'banking and insurance' serve both capital circulation and production, as well as consumption. Each of these markets requires quite different corporate, technological and employment strategies. Thus the 'arena' of capital circulation, as defined here, does not contain all of the conventionally defined financial services: they are more specifically concerned with those functions, usually associated with 'the City', that support capital accumulation, manipulation and speculation.

The most distinctive characteristic of the modern growth of these activities is their domination by trends in international financial markets. They have also been subject to particularly rapid recent processes of regulatory and corporate restructuring, and face the prospect of further accelerated change as a result of the evolution of the European single market in the 1990s. Within Britain, their growth, and the increasingly complex division of labour that they support, also dominates the recent economic development of the South East, stimulating growing regional inequalities, and the rising dominance of the service class based in that region (Lash and Urry, 1987).

While international macroeconomic and corporate relationships dominate the capital circulation arena itself, developments in the other arenas also impinge upon it. For example, the growth of multinational *production* has particularly stimulated world capital circulation functions during the past twenty years. Also, the very technology that has encouraged integration of world financial markets comes, of course, from the production arena (Howells, 1988; Howells and Green, 1988). In the *domestic* arena, the growth of insurance, pensions and savings has injected huge amounts of capital into financial markets, providing a stable income base for core institutions. Even the *public service* arena, whether as a purchaser of credit for infrastructure investment or as a regulator, impinges significantly on capital circulation activities.

Thus, while a distinctive complex of internal markets makes up the capital circulation arena, its dynamism also depends upon its relationships with other elements in the economy. For example, the proposed post-1992 liberalization of services in the EC may be as significant for the links between the capital circulation and other service arenas as for the evolution of European capital markets themselves. While global trends may remain beyond the scope even of united European influence, quite new internal conditions for the development of financial services will be created. In the production arena, for example, technical standardization in communications and electronics infrastructure will greatly assist the integration of financial markets. The progressive unification of domestic markets will also release new resources and create new forms of organization in the capital circulation arena. Thus, its future will probably increasingly depend on relationships with these other service arenas.

Domestic services

The domestic service arena is frequently characterized simply as the target for the production of consumer goods. In employment terms, it is assumed that patterns of formal disposable income are translated more or less directly into local demand, thereby creating predominantly local jobs. This view is, of course, too simple. Much more complex relationships within this arena, responding to pressures from technological and corporate change, and dependent upon changing social behaviour and attitudes to work, affect the ways in which domestic consumption is translated into demand. At the regional scale this has implications for both the quality and distribution of employment.

A distinction must first be made between direct and 'intermediate' consumer services (Gershuny, 1978). Both have been influenced by manufacturing innovation, and both are increasingly being served by dominant groups of nationally based organizations. Even in the former, the traditional close relationship between the location of consumption and service employment has been significantly loosened in recent years. Major corporate and technical change in retailing, in particular, has reduced labour inputs through investment in new manufacturing technology.

Consequently, dependence has grown on the other service arenas to provide supporting expertise in technical innovation, financial management and distribution. The influence of some retailing companies has also been significantly extended into the manufacturing, transportation, wholesaling and financial sectors. These trends have impinged in different ways on different retail sectors, of course. Generally, however, while locally dispersed patterns of retail employment have thinned, regional and national concentrations into larger outlets, and supporting research, administration and warehouse functions, have emerged more strongly.

Increased domestic dependence on what Gershuny has called 'intermediate' consumer services is also a consequence of manufacturing innovation. These activities depend on the use in the home itself of often complex manufactured goods. Direct service employment has fallen over many decades, for example in domestic work, transportation, entertainment, and decoration and repair, as consumer spending has shifted towards manufactured substitutes, operated ('self-service') by domestic consumers. Functions supporting 'intermediate' consumer demand have grown instead, serving the domestic acquisition and operation of goods such as washing machines, central heating, motor vehicles, radio and television, and DIY gadgetry. These functions include advertising and sales, consumer finance, rental, distribution, equipment repair and maintenance, and the provision of related products such as radio and television programmes.

Economic changes driven by the growth of intermediate demand in the domestic arena therefore reflect the availability and rate of adoption of domestic manufactured goods. Direct service labour is displaced, at least to the extent that householders are prepared to acquire and operate the new technology themselves. The provision of many intermediate consumer services is dominated by large manufacturing/consumer service corporations, although small firms and the informal sector also play a significant role. The large firms operate through national hierarchies of headquarter, divisional and local service centres, linked by developing information and communications technology.

The domestic arena is therefore characterized by changing patterns of inter-action between direct and intermediate consumer demand, employment in the formal and household sectors, and the large- and small-firm segments of the economy. The general effect is to loosen the traditional close relationship between the domestic location of consumption and the demand for services, especially for the higher-quality technical and managerial occupations. There are also other employment consequences of these trends, arising from the variable ability of households to realize the benefits either of greater domestic mechanization or of large-scale, high-technology retailing. These favour regions and sub-regions with high disposable incomes, compounding the disadvantages of low-income areas.

Large companies serving national markets have become increasingly domi-nant in both direct and intermediate domestic servicing. These markets include food retailing, domestic appliances, vehicle and other non-food goods distribu-tion, domestic and automobile repair and maintenance, banks, other finance agencies, advertising and media production. A division of labour more regionally differentiated than in the past is emerging, reinforced by, and perhaps reinforcing, income and employment inequalities. Some regions may increasingly come to export the higher levels of technical, computational and managerial expertise in consumer marketing to others.

Public services

The most distinctive feature of public services is the non-profit basis upon which they are supposed to be provided. The coherence of the public service arena, including diverse state-owned or managed activities, derives from public owner-ship and the criteria by which this is exercised. Its realm of activities has been reduced in recent years as a result of privatization measures, transferring owner-ship and management to the private production or service arenas. The wider significance of public services is greatest for the domestic arena, through health, education and other welfare functions. It also makes an integral contribution to the commercial sectors, however, especially through its provision of welfare, infrastructure and some utilities, its control of the nationalized industries, its role as a huge market and its regulatory functions.

Like consumer services, the local orientation of many public administrative and social services is often taken to suggest that they cannot create significant differences in regional economic prosperity. Nevertheless, there is obvious scope for 'import substitution' of any such services supplied from outside a region. The devolved element of administration already present in Northern Ireland, Scotland and Wales illustrates these possibilities.

As well as serving these needs, governments in the past have supported private economic activity through infrastructure investment. The direct responsibility of the public sector for such services has been reduced in recent years, although inherited patterns of electricity and gas provision, and of road and telephone networks, remain almost wholly the product of public sector activities. Public regulation remains strong even after privatization. Through their influence on these types of service, including new networks such as cable and satellite communications, public policies can exert a significant effect on the overall rate, structure and spatial pattern of many private sector developments (Gershuny, 1978).

Even where governments seek to distance themselves from direct intervention in economic management, their own patterns of activity, through housing and transport investment, research and development, and defence are highly influential in creating economic change and in stimulating private sector investment (Johnston, 1982; Lovering, 1985). The control of common information and advisory services, and of educational and training networks, also gives public bodies great leverage on patterns of change. The nationally uneven distribution of many public service functions in general favours the more prosperous southern areas of the UK. This substantial 'hidden' public contribution to regionally unequal growth has become more significant recently as formal regional policy has declined (Lovering and Boddy, 1988).

The most pervasive general changes that have affected the public service arena in recent years arise from economic and political pressures towards increased scale and capital intensity of provision. These pressures have significantly reduced public sector employment since the mid-1970s. Employment has also been increasingly restructured as the result of technical innovation and administrative concentration. The detailed effects of these pressures vary according to the diverse administrative structures of public bodies. Generally, however, there has been a trend towards centralization, at least at the regional scale, and, like consumer services, increased pressure towards a concentration of strategic control functions in certain regions.

These processes of centralization will almost certainly be enhanced by current policies intended to shift the boundary between the public and private sectors. Two basic changes in public sector activities are involved: the privatization of public corporations and nationalized industries, and new requirements for public bodies to tender or contract out certain services to private companies (Department of the Environment, 1985). A third element of policy is also regarded as significant by Howells and Green: reduced government regulation of the private sector, especially of the financial services. Within the capital circulation arena, this will enhance the rate at which international conglomerates will come to dominate the financial scene compared with regionally based companies (Howells and Green, 1988, 32).

Among the most important state-owned service monopolies, privatization has so far introduced a new mode of organization into telecommunications, airport management, and gas production and distribution. Similar changes are imminent for water and electricity supply. The differential economic impacts of these changes between regions will depend on the strength with which 'social' requirements are imposed on the new private operators. In general it is to be expected that regions of high-density demand will be favoured under a private sector regime, for example through the introduction of new services, rather than the more peripheral regions, where predominantly cost-cutting, labour-saving investment is more likely. The pervasive influence of public investment on the other arenas suggests that these changes will have widespread multiplier effects on regional economic inequality, both through material production and other services.

The contracting-out of services by public bodies, including central government departments, local authorities, educational services and the National Health Service, will reinforce these trends. The new emphasis on private education and health provision may be seen as having already initiated the move. Formal contracting-out, in cleaning, catering, security, vehicle maintenance, and computing and data processing, has taken place most rapidly in the South. The work has gone largely to nationally and even internationally based companies, operating their technical and sales functions on an interregional rather than a local basis. As well as reducing the public sector, therefore, the influence of these changes will not particularly favour local service firms. They may also reduce the numbers, pay levels and working conditions of manual workers in the sectors and regions involved (Howells and Green, 1988, 130–8).

Thus, the public sector has been responsible in the past for marked inequalities in growth potential between different parts of the country. Further, current radical changes in management and control may stimulate growth in some regions rather than others. This will occur in spite of any continuing attempts to decentralize the declining proportion of routine public sector jobs from London. With a long-term squeeze on the numbers of manual workers and the conditions under which they work, there may also be increasing polarization in the quality of the public sector job opportunities available in different areas.

The prospects for service change

The case has been presented here for considering *any* 'service' function as offering, directly or indirectly, a potential source of regional, and sometimes of national, income and employment change. Essentially, the various elements and arenas of modern economic activity are so functionally and geographically interdependent that the contribution of none of them to economic development can be discounted. The complexities of each arena of change, and its dependence upon other arenas, have moved service studies away from the traditional concern with patterns of consumer behaviour. This is self-evident in the cases of production-related and capital circulation services. The provision even of domestic and public services, however, is now governed by corporate developments and affected by new technology to create varied regional economic and employment outcomes.

Thinking ahead, it seems clear that we shall enter the 1990s with a very different view of the economic significance of services from that generally held a decade earlier. This may accord with either a pessimistic, 'de-industrialization' or a more optimistic, 'post-industrial' perspective on economic developments in the 1980s. Whichever is adopted, however, there is an urgent need to improve the monitoring and interpretation of service change in relation to other economic developments. The range of service products will continue to evolve rapidly. Employment in some services, including new services, will grow, while others, perhaps thriving at present, decline. These patterns will depend on trends in demand and market differentiation, structured by the pressures for change arising within and between various arenas of activity. Diverse influences will be at work from changing manufacturing technology, international financial markets, domestic social behaviour, political ideology and the strategies of conglomerate and other large organizations.

For production-related services, the impact of technical changes, summarized in the move towards 'flexible manufacturing', will place increasing emphasis on the independent service sector and its relationship with 'in-house' functions. The capital circulation services, having experienced various transformations in both international and national conditions in the past decade, face difficult new choices in relation to European integration in the 1990s. Both of these arenas will undoubtedly move significantly towards European-orientated market developments in the 1990s.

Perhaps in the domestic arena, even assuming continuing general prosperity, limits may be reached to the growth of services, and especially of employment, arising from the key social developments of recent decades. These include increased home ownership, female employment levels, car ownership, and holiday and leisure time. On the other hand, a continuing switch to the private provision of formerly public services is likely, as is a greater interest in ecologically more conservationist economic processes. These developments suggest a changing, although not necessarily diminished, role for the public sector. Although less directly involved in service provision, it will exert its control in a more centralized manner, and public spending will still have an indirect influence on patterns of economic development. More emphasis also seems likely on regulation, for example over the activities of financial services, in environmental management or in health and education.

Many commentators fear that the growth of the services-led economy over the next decade will be dominated by the continuing polarization between the highly rewarded 'service class' and other workers relegated to low-skill, poorly paid employment. Powerful trends throughout the service sector seem to be increasing the uneven regional distribution of key activities, often but not invariably favouring 'core' regions at the expense of the periphery. Such inequitable pressures are very real, and they will be reinforced by trends in the organization of service provision. Nevertheless, the growing range and variety of both white- and blue-collar service skills, and the segmented labour markets within which they operate, suggest a much more complex outcome than is implied by a simple polarization model. In addition, with declining workforce numbers in the 1990s, greater emphasis will need to be placed on improved worker training and wage structures to attract recruits. Acute labour shortages may also favour areas outside the greater South East. The social effects of these changes are difficult to predict, but the expertise required to sustain the economy is much broader than that usually ascribed simply to the innovators, managers and bureaucrats of the service class.

Conclusion: service practice

Those working in any so-called service activity have peculiar problems of perceiving their wider role in the scheme of things. Service expertise, however vital, is supposed to be impermanent, short-lived and marginal to the real production of wealth. This chapter has been devoted to challenging such a view. One result of a 'dis-integrated' perception of services is that practitioners find it difficult to see beyond the immediate market they serve, whether in banking, transport, tourism, leisure or education. Strategies for the future, especially in the private sector but also often sadly in public planning, are usually based only on recent, short-term trends. What the 'integrated' view of this chapter has attempted to offer is a hint of the full range of economic pressures that may affect individual or linked groups of services. It has also emphasized the general economic importance, both nationally and regionally, of efficient service provision, although the impacts of this efficiency may not always benefit other competing activities.

Efficient service practice requires criteria of its economic value and efficiency that go beyond the limited horizons of short-term, localized commercial or public sector management. This is not simply to benefit economic planners and forecasters, an unfashionable breed in any case. The morale and coherence of those working in the service sector also require a better informed public and political appreciation of their worth. In practice, moreover, service change must be seen as the outcome of the interaction of competitive, public sector and domestic requirements on the various arenas of provision. The economic importance of some parts of the service sector has been recognized in recent years. The time is now ripe for all service activities to be subject to the type of detailed and continuous functional analysis that will illuminate their basic contribution to economic change in the 'post-industrial' era.

References

Allen, J. (1988) 'Service industries, uneven development and uneven knowledge', *Area*, 20, 15–22.

Daniels, P.W. (1985) *Service Industries: A Geographical Appraisal*. London: Methuen.

Department of the Environment (1985) *Competition in the Provision of Local Authority Services*. London: HMSO.

Gershuny, J. (1978) *After Industrial Society? The Emerging Self-Service Economy*. London: Macmillan.

Howells, J. (1988) *Economic, Technological and Locational Trends in European Services*. Aldershot: Avebury.

Howells, J. and Green, A. (1988) *Technological Innovation, Structural Change and Location in UK services*. Aldershot: Avebury.

Johnston, R.J. (1982) *Geography and the State: An Essay in Political Geography*. London: Macmillan.

Key, T.S. (1985) 'Services in the UK economy', *Bank of England Quarterly Bulletin*, 25, 404–14.

Kumar, K. (1978) *Prophecy and Progress: The Sociology of Industrial and Post-industrial Society*. Harmondsworth: Penguin.

Lash, S. and Urry, J. (1987) *The End of Organized Capital*. London: Polity Press.

Lewis, J. (1988) 'Employment matters: a comment', in Marshall, 1988.

Lovering, J. (1985) 'Regional economic development and the role of defence procurement: a case study', *Built Environment*, 11, 193–206.

Lovering, J. and Boddy, M. (1988) 'The geography of military industry in Britain', *Area*, 20, 41–51.

Marshall, J.N. (1979) 'Ownership, organization and industrial linkage: a case study of the Northern Region of England', *Regional Studies*, 13, 531–57.

Marshall, J.N. (1985) 'Business services, the regions and regional policy', *Regional Studies*, 19, 353–64.

Marshall, J.N. (ed.) (1988) *Services and Uneven Development*. Oxford: Oxford University Press.

Marshall, J.N., Damesick, P. and Wood, P.A. (1987) 'Understanding the location and role of producer services', *Environment and Planning A*, 19, 575–95.

Massey, D. (1984) *Spatial Divisions of Labour*. London: Macmillan.

Ochel, W. and Wegner, M. (1987) *Service Economies in Europe: Opportunities for Growth*. London: Pinter/Boulder, Colo.: Westview.

Piore, M.J. and Sabel, C.F. (1984) *The Second Industrial Divide*. Basic Books, New York.

Postner, H.H. and Wesa, L. (1984) *Canadian Productivity Growth: An Alternative (Input–Output) Analysis*. Economic Council of Canada, Ottawa.

Walker, R. (1985) 'Is there a service economy? The changing capitalist division of labour', *Science and Society*, 49, 42–83.

Wood, P.A. (1986) 'The anatomy of job loss and job creation: some speculation on the role of the "producer service" sector', *Regional Studies*, 20, 37–47.

Wood, P.A. (1987) 'Producer services and economic change: some Canadian evidence', in Chapman, K. and Humphrys, G. (eds) *Technological Change and Economic Policy*. London: Blackwell.

Wood, P.A. (1988a) 'The economic role of producer services: some Canadian evidence', in Marshall, 1988.

Wood, P.A. (1988b) 'Non-production employment in manufacturing', in Marshall, 1988.

Chapter 2

Geographical perspectives on the development of producer services

Peter Daniels

Introduction

The transition to a service economy or a 'post-industrial and information society' has been less smooth than expected (Bell, 1973; Blackaby, 1979; Hall, 1987; Rajan, 1987). The current state of conceptual and empirical research on many service industries is still inadequate for a proper evaluation of location patterns or policy proposals. In the past this was explicable in terms of academic neglect. But it now coincides with a good deal of debate about the role of services in national economies and at more specific regional and local scales. Indeed, there has been growing uncertainty recently about the advantages and disadvantages of service sector growth at all scales of analysis: international, national, regional and local (see, for example, Petit, 1986; Gemmell, 1986; Ochel and Wegner, 1987). This is encapsulated in the ongoing debate about the measurement and significance of de-industrialization (Martin and Rowthorn, 1986).

Before embarking on an overview of some of the research on producer services undertaken by geographers in recent years, it is helpful to consider briefly some of the wider issues confronting research on services in general. Although far from exhaustive, the following provides an indication of some of the questions arising from the strong development of the service sector during the last decade:

- Is the growing share of services in GDP and employment an indication of de-industrialization and of weakening manufacturing strength or only the expression of complexities created by increasingly interdependent national economies?
- Are service activities a force against improvements in labour productivity or are services that are labour intensive the main hope for resolving unemployment problems?
- To what extent will information technology put future expansion of service jobs at risk?
- Are services the main avenue for technical progress and for more efficiency and flexibility in the most industrialized countries?
- What is the role of services in the process of economic development, especially in lagging industrial or rural regions?
- How close are the links between the production of goods and the production of services, and what determines the way in which the relationship evolves?
- What are the main determinants of the expansion of services within firms and the reasons for the contracting-out of services?

Numerous statistical, definitional and classification problems continue to plague research on services (see, for example, Coppieters *et al.*, 1986; Boulianne and Thevoz, 1985; Moulaert *et al.*, 1986; Ochel and Wegner, 1987; Howells, 1988). One of the principal problems with official statistics is inadequate disaggregation: service activities are at least as diverse as manufacturing but occupy less than a quarter of the list of activities in most census and similar data sources. Survey-based research, supplemented with the plentiful literature available from trade and professional associations, trade unions, consultancy organizations and specialist publications on service industries, is therefore an important source. But in some respects this has also become more difficult as many services have become large and diverse multinational enterprises (Dunning, 1989). There is undoubtedly a need for more international comparative research which is conducted in parallel with more detailed monitoring of the impact of developments in services on local economic and social structure (see, for example, Cooke, 1986; Thrift, 1986). The range and volume of recent research on service industries is demonstrated in various bibliographies (see, for example, Illeris, 1985; P.O. Pederson, 1986; Centre de Documentation et d'Echange sur les Activités de Service, 1985).

A good deal of geographical research has been directly concerned with aspects of the service sector. Retailing has probably received the most detailed and longstanding attention (see, for example, Davies, 1976, 1984; Dawson, 1983; Treadgold and Davies, 1988). Other services such as wholesaling (McKinnon, 1983, 1989), research and development (Howells, 1984) and producer services such as accountancy, commercial property consultancy and investment banking (Marshall, 1988) have recently been the subject of greater scrutiny. Analyses of specific services are complemented by studies of the relationship between information technology and the location of services (Howells, 1988), trade in services (Harrington, 1988), the role of services in regional development (Illeris, 1989; Harrington and Lombard, 1988), the effects of organizational and structural changes within services on cities and regions at national and international level (Rimmer, 1988) and the role of services in regional policy (Marshall and Bachtler, 1987). Common to both sectoral and thematic research on services by geographers is a concern to understand better and to explain the influence of location and space on the dynamics and patterns of growth and change which have been such a prominent characteristic of services in general, and producer services in particular, during the last decade. Equally important is the geographer's substantive interest in the relative performance of regions or metropolitan areas (at various scales) as a result of the behaviour of service organizations.

Producer services

Heterogeneity is a hallmark of the service sector (see, for example, Price and Blair, 1989). In order, therefore, to make the task of summarizing some of the recent work by geographers more manageable, this chapter deals exclusively with producer (or intermediate) services. These services are marketed to firms and public institutions (rather than to final consumers) in all economic sectors for incorporation in the production of a good or another service. A useful review of alternative ways of classifying services is provided by Illeris (1989). It is evident from this and other work (see, for example, Marshall, 1988; Allen, 1988) that universal agreement on the activities to be included in the producer services is some way off. For the purpose of the present discussion they will be taken to include professional and business services, financial services, insurance and real estate.

Producer services employment has been growing at 2 to 3 per cent per annum for the last decade (Elfring, 1988). Although the recession during the early 1980s slowed down the rate of employment increase (Howells and Green, 1988), UK services, for example, have consistently expanded since 1971. However, while transport and communication services have contracted in absolute and percentage terms, banking, finance and insurance have largely maintained their growth momentum. Absolute increases of 154,000 between 1971 and 1976 had expanded to 284,000 between 1981 and 1984. The relative change of amost 17 per cent during this latter period for the group as a whole was exceeded by business services (24.7 per cent), renting of movables (18.9 per cent) and owning/dealing in real estate (21 per cent) (Howells and Green, 1988). Whether ranked by absolute employment change or by relative change in 1976–81 or 1981–4, producer services are dominant amongst the top ten classes of activity. In this respect the recent growth performance of producer services far outstrips that of other sectors of the UK and other advanced economies. This raises questions about the role of producer services in the process of economic and social change, particularly the causes and the consequences of observed differences between regions or cities.

Uneven growth: a recurring theme

The highly uneven spatial distribution of producer service growth is a recurring theme in geographical research. This distribution has happened even though the economic and technological environment within which the growth has been taking place has offered the prospect of greater locational flexibility than at any time in the past. The revolution in telecommunications and computing (information technology) which some see as relegating space, distance and time to a lowly position in the location decision-making process has had mixed effects. Such is the potential that producer services (amongst others) could be supplied from 'electronic cottages' whose location is determined by the lifestyle preferences of their occupiers (whether employees or self-employed). Yet a good deal of the evidence about the spatial distribution of producer services (whether measured by employment, number of establishments or transaction flows) clearly demonstrates that certain regions, particular cities and specific locations within cities have attracted a disproportionate share of recent growth (see, for example, Howells, 1988; Illeris, 1989; Leyshon et al., 1989). Similar differentiation is also apparent at the global scale as major financial centres such as London, New York, Tokyo, Paris or Singapore have become the demand focuses for office space and employment in the wake of the internationalization of services (Noyelle, 1988; Nusbaumer, 1987).

It is not surprising, therefore, that geographers have examined the distribution of producer services at different scales in relation to other economic and social indices. The spatial patterns of producer service employment at regional and urban level, particularly with reference to metropolitan/non-metropolitan distributions (Gillespie and Green, 1987 (UK); Kirn, 1987; Beyers and Hull, 1988 (USA); Van Dinteren, 1989 (Netherlands)), have been extensively examined. Of interest is the degree to which these services are subject to the processes of decentralization which have dominated metropolitan/non-metropolitan relationships since 1945 in relation to population distribution and the location of manufacturing, retailing and wholesaling activities. By comparison, the producer services have lagged behind substantially and may, at certain scales of analysis and for certain types of service (such as corporate financial services), be recentralizing and reinforcing agglomeration in large cities. Even where decentralization of producer services from metropolitan areas is taking place it tends to occur as 'concentrated decentralization' (i.e. within the same metropolitan region and its immediate environs) rather than as interregional migration. This is well documented, both in a historical context (Location of Offices Bureau, 1975) and in more recent data on corporate headquarters location, assets and employment which can, to a limited degree, be used as a surrogate for producer services to explore interregional shifts or changes in the metropolitan hierarchies within national urban systems (Wheeler, 1987; Semple *et al.*, 1985 (US); Evans, 1973 (UK)). It is, however, somewhat dangerous to make such sweeping generalizations: Illeris (1989) has assembled comparative statistics for Europe and the United States and shows, for example, that large cities are attracting a disproportionate share of producer service employment growth in the UK, Sweden, Canada and the Mediterranean countries but that the differential is less clear in the United States or in some other European countries. In some countries higher growth has occurred in southern than in northern regions (United States, UK, West Germany, France).

One of the central questions derived from these trends is whether they inhibit economic development and structural adaptation in cities and regions which have not figured prominently in the growth of producer service activity. This requires research on:

- the way in which producer services are incorporated into the production process (in relation to manufacturing and services);
- whether inability to use (or lack of knowledge of) such services places limits on the effective production of a good or service;
- whether quality of the service available is at least as important as access or availability for maintaining firm competitiveness;
- the factors influencing decisions whether or not to use producer services;
- whether proximity is a prerequisite for use or whether knowledge of potential value added or simply the presence/absence of specialist services (irrespective of where they are located) is enough to ensure consumption;
- the significance of size and status of firms/establishments for producer service consumption;
- the extent to which the characteristics of smaller firms (in particular) such as product type, market or owner attributes (educational qualifications, age,

occupation, reasons for setting up business) influence decisions to use producer services.

Some guidance on the answers to some of these questions is provided by
several small-scale empirical studies of the supply and demand for producer
services (E.O. Pederson, 1986; Daniels, 1986; Beyers *et al.*, 1986; Sjoholt, 1988).
Large establishments use a wider range of producer services more frequently than
small establishments (both in manufacturing and services). The local orientation
of consumption varies according to the kind of service required: the more
specialized it is, the less likely that it will be obtained from the local area. Market
research is usually acquired from sources outside the region, but the findings
derived from studies of research and development, marketing, advertising or
computing services, for example, do not reveal a clear tendency one way or the
other. It does seem, however, that services not obtained from local sources will
tend to be purchased from the highest-order metropolitan area within a national
urban system, especially if purchasing establishments are part of multi-site
organizations controlled from outside the local area. There are indications that
externally controlled service establishments are more likely to be supplied with
producer services from within their organization than are externally controlled
manufacturing plants.

Nevertheless, an encouraging level of complementarity is evident in the results
of recent research. Of course, allowances for differences in scale and economic
structure must be made, and they inevitably give rise to differences in detail. Some
of the commonalities may be summarized as follows (Daniels, 1987a; see also
Illeris, 1989):

- the use of producer services generally increases with firm size and complexity
  of organizational structure;
- certain producer services such as management consultancy or advertising
  agencies are used infrequently, especially by small firms;
- such services are most likely to be imported from higher-order centres or
  supplied via headquarters that are usually also located in higher-order
  corporate complexes;
- externalization of service demand is most frequently associated with large
  firms, mainly for producer services that will be purchased from elsewhere if
  not available locally;
- external provision of all but industry-specific services is the preferred strategy
  of most firms in order to reduce fixed costs;
- small firms make do with local services, tend not to require producer services
  (often because they are perceived as being high cost) and therefore hold back
  any prospect of stimulating the local supply of such services;
- specialization requires recruitment of specialist personnel which, unless a city
  or region is already specialized in specific sectors, will probably be difficult;
- an improvement in the supply of sophisticated business services in under-
  provided locations requires an investment in human resources in the form of
  more labour force retraining and education;
- there are varied (but underdeveloped) links between producer services and

local higher-education establishments with positive economic development effects.

Finally, some of the research by geographers on the markets for producer service outputs has begun to dispel the myth that they are essentially part of the non-basic sector of metropolitan or regional economies. This longstanding, and essentially continually pervasive, assumption has long been used to defend the research attention devoted to manufacturing. From a policy standpoint it is believed that investment in manufacturing is a prerequisite for service sector expansion. Research by, amongst others, Ley and Hutton (1987) in Vancouver, Bailly, Maillat and Rey (1984) for two regions in Switzerland, Beyers, Alvine and Johnson (1985) in the Puget Sound Region (Seattle), and E.O. Pederson (1986) in Esbjerg shows, for example that:

- sales by producer services to other services are very similar to those to manufacturing;
- less than half of the output of producer services goes to local clients (i.e. within the same city) and 25 to 30 per cent (on average) is exported outside the city or metropolitan area to other parts of the same country or overseas (about 5 to 6 per cent of the total goes overseas);
- the number of jobs resulting from services sold outside the local area may be larger than the corresponding number of manufacturing jobs.

Role of structural and organizational change in producer service firms

Some inferences about the forces shaping the geography of producer service development can be made using secondary sources or primary data of the kind generated by establishment surveys. But what of organizational behaviour and the way in which its development is translated into spatial outcomes which may also incorporate significant temporal trends? Archival and related material held by producer service organizations can be used to trace where growth has been taking place during the last decade, the strategies which it represents and the factors that have influenced location decision making (see, for example, Rimmer, 1988; Daniels *et al.*, 1988a, 1988b; Perry, 1989; Harris, 1984). While details may vary there are undoubtedly some underlying similarities in the recent organizational changes undertaken by these activities which have also been reflected in location behaviour. These can be summarized as follows:

- organizational
    concentration of ownership
    demise of intermediate-sized firms
    diversification
    specialization
    internationalization
    information technology adoption

- spatial
    locational centralization
    expansion of 'provincial' office networks within UK
    selective expansion into 'global' cities such as New York, Tokyo, Hong
    Kong, Singapore, Sydney

The organizational and spatial changes represent efforts to achieve a number of goals. Concentration of ownership through merger with, or takeover of, competitors helps to sustain market share, to capture the clients (and possibly the expertise or products) of vulnerable firms. Where this activity involves widely spread geographical locations, it will probably allow improvements in the services offered to corporate clients who may also have manufacturing or service operations in similar areas (Dunning, 1989; Enderwick, 1989). Such is the dynamic of competition amongst producer service firms that it is no longer adequate to wait for demand to express itself or for relationships with long-established clients to be enough to remain profitable. Some producer services such as accountants, management consultants or even investment banks have become geared up to making or seeking markets through advertising (where professional rules permit) or the establishment of new offices without an established client base. The possibilities for operating in this way are increased as organizations have become larger and can therefore benefit from economies of scale in the supply of some services which, as in some areas accountancy for example, are essentially the same everywhere but which do require some 'tailoring' to specific client needs. Extending the geographical coverage also allows producer service firms to keep in touch with the latest ideas and innovations, especially if they choose locations that are universally regarded as significant 'corporate complexes' (such as New York or London). Some of the restructuring which has characterized large producer service organizations recently could therefore be interpreted as a response to the locational decisions taken by competitors. There seems to be a good deal of old-fashioned 'follow-the-leader' behaviour with respect to location choices. Thus, all ten of the largest international design consultancies (all but one of which have their headquarters in London) are represented in London, six in New York and San Francisco, four in Los Angeles and three in Tokyo, Sydney and Madrid (*Financial Times*, 1989).

Many of these trends have, of course, been underpinned by information technology. At international level at least, deregulation of telecommunications services may be helping to reinforce the already strong agglomeration tendencies revealed by producer services. Investments in new fibre optic networks or teleport facilities are likely to be made first in locations where expressed demand is already substantial. This further reinforces the comparative advantage of the major producer service complexes.

The example of financial services

The growth and location of financial services (insurance, banking, finance, leasing) is related to a number of factors. Developments in information technology have greatly improved both the internal and external efficiency of financial markets. External efficiency has been enhanced by the increased speed and capacity of financial information systems; data production and distribution is increasingly subject to computer applications and is supplied 'on-line' by a growing number of financial information companies. Internally, efficiency has been improved through better links between markets and between geographically separate parts of the same firm, between institutions and individuals; dealing and settlement systems are increasingly being automated; remote trading is practicable. Consequently, turnover in financial markets has increased dramatically, aided by the development of automatic execution systems for trading of small lots, the progressive introduction of expert systems and the reduction in deal execution time and costs. All of these technology-related developments encourage institutional investors to be more 'active'.

Although technical advances have increased the locational flexibility of financial services, in practice they have displayed a clear trend towards spatial concentration. This is true in relation both to international patterns of growth and location and to the situation within the UK, Tokyo, New York and London, along with a larger number of 'second tier' cities, are attracting the lion's share of international financial services: in the UK there is well-documented evidence for the concentration of financial services in and around the City of London. With one or two exceptions, such as the headquarters of insurance offices, most of the major provincial cities are heavily dependent on financial services provided via branches: some overseas banks, for example, have established branches outside London, but there has been little change in the numbers represented (1981–6) when closures are taken into account. Most make location decisions which reflect the distribution of certain ethnic groups or foreign direct investment in certain regions, for example Japanese banks are represented in Manchester. It is necessary to infer relationships of this kind, however, because the client balance (between consumer and corporate, for example) is not known.

Globalization of markets (linked to information technology, 24-hour trading) has influenced both the location and pace of growth of financial services. Securities dealing, foreign currency dealing, investment banking and related services have expanded along narrowly defined pathways that connect a small number of international financial centres. In many ways this has been encouraged by the diversification of financial instruments made possible by technology and encouraged by competition which is most readily assessed and responded to in cognate locations. The expansion of financial services has also been encouraged by demand, especially from large national and multinational firms, for participation in highly dynamic financial markets using the best methods available to ensure that capital, securities, loan raising, etc. take place in a way that maximizes the benefits. Investors, notably pension funds and insurance companies, have amassed large capital funds that need to be invested to cover future disbursements and have developed into highly professional institutional investment vehicles. Finally, deregulation of financial markets such as allowing outsiders to take 100 per cent ownership in Stock Exchange firms, the removal of fixed commission rates and the ending of the demarcation between jobbers and brokers has enabled financial services to engage in even more extensive cross-border transactions and representation.

Many of these developments have triggered new alliances between financial service firms, with some adopting 'global' strategies, i.e. providing a full suite of financial services, and others (often the smaller firms) going for a niche strategy, i.e. identifying a particular gap in the market or refining an existing service to a level far superior to that of competing suppliers. Little wonder, in either case, that growth of financial services has been so place-specific since, for example, the increasingly specialized labour demand, the specialist information and knowledge, or simply a heightened awareness of trends and innovations are most readily realized in or very near to large-scale agglomerations. The buoyancy of office markets in major cities has been clearly linked to the demands generated by financial services during the past five years. However, the impact on provincial office markets has been much more limited despite recent claims by cities, such as Bristol, that they are now significant financial service centres (Leyshon *et al.*, 1989).

The stock market crisis on 'Black Monday' (19 October 1987) has introduced much uncertainty into the future prospects for financial services. Geography and distance may in the past have delayed the transmission of information from New York to the other major financial centres, and modern telecommunications probably contributed to a domino effect in London and Tokyo which accelerated the loss of business confidence. Over-capacity and too many firms and banks chasing business were identified as problems before the crash occurred, and it has brought forward the labour shedding and consolidation that observers considered inevitable as intense competition pushed commissions so low that it would be impossible for some firms to survive. Both foreign and UK investment banks have shed labour: 50,000 jobs (out of 200,000 + in financial services in the City) are expected by some analysts to disappear by 1990. It is difficult to know how to translate these losses to provincial cities; perhaps much will depend on the importance attached by the financial services already there to a physical presence in regional markets. The fall in financial services jobs may, in turn, reduce the demand for office space (it has recently been estimated that job losses following the crash on Wall Street have been accompanied by a fall in office rents and rental values of 20 to 25 per cent), cause a slowdown in office rent growth and therefore reduce the pressure to search for less costly locations for back office functions. Much will depend on trends in floorspace–worker ratios or, perhaps more accurately, in floorspace–information technology ratios. A record 4.8 million ft^2 of office space was completed in central London in 1987. With more than 50 per cent of occupier demand emanating from banking and finance, it is not difficult to anticipate some slack in the market. There is some 30 million ft^2 of office space proposed for central London and adjacent areas such as King's Cross and Docklands (Dudman, 1988; see also Cundell, 1988). It seems likely that the take-up of such a large volume of office space will depend upon London maintaining its status as an attractive centre for overseas services and, in particular, for financial services headquartered in Japan and Europe (Edward Erdman Research, 1989).

Notwithstanding the particular circumstances surrounding the future of financial services growth, office relocation remains an attractive proposition for many firms, especially those located in the cores of major cities. There are a number of push factors:

- Rent and rate differentials: the cost of leasing Grade A office space in major financial centres is two or three times as high as elsewhere and may be as much as 6–7 times as high as in a provincial city centre. The gradient within provincial conurbations is much lower and in some instances is hardly present.

- Cost of labour: secretarial and clerical staff, still a significant labour input, command salaries of £8,000–12,000 in London compared with £5,000–9,000 in places outside the South East, for example. Add to this the need to provide additional incentives such as luncheon vouchers, a company restaurant or low-cost loans towards season tickets for commuting (caused by intense competition for the best labour), the overall cost of retaining one employee in central London will range between £20,000 and £30,000 per year. In relation to the value of their output, this is an avoidable cost if 'back office' activities are relocated.

- Consolidation: many financial service firms occupy more than one office building, which can create serious internal communication problems as well as make them vulnerable to frequent changes in accommodation costs. However, it may be difficult to find an office building in a suitable city centre location, of the right size, with an appropriate internal configuration, at an acceptable rent, adequate for the corporate image and at the time required.

- Long, expensive, tiring journeys to work, together with congestion on the routes and at the destinations, which lead to higher staff absenteeism rates and less effective use of working hours (lower productivity).

- Difficulties of finding housing at affordable rents/purchase prices: lower-paid office workers, in particular, are unable to live in lower-cost inner urban locations because demand from highly specialized, highly paid office workers (many of them in financial services) has partially transferred to inner city (gentrified) locations within easy reach of downtown office areas.

- Mismatch between the quality of office accommodation required and that available: this factor has become more acute as the specifications for office buildings have changed in line with the evolution of information technology.

- Growth in the number of employees beyond the capacity of existing office buildings: this prompts firms to consider locational alternatives that may include places outside London.

- In the case of government offices, policy decisions to disperse work: for example, the recent announcement that the Patent Office is to be transferred from London to Cardiff (1,100 jobs: 600 created in Cardiff, 500 transferred from London) as part of a drive by the DTI to disperse some key divisions to the regions. The Office's headquarters in Holborn has a rent bill of £6 million compared with a possible £1 million (per year) in Cardiff.

Set against these 'push' factors for financial services (and other office-based services) are a number of 'pull' factors, many of which are the converse to the circumstances causing firms to look again at their (central London, metropolitan region) locations:

- Overhead savings: rents, rates, personnel recruitment costs, salaries (especially for less skilled office workers).
- Improved access to labour, especially to female office staff seeking part-time positions, a growing proportion of the jobs in offices.
- Less congested, shorter, less expensive journeys to work for most employees, and easier parking at destination (for employees and clients).
- Improvements in the working environment, both within office buildings and in terms of the physical surroundings.
- More loyal, reliable, productive labour force.
- Where a firm wishes to construct its own office building, rather than lease, it will be less costly to purchase a site and construction costs may be lower, especially if the firm does not require a building that is 'tailored' to a very demanding specification.
- Centralization of a firm's establishments at one location: this is especially applicable to manufacturing firms where ownership of an industrial site outside a high-cost location may make it very attractive to move an office next to a production plant even though there are no direct links between the two establishments.

Since the closure of the Location of Offices Bureau it has not been at all easy to measure the volume of recent office relocation within or between any British cities (see, for example, Richard Ellis Research, 1985). Occasional reports in the business press suggest that relocation is continuing to take place and mainly over short distances, i.e. within the same metropolitan region. There have been exceptions, of course, such as the recent relocation of some of Marks and Spencers administrative functions to Chester and a similar relocation of some London staff by Shell to a location near its Stanlow Refinery in Cheshire. Publicity tends to be given to location changes by large firms. There is no information about office relocation by smaller enterprises, but if their behaviour follows that of similar firms during the 1970s they will tend to relocate over even shorter distances.

Local impacts of recent producer service growth

There is one other facet of the spatial behaviour of producer services that has also received some attention. This it the local and sub-regional impact of centralization on property markets (commercial and residential), on labour markets, on access to housing and jobs in inner cities, and on planning mechanisms for coping with the high level of demand for new buildings and infrastructure (see, for example, Leyshon et al., 1987). A related issue is the spatial manifestation of the demand generated by rapidly growing activities for a wide range of intermediate inputs. Evidence from foreign banks in the City and in Manhattan suggests that well over half the linkages generated are with suppliers, etc. in the same small area of the city; very few purchases are made from firms located outside the metropolitan region (Daniels, 1987b). The result is a further reinforcement of a small number of established corporate/service complexes. In most cases the local demand for staff translates into technical and clerical requirements rather than managerial and professional positions, which are often filled by expatriates. Such international movements of highly skilled, high-income labour have also accompanied the internationalization of accountancy, advertising and property services, and will lead to location-specific effects on residential and commercial property markets.

Conclusion

There are some interesting and significant spatial outcomes associated with the recent and rapid expansion of producer service functions. Some of the key features of interest to spatial analysts have been summarized. Spatial considerations may not be explicitly included in the evolving organization and structure of producer services, but there is no doubt that the cumulative effects of their decisions do have a clear spatial expression. This, in turn, leads to other spatial effects which are manifest in a number of different ways at local, national and international levels of analysis. The challenge for geographers is not just to chart the changing geography of producer services and the demand for closely related requirements such as office space, but to enhance our understanding of the processes that determine the way in which space is absorbed into the development and location equation. Interdisciplinary research could well have an important role in efforts to further some of the work already undertaken, and international comparative research is also likely to become more significant if we are to understand properly and anticipate future trends in the behaviour and location of these services. Nowhere is this likely to be more important than in Western Europe. The imminent creation of a single market within the EEC (1992) and the continuing concentration of ownership and international orientation of many producer services may well rewrite the geography of these activities, notably the dominance of London for financial services and the level of provision in lagging regions.

References

Allen, J. (1988) 'Service industries: uneven development and uneven knowledge', *Area*, 20, 15–22.

Bailly, A., Maillat, D. and Rey, M. (1984) 'Tertiaire moteur et développement régional: les cas des petites et moyennes villes', *Revue d'Economie Régionale et Urbaine*, 5, 757–76.

Bell, D. (1973) *The Coming of Post-Industrial Society*. New York: Basic Books.

Beyers, W.B., Alvine, M.J. and Johnson, E.K. (1985) *The Service Economy: Export of Services in the Central Puget Sound Region*. Seattle: Central Puget Sound Development District.

Beyers, W.B., Tofflemire, J.M., Stranahan, H.A. and Johnsen, E.G. (1986) *The Service Economy: Understanding the Growth of Services in the Central Puget Sound Region*. Seattle: Central Puget Sound Economic Development District.

Beyers, W.B. and Hull, T.J. (1988) 'Understanding the growth of producer service employment in the United States: 1974–85', Paper presented at 35th North American Meetings of the Regional Science Association, Toronto, November (mimeo).

Blackaby, F. (ed.) (1979) *De-industrialization*. London: Heinemann.

Boulianne, L.M. and Thevoz, L. (1985) *Nouvelle nomenclature du système de production et rôle des activités de services*. Lausanne: Communauté d'Etudes pour l'Aménagement du Territoire.

Centre de Documentation et d'Echange sur les Activités de Service (1986) *Orientations, Outils, Activités de la Recherche sur les Services*. Lyons: CNRS–Economie et Humanisme, No. 3.

Cooke, P. (ed.) (1986) *Global Restructuring, Local Response*. London: Economic and Social Research Council.

Coppieters, P., Delauney, J.C., Dyckman, J., Gadrey, J., Moulaert, F. and Tordoir, P. (1986) *The Functions of Services and the Theoretical Approach to National and International Classifications*. Lille: Johns Hopkins European Centre for Regional Planning and Research.

Cundell, I. (1988) 'Planning for city offices in the 1990s', Geography Discussion Papers New Series No. 22, Graduate School of Geography, London School of Economics.

Daniels, P.W. (1986) 'The supply and demand for intermediate services by Merseyside firms', Department of Geography, University of Liverpool (mimeo).

Daniels, P.W. (1987a) 'The geography of services', *Progress in Human Geography*, 11, 433–47.

Daniels, P.W. (1987b) 'Foreign banks and metropolitan development: a comparison of London and New York', *Tijdschrift voor Economische en Sociale Geografie*, 77, 269–89.

Daniels, P.W., Leyshon, A. and Thrift, N.J. (1988a) 'Large accountancy firms in the UK: operational and adaptation and spatial development', *Service Industries Journal*, 8, 314–43.

Daniels, P.W., Leyshon, A. and Thrift, N.J. (1988b) 'Trends in the growth and location of professional producer services: UK property consultants', *Tijdschrift voor Economische en Sociale Geografie*, 79, 162–74.

Davies, R.L. (1976) *Marketing Geography: With Special Reference to Retailing*. London: Methuen.

Davies, R.L. (1984) *Retail and Commercial Planning*. London: Croom Helm.

Dawson, J.A. (1983) *Shopping Centre Development*. London: Longman.

Dudman, P. (1988) 'Wet fingers in the air', *Property Now*, Winter (published by Edward Erdman Surveyors).

Dunning, J.H. (1989) 'Multinational enterprises and the growth of services: some conceptual and theoretical issues', *Service Industries Journal*, 9, 5–39.

Edward Erdman Research (1989) *London's Office Market: The Overseas Influence*. London: Edward Erdman.

Elfring, T. (1988) *Service Employment in Advanced Economies*. London: Gower.

Enderwick, P. (ed.) (1989) *Multinational Service Firms*. London: Routledge.

Evans, A.W. (1973) 'The location of headquarters of industrial companies', *Urban Studies*, 10, 38–95.

Financial Times (1989) 'The top ten international design networks', 22 February.

Gemmell, M. (1986) *Structural Change and Economic Development: The Role of Services*. Basingstoke: Macmillan.

Gillespie, A.E. and Green, A. (1987) 'The changing geography of producer service employment in Britain', *Regional Studies*, 21, 397–411.

Hall, P. (1987) 'The geography of the post-industrial economy', in Brotchie, J.F. *et al.* (eds) *The Spatial Impact of Technological Change*. Beckenham: Croom Helm, 3–17.

Harrington, J.W. (1988) 'Towards an understanding of trade in services: Canada and the US', Canada–United States Trade Center, Department of Geography, University of Buffalo.

Harrington, J.W. and Lombard, J.R. (1988) 'Producer service firms in a declining manufacturing region', *Environment and Planning A*, 20, 65–80.

Harris, G. (1984) 'The globalization of advertising', *International Journal of Advertising*, 3, 223–34.

Howells, J.R.L. (1984) 'The location of research and development: some observations and evidence from Britain', *Regional Studies*, 18, 13–29.

Howells, J. and Green, A.E. (1988) *Economic, Technological and Locational Trends in European Services*. Aldershot: Avebury.

Illeris, S. (1985) *Bibliography of the Role of Services in Regional Development*. Brussels: Commission for the European Communities, FAST Occasional Paper 67.

Illeris, S. (1989) *Services and Regions in Europe*. Aldershot: Avebury.

Kirn, T.J. (1987) 'Growth and change in the service sector of the US: a spatial perspective', *Annals, Association of American Geographers*, 77, 353–72.

Ley, D. and Hutton, T. (1987) 'Vancouver's corporate complex and producer service sector: linkages and divergence within a provincial staples economy, *Regional Studies*, 21, 413–22.

Leyshon, A., Thrift, N.J. and Daniels, P.W. (1987) '"Sexy greedy": the new financial system, the City of London and the SE of England', Working Papers on Producer Services 8, University of Liverpool and St David's University College, Lampeter.

Leyshon, A., Thrift, N.J. and Tommey, C. (1989) 'South goes north: the rise of the British provincial financial centre', Working Papers on Producer Services 10, University of Bristol and Service Industries Research Centre, Portsmouth Polytechnic.

Location of Offices Bureau (1975) *Office Relocation: Facts and Figures*. London: Location of Offices Bureau.

McKinnon, A.C. (1983) 'The development of warehousing in England', *Geoforum*, 14, 389–99.

McKinnon, A.C. (1989) *Physical Distribution Systems*. London: Routledge.

Marshall, J.N. (1988) *Services and Uneven Development*. Oxford: Oxford University Press.

Marshall, J.N. and Bachtler, J. (1987) 'Services and regional policy', *Regional Studies*, 21, 471–75.

Martin, R. and Rowthorn, R. (1986) *The Geography of De-industrialization*. Basingstoke: Macmillan.

Moulaert, F., Tordoir, P., and Dyckman, J. (1986) 'The international division of services: theoretical issues', Paper presented at 33rd North American Meetings of the Regional Science Association, Columbus, Ohio, November.

Noyelle, T.J. (ed.) (1988) *New York's Financial Markets: The Challenges of Globalization*. Boulder, Colo.: Westview Press.

Nusbaumer, J. (ed.) (1987) *Services in the Global Economy*. Boston: Kluwer.

Ochel, W. and Wegner, M. (1987) *Service Economies in Europe: Opportunities for Growth*. London: Frances Pinter.

Pederson, E.O. (1986) 'Office location: a bibliography', Vance Bibliographies No. P2055, Monticello, Ill.

Pederson, P.O. (1986) *Business Service Strategies: The Case of the Provincial Centre of Esbjerg*. Brussels: Commission of the European Communities, FAST Series FS19.

Perry, M. (1989) 'The international and regional context of the advertising industry in New Zealand', Occasional Publications 24, Department of Geography, University of Auckland.

Petit, P. (1986) *Slow Growth and the Service Economy*. London: Frances Pinter.

Price, D.G. and Blair, A.M. (1989) *The Changing Geography of the Service Sector*,

Rajan, A. (1987) *Services: The Second Industrial Revolution*. London: Butterworths.

Richard Ellis Research (1985) *Suburban London Offices: The Occupier's View*. London: Richard Ellis.

Riddle, D. (1986) *Service-Led Growth: The Role of the Service Sector*. New York: Praeger.

Rimmer, P.J. (1988) 'The internationalization of engineering consultancies: problems of breaking into the club', *Environment and Planning A*, 20, 741–59.

Semple, R.K., Green, M.B. and Martz, D.J.F. (1985) 'Perspectives on corporate head-quarters relocation in the United States', *Urban Geography*, 6, 370–91.

Sjoholt, P. (1988) 'Use of producer services by manufacturing industry: a comparative pilot study in metropolitan and non-metropolitan Norway', NORAS Program Forksning for Regional Utvikling Report No. 6, Institutt for Geografie, Norges Handelshoyskole, Bergen.

Thrift, N.J. (1986) 'Localities in an international economy', paper presented at an ESRC Workshop on Localities in an International Economy. Cardiff, September (mimeo).

Treadgold, A.D. and Davies, R.L. (1988) *The Internationalization of Retailing.* Harlow: Longman.

Van Dinteren, J.H.J. (1989) 'The enlargement of the Dutch metropolitan complex', *Tijdschrift voor Economische en Sociale Geografie* (in press).

Wheeler, J.O. (1987) 'Fortune firms and the fortunes of their headquarters metropolises', *Geografiska Annaler*, 69B, 65–71.

Part 2

Strategic Developments for the 1990s

Introduction

Luiz Moutinho

Knowledge of the market and environment are fundamental to the processes of management. However, rapidly changing markets and increasingly complex and uncertain environments have been a feature of the 1980s. If managers are to be proactive, they need to be developing a knowledge base which will help them to predict future conditions and to plan their business strategies accordingly. Part 2 focuses on this requirement by identifying some of the approaches, analytical techniques and strategies that managers and marketers will need to consider in the 1990s.

The rate of growth in size and importance of the service sector has created problems which are only now being addressed. Managers in service firms often have backgrounds in the longer-established manufacturing sector, and even those who are familiar with service management methods have had to rely on imported management philosophies and techniques. Marketing organization is also different in service firms because of the need for close co-operation between line management and marketing functions in the design and delivery of services. This is an important theme in Part 2 which is developed in several chapters.

An effective services marketing strategy will have at least four characteristics. It will: be based on a detailed understanding of the market-place; exploit the key competencies of the organization; employ valid assumptions about environment trends and market behaviour; and offer a realistic basis for gaining and sustaining competitive advantage. A cohesive, integrated approach to the formulation of strategy also prevents the various functions within the organization from overlapping or conflicting with each other.

The intensification of competition, deregulation, technology transfer and innovation among other things has led to structural changes in the service sector. Consequently, service firms are having to develop their own mechanisms for responding to the agents of change, and this will be reflected in the design and delivery of services in the 1990s. As service firms seek new business and profit opportunities, the need for realistic and effective strategies will become more pressing, and the ability to manage change will increasingly differentiate successful firms from those that rely on more traditional reactive or passive policies.

Chapter 3

Marketing organization in service businesses: the role of the part-time marketer

Evert Gummesson

Introduction: The tale of the CEO and the organization hologram

Let me begin by telling a modern tale. Tales are frequently told at conferences, but then they are usually labelled 'research reports' or 'studies'; the annual reports of companies are sometimes modern versions of Hans Christian Andersen's *The Emperor's New Clothes*. This one I call *The Tale of the CEO and the Organization Hologram*.

It is about a man who created a service conglomerate. He is dynamic, well dressed and plays squash. On the rare occasions when he is free in the evening, he spends time in his cellar working on his vintage wine collection. Every weekend and holiday, or at least the more important ones like Christmas, he devotes solely to his family.

At the beginning of his career he managed all his own business affairs. He designed, manufactured, bought, sold and went to the bank to pay invoices. The company grew and he went public, first on the London Stock Exchange and soon afterwards on the New York and Tokyo exchanges. He went to executive training centres in the USA and Europe and was taught that he was not selling but marketing his services. He was taught how to split up the firm into profit centres, to organize matrices, to engender a corporate culture and to engage in business development, strategic management and telemarketing.

'The CEO cannot delegate,' said some of his MBAs whom he had been advised to employ by an executive search firm. 'Delegate?' pondered the CEO when playing with his new Apple Macintosh SE with a built-in 40 megabyte hard disk. 'These young whizzkids do not understand what keeps this company together. They are stuck in the narrow world of organizational boxes and specialization.'

He read a study from INSEAD, the prestigious international school for executives, which ranked key strategic marketing issues for the 1990s. It reported that issues on marketing organization ranked highly, particularly among service firms. 'Adapting the company structure to implement new market strategies', 'Creating a marketing culture throughout the organization', and 'Recruiting and retaining high-calibre marketing professionals' ranked numbers 2, 4 and 7 out of a total of 18 strategic marketing issues. 'Obviously I am not the only one with a problem,' he sighed.

He had begun to think about a solution. On a wall in his boardroom he had an oil painting of himself. He had the idea that if he replaced the painting with a holo-gram of himself, it would help him to adjust to the high-tech image of his company.

As you may know, holograms are three dimensional. 'Better than the matrix organization,' the CEO thought, 'which is just two dimensional. Better than our chartered accountants who are one dimensional,' he added with a wry smile.

But holograms have yet another quality, the CEO read in the accompanying instruction manual. 'If you take a holographic picture,' it said, 'and cut out a piece of it, you will get a new and complete picture.' In other words, each little piece of the hologram holds complete information about the whole picture.

'If I cut my oil portrait into pieces,' the CEO thought, 'each will only represent small fragments. One might show my nose, another part of my chin, a third a pimple on the neck.' But when he cut up the hologram he got a new picture of the whole of himself. All of a sudden he was two, then four, then sixteen, then two hundred and fifty-six, then sixty-five thousand five hundred and thirty-six, then . . .

'Imagine if my organization could have the characteristics of a hologram,' he said. 'Then I could duplicate myself, at least my spiritual self, so that each and every person understood the mission of my company and their part of the whole. They would be the bearers of a desired company culture that would provide a focus for the business and its customers. In essence every employee would be a microcosm of the company. I would not need the organizational chart that McKloskey & Company Management Consultants designed, and for which they invoiced £215,000 (plus copying costs). What I need is an organization hologram.'

With this vision in his mind, and the fact that marketing organization is so highly ranked as a strategic issue for the 1990s, the CEO went out to ask advice from the gurus of marketing. He went to universities in the UK and the USA, to 'the Nordic School of Services' in Sweden and Finland, to prestigious consulting companies, to IMEDE and INSEAD, to MSI and PIMS, to MCE and EIASM, to EMAC and AMA, even to the trendiest of advertising agencies.

The question is: Did he get any advice?

The purpose of this article is to make a modest contribution to resolving some of the CEO's concern.

Overview

The tale of the CEO provides the clues to the state of the art of marketing organization in service businesses.

In getting companies, and of late also governmental bodies, marketing orientated one has to abandon the belief that marketing can be left to a marketing department. The department can do certain things but not others. This is partic-ularly true in service businesses where marketing is embedded in the service production process of which the customer is also a part. Thus, in order to under-stand the marketing of services and to find an organizational solution, one has to understand both the general principles of service production and the unique characteristics of the specific service operation to be organized. There is a need for a total marketing orientation of the whole company, a marketing culture.

The mechanistic view holds that organizations could be structured around specialist functions and that these functions could be assembled into a functioning whole, just like different metal pieces are welded and bolted together to become an engine. In reality, companies work with processes that cut across hierarchical tiers and departmental boundaries. The interfaces are not, and never will be, clear. Responsibility is seldom given for a process as such, but only for a specific activity. Thus implementation becomes inefficient, leading to low productivity and unsatisfactory quality.

Organization theory provides limited assistance on marketing organization. It provides sets of general principles, but they are so general that their application to specific departments and functions is jeopardized.

This chapter suggests new approaches to organizing marketing in a service firm. It is an effort to conceptualize services marketing organization based on the unique features of the service production and delivery system. A central issue is the role of the full-time marketer vs the part-time marketer, and also the marketing opportunities created during the service production/delivery process, the points-of-marketing. This chapter presents the author's own conclusions, based on research as well as on practical experience.

The full-time marketer vs the part-time marketer

In service firms especially, only part of the marketing is handled by the marketing and sales department. In fact, the department is not able to handle more than a limited portion of the marketing, as its staff cannot always be in the right place at the right time with the right customer contact. This poses an organizational dilemma because the employees who produce and deliver services also carry out marketing activities for those services. In this situation, whether they are aware of it or not, responsibilities may be unclear or even confused (Gummesson, 1979, 309–13).

In order to make this dilemma manageable, I have distinguished between the marketing department (including sales) and the marketing function (310). The marketing department is the unit designed to work solely with marketing and sales activities: they are the full-time marketers. Such work is also carried out by external contributors, mainly distributors and consultants (e.g. advertising agencies and market research bureaux).

But all activities that influence customer relations and the generation of revenue are part of the marketing process. With this approach to marketing, members of top management as well as of all other departments of the company become part-time marketers (Gummesson, 1987, 1989). In fact it does not stop here. There are also external part-time marketers – customers, suppliers, trade unions, environmentalists and, of course, the media – who can reinforce our position in the market or weaken it, even destroy it. For example, McKenna (1985) states that by far the most important factor influencing corporate image and sales in the USA is the company's degree of financial success, which will be constantly evaluated by investors, banks and the financial press. Only those companies that are financially sound and that preferably top the league of growth and earnings will have credibility in the market. Although McKenna's experience relates to Silicon Valley firms, it has direct implications for services: when you buy a computer you want to be sure that the supplier will exist in the future and will provide spare parts, maintenance and new software.

So the marketing function includes full-time marketers as well as part-time marketers, and both can be internal as well as external. The distinction between the marketing department and the marketing function is relevant in any type of company, but in service businesses it is particularly important. Two examples will illustrate.

The first example concerns the marketing organization of a bank. The full-time marketers are those working in the marketing department. Their role may be limited to handling marketing research, advertising, sales promotion and part of the public relations. But marketing activities are also carried out part time by different organizational units at different levels. Marketing strategy can be designed by the board, the top executives, the 'product management' and the regional management. The sales force consists of those people who are in direct contact with customers, among them branch office managers and cashiers. However, with the exception of members of the marketing department, the staff are hired not for their marketing know-how but for their ability to produce the bank services.

Professional service firms – management consultants, accountants, architects, etc. – provide the second example. The professional tries to spend as much of his or her time as possible on service delivery, but has to allocate some time for contract negotiations. In smaller professional firms the marketing is handled by partners and senior professionals, and may often be seen as a nuisance that steals time from 'productive' work. In larger professional service firms, however, a specialized marketing and sales department may exist. This department has to include people who have had client service responsibilities, and thus have a gut feeling for the service production and delivery process. In order to get leads and introductions to prospective clients, information on competitors, etc., the department has to draw on the skills and contacts of the professionals who do not belong to the department.

For accounting firms ('CPAs'), Congram and Dumesic (1986, 66–8) suggest different combinations of the following five possible organizational positions:

- partner in charge of marketing representing the know-how of the production and delivery of auditing services (this may be a full-time or a part-time position);
- marketing director, with a background in services marketing, but not necessarily in auditing services;
- marketing co-ordinator, with a general background in marketing;
- marketing assistant, with some experience in administrative work;
- outside consultants, mainly used in a supportive role.

The first two are senior positions concerned with marketing strategy, planning and resource allocation, while the third and fourth are geared towards the implementation and monitoring of marketing programmes.

The most important part-time marketers, however, are likely to be, first, the accountants themselves who are in daily contact with clients and, second, the clients themselves and their referrals or non-referrals.

The last example is from the United States, but in some countries accountants and other professionals are not allowed actively to canvass clients. That means that they are even more dependent upon the external part-time marketers. Although the illustration relates to accounting firms, it may well give guidance to other professional service firms.

These two examples illustrate that service firms have full-time marketers but at the same time are heavily populated by part-time marketers; they have internal contributors to marketing as well as external ones. This has to be recognized by management as well as by each individual employee.

My conclusion is the following: what at first glance may be considered an organizational dilemma can be turned to an advantage: the fact that so many people in a service business have customer contact creates multiple chances to influence customers.

The remainder of this article will deal with the following issues. First, a brief description of the service production/delivery system will be made from the vantage point of the customer. The description is based on the customer's interaction with the service provider, and marketing opportunities are identified. Secondly, the impact of these interactions on the marketing organization is defined in terms of four types of part-time marketer. The chapter ends with views on emerging issues for the 1990s, implications for practitioners and a postscript.

Understanding the service production system

The product company has a sales force that is responsible for the direct contact with customers. Some service companies have sales forces as well, for example insurance companies. In services marketing, relationships and interactions arising from direct contact between the customer and the service provider are key phenomena. These face-to-face contacts, for example the contact between a waiter and the guest, are necessary in order to produce and deliver the service or part of it. Moreover, the customer partly consumes the service at the same time as it is produced and delivered. During this simultaneous production, delivery and consumption process, a number of natural marketing opportunities emerge and these must be recognized and utilized.

The direct contacts between the customer and an employee of the service firm are referred to as the *service encounters* or *moments of truth* (Carlzon, 1987; Petersen, 1988). IBM Canada, just 5 per cent of IBM world-wide but as big as the whole of Apple, started recently to identify their moments of truth (Myles, 1988). They asked themselves how many phone calls they received from customers. No one knew and no one knew what the calls were about and how they were handled. A study revealed that, in one year, ten million phone calls were made by customers! Moreover, six million of these calls were handled by non-salespeople, i.e. by part-time marketers.

The moments of truth refer to the customer's contact with a member of staff.

In order to emphasize marketing opportunities, I would like to include other types of contact as well and talk about *points-of-marketing*, defined as opportunities to influence the customer's present and future purchases. In order to identify the points-of-marketing, the service production system has to be fully understood by the service provider. Its characteristics are explained below.

Service production from the supplier's point of view: the degree of controllability

In my view the real difference between products and services lies in the way they are produced and delivered. In the goods manufacturing company, the environment – the factory – is highly controlled by the company. It employs the people, selects the machinery, designs the factory, etc., and the customer does not have to go to the premises. Service production is characterized by a lesser degree of controllability. The customer is involved in part of the production process, and the customer can range from a skilled co-producer to a complete amateur. The service is sometimes produced on the customer's premises where the service provider has little control over the environment (e.g. installing or repairing equipment, a doctor at an emergency site).

Service production from the buyer's point of view: the quality experience

I would like to suggest a division of the 'service product' into two distinctive elements:

- the service production and delivery process;
- the future benefits of the service to the customer.

Similar divisions have been discussed mainly in relation to quality of services (Grönroos, 1983; Lehtinen, 1985). The customer will judge the quality of the service and form an attitude towards the service provider both from experience of the process and from an assessment of the potential benefits. During this process, there are unique opportunities to influence the customer's present and future purchases by direct contact, utilizing the naturally occurring points-of-marketing.

Four types of contact and interaction occurring during the service production process are described below, each with specific points-of-marketing.

Interaction 1: Between the service provider's contact person and the customer

Examples of the interaction between a contact person and the customer are the interactions between a doctor and a patient, between an advertising agency and a product manager, and between a passenger and a flight attendant. The customer is a co-producer: if the customer does not co-operate – the patient does not take the prescribed medication, the product manager does not brief the ad agency properly, the air passenger does not appear at the gate on time – the services cannot be properly produced.

The quality of the service – the process as well as the future benefits – is often greatly enhanced if the service is produced in close and constructive interaction between a knowledgeable customer and the service provider. The contact is some-times extremely intense and intimate and includes risk for the customer, such as in surgery, in a divorce case, or in an investment decision. The shared experience can cement (or prevent) longlasting relationships. In other cases, such as taxi services and postal services, each service encounter can be trivial but, because of the repeated need for the services, they are perceived to be important by the customer.

All these contacts provide opportunities to influence the customer's percep-tion of the service. The customer may find the service provider friendly and pro-fessional, and may feel at ease – or the opposite. The experience of this contact can be totally decisive for future purchases and referrals to other customers.

Interaction 2: Between customers

Customers partly produce the service between themselves if the seller provides the right systems, the right environment and the right staff. An obvious example is a dinner dance. If the customers refuse to dance with each other, there will be no service produced; if the setting is right the customer will be stimulated to co-produce high-quality services and will come back as well as recommend the place to others. Customers who line up in front of a box office, travel business class or listen to a concert interact and jointly influence the image of the service provider and the perceived quality.

The choice of customers becomes important as a market segmentation factor, for example business travellers and tourists occupying different sections in the aircraft, or a law firm accepting only business firms as clients. The overt inter-actions between customers are sometimes non-existent, for example when the service is carried out on the customer's premises, such as cleaning services. On the other hand, the waiting time for a service may be dependent upon the other customers and the number of them that want the service at the same moment. This is particularly significant for emergency services: down time of computers can keep a whole factory still; the rapid delivery of security services could be a matter of life or death.

The interaction between customers should therefore be considered in the design of the marketing strategy as well as in the design of the production system: customers who fit together reinforce the positive experience and the image of the service supplier.

Interaction 3: Between the customer and the provider's physical environment

The physical environment includes buildings, machinery and furniture. In a super-market, for example, the positioning of the merchandise, the way it is displayed and the attractiveness of the premises, including such things as the car park, influence the buyer's purchases. The marketing director of a hamburger chain stated that his most important marketing staff are the group of architects who design the restaurants. They influence the visibility of the restaurant through the architecture of the building and the signs, attract the desired customer segment through the right interior decoration and affect the number of customers that can be seated through an optimal layout of tables and chairs. The physical access is important: is the service operation conveniently located for the customer and are the opening hours right? The physical environment is also perceived as evidence of the price class and of the professionalism of the service provider.

The term *ergonomy* is used to emphasize the significance of 'harmony' in the man–machine interface, but it has to my knowledge primarily been used as a term that identifies work hazards for employees. Companies seem to have viewed this as a problem of employee relations rather than as a vehicle for increasing productivity, quality and profits. The term is now being replaced by *human factors engineering*, which sees the interface in a wider perspective and also attaches increased importance to it.

Interaction 4: Between the customer and the provider's systems and routines

The interaction between a customer and the service provider's systems and routines is as important as the person-to-person and man–machine interaction: for example, the taxpayer and the taxation system, the credit card user and the system for credit clearance, the checking-in and checking-out procedure at a hotel, the way of ordering tickets for a theatre.

From a marketing point of view, systems should be customer friendly. Security, the ease of access to the system and the know-how needed to enter the system are some of the important features. Systems may scare away customers and make them avoid the services even if they need them. Part of marketing may be educational, informing and training the customers to use the system to their advantage.

Designed-in marketing

In the preceding paragraphs four types of interaction have been identified. These are unique to the way that services are produced and delivered. In these inter-actions, marketing opportunities – points-of-marketing – exist either through direct or through long-term influence on sales: we want to sell now but we also want to maximize customer retention and create positive word-of-mouth.

The customer's style of participation is important, particularly in the most intense phase of the service production/delivery (Lehtinen, 1985), as well as the seller's ability to design and produce the service so that the contribution from the buyer becomes a good one. The customer should feel welcome and find the provider responsive to customer needs. (Some customers are not nice though, which adds an extra burden to the contact person's job.)

The importance of prevention and designed-in quality is stressed by the literature on quality management. It is also stressed in the suggested approaches to the design of services (Shostack, 1981; Dale and Wooler, 1989; George and Gibson, 1989). In a similar vein, the service production/delivery process is actually designed-in marketing. The more marketing is built into the service production/delivery process, the less you have to worry about the marketing organization: the major part of the marketing is already prepared for at the design stage.

From marketing management to marketing-orientated management: four types of part-time marketer

Who in the marketing organization influences the interaction and who can act upon the points-of-marketing?

As the marketing function is spread throughout the service company, it is essential that the whole organizational structure is supportive to marketing. In service firms particularly there is extreme interdependence between traditional departments – production, delivery, personnel, administration, finance, etc. – and marketing. Therefore, it is more appropriate in the service firm to talk about *marketing-orientated management* than to use the traditional label 'marketing management'.

An example of an organization that is based on marketing-orientated management, thus giving total support to marketing, is Scandinavian Airlines System, SAS (Carlzon, 1987). The airline went through a major turnaround into a customer-orientated company in the 1980s. From being loss making it went into the black within one year, and it has remained there. A basic change was that the organizational structure was turned into a structure that supports excellence in customer relations.

The old SAS organization suffered from several deficiencies that hampered customer contact and the continuing adjustment to market needs. The organizational structure was centred around the technology of operating and maintaining aircraft. Further, there was one-way communication from management down the organization and thus neither the experience of front-line staff nor customer reactions were fed back to decision makers. The passenger became a residual in the system, maybe even a nuisance.

To get rid of these deficiencies, an organization was introduced which identified the roles of the customer (who was promoted from the bottom of the organizational pyramid to the top), front-line personnel, support personnel and company management. Each of these four roles contains part-time marketing activities. The last three may include full-time marketers as well, but these will not be dealt with here.

Part-time marketers 1: Customers

The customer is part of the production/delivery process; this has been clearly pointed out in the above description of the interactions. As a participant in the production process, the customer could be seen not only as a part-time marketer but also as a part-time employee, sometimes even a part-time supervisor.

The role of the customer as part-time marketer is often carelessly handled. In a recent study by the management consulting firm Arthur D. Little (Krauss, 1988), it was revealed that the average business does not hear from 96 per cent of its unhappy customers, and 65 to 90 per cent of those will not go back to the same company. This, of course, is a major problem as the suppliers will not know what they have done wrong and will repeat the same mistake. But the consequences for part-time marketing are even more alarming: customers who have a complaint tell on average nine or ten other people; 13 per cent tell twenty or more; and those who had their complaint resolved tell five people on average. The results are not surprising and confirm earlier studies, but they clearly indicate the customer's key role as a part-time marketer.

Part-time marketers 2: Front-line personnel

In the discussion relating to the interaction between front-line personnel and the customer, it was established that direct contact creates natural points-of-marketing. But front-line personnel also play an indirect role in marketing. For example, in the design of the service production/delivery system, new service development and the redesign of existing services their hands-on experience of the process means that they can help in giving advice and ideas, suggesting improvements and testing new ways of operating. In marketing research, the contact person learns about customer attitudes, behaviour, needs and complaints.

Part-time marketers 3: Support functions/back office

Each service organization needs support functions, sometimes referred to as the back office. These are people that give support to the production/delivery process but are usually invisible to the customer: they work in the kitchen of the restaurant, they service the car rental company's vehicles, they maintain the computer systems. Their jobs are essential both to the front-line staff and to the customer.

The support staff therefore primarily influence the external customer via internal customers, the front line. The staff should be supportive in the right sense; unfortunately all too often that support turns into administration and middle management, taking away decision power from the front line, and complicating and delaying matters.

Part-time marketers 4: Company management

The role of company management should be concentrated on strategic issues, company policy, the provision of resources and other long-term and structural issues. The behaviour of contact personnel, the interaction between customers, the physical environment and the systems can be changed only partly by the front line and the support functions. The task of management becomes that of providing a platform for the front line and the support functions, based both on the know-how of these two categories and on other conditions such as company mission and long-term goals. Management should delegate authority and make sure that the conditions of operating are known throughout the organization. This requires communication up and down the hierarchy. If the communication chains are broken, the company will end up with unworkable policies, weak support and missed marketing opportunities.

Emerging issues for the 1990s

The basic theme throughout this chapter has been that marketing activities, particularly in a service company, are ubiquitous in the organization, they are part of the company culture. Let me now give some reasons why service organizations, private as well as public ones, have to show more muscle in the market in the future.

First, it is already a fact that services, including the public sector which, in the Western world, is almost exclusively a service producer, account for the larger share of the GNP in industrialized countries – usually 60 to 70 per cent. Thus it is obvious that efficiency in service production and marketing affects the wealth of a nation. The current wave of privatization is a consequence of the fact that governments, both central and local, have failed in providing the services they have been appointed to handle. However, the quality of services rendered by private companies is highly variable and the need to develop service production and marketing practices is just as essential there as it is in the public sector.

Secondly, services are little traded as compared to products, especially on the international arena. Export of services is different from export of goods: internationalizing a service operation could mean selling a concept through a franchise or a licence, it could mean importing the customer as is the case in tourism. One example is Japan. The 1970s meant a breakthrough for Japanese products on the world market. Japan became market leader in cars, motorcycles, cameras, colour televisions and a long range of other products. Quality, productivity and aggressive marketing were key factors in building their market position. We seem, however, to close our eyes to the fact that the same thing is now happening in services; it has already occurred in financial services. Out of the ten largest banks in the world, seven are Japanese. Tokyo is the largest stock exchange, followed by New York and then Osaka. Japanese companies account for 23 per cent of the banking assets and 40 per cent of the international business in the City of London (Pauli, 1987, 74). Not only will the Japanese increase their international trade of services, but it is likely to grow everywhere. An efficient marketing organization is necessary to meet these challenges.

Thirdly, the service infrastructure is developing, making it possible to trade services more efficiently, more freely and in different ways then previously. Cheap and powerful computers, telefax and other types of information technology are part of this infrastructure. So is the fact that the Common Market opens borders for the free movement of capital and people, making it easier to expand a service operation overseas.

Fourthly, innovative organization solutions for service firms are emerging around the world. Sadly, satisfactory research on marketing organization is almost non-existent: the only book I know which deals specifically with marketing organization is by Piercy (1985). Companies as well as public authorities should be alert to new approaches to service production and service marketing. This will require rethinking of their traditional organizational designs.

Summary: implications for practitioners

How does the approach to marketing organization presented in this chapter affect the practitioner? In order to apply the approach properly, one has to know the specific characteristics of the service operation to be organized: the production of the service, the type of customer, the competition, etc. Let me, however, summarize the approach into general guidelines for marketing organization.

A service firm should consider the following nine issues in order to take advantage of the points-of-marketing:

(1) The customer should be seen as part of the organization.
(2) The front-line staff should know the mission of the firm but should not be curbed with unnecessary and stifling regulations. They need freedom to make those decisions that can be made only in the service encounter, and they should be used as points-of-marketing.
(3) The hands-on experience of the front line and the support units should be valued. They should be stimulated to make suggestions, receive assignments and make quick decisions. Fancy solutions based on reports and research are unnecessary: let loose the knowledge within the organization.

The next two issues concern the full-time marketers:

(4) The respective fields of marketing superiority of the full-time and part-time marketers should be identified.
(5) When the need for full-time marketers has been established, one or several marketing departments could be created.

In order to utilize the opportunities of the part-time marketers, who may form the core of the service company's marketing:

(6) Employees should be recruited who have the potential to take on the role of part-time marketer as well as the professional role of their core job.

(7) They should be trained to understand their role in influencing customer relationships.
(8) They should be motivated to strengthen customer relationships and to use sales opportunities.
(9) The service production/delivery system should be designed to support marketing activities.

Finally, let's see how the CEO conceived his organizational problem after his study tour.

Postscript

When the CEO returned from his grand tour of the marketing gurus we were lucky to catch him stepping out of his executive jet at Heathrow Airport.

'Did you get advice concerning your vision of the organization hologram?' we asked.

'To a degree,' said CEO. 'I have learnt about the significance of the part-time marketer in the service organization. I have learnt that it is essential that marketing opportunities, the points-of-marketing, are considered in the design of the service production and delivery system. I have noted the role of the external marketers, particularly the customers. I didn't, though, find very much in the conventional research and education or textbooks that enlightens me. I wonder why that is so?'

With this unanswered question – which echoed against a Concorde and disappeared into the London Tube where it is still echoing about – the CEO indicated that the interview was over and he boarded his executive helicopter for a quick ride to his new Docklands office.

References

Carlzon, J. (1987) *Moments of Truth*. Cambridge, Mass.: Ballinger.
Congram, C.A. and Dumesic, R.J. (1986) *The Accountant's Strategic Marketing Guide*. New York: Wiley.
Dale, A. and Wooler, S. (1990) 'Strategy and organization for service: a process and content model', in Brown *et al.* (eds.) *Quality in Services—Multidisciplinary and Multinational Perspectives*. Lexington, MA: Lexington Books.
George, W.R. and Gibson, B.E. (1990) 'Blueprinting: a tool for managing quality in services'. In Brown *et al.* (eds) *Quality in Services: Multidisciplinary and Multinational Perspective*. Lexington, Mass.: Lexington Books.
Grönroos, C. (1983) *Strategic Management and Marketing in the Service Sector*, Cambridge, Mass.: Marketing Science Institute.
Gummesson, E. (1979) 'The marketing of professional services: an organisational dilemma', *European Journal of Marketing*, 13, 5, 308–13.
Gummesson, E. (1987) 'The new marketing: developing long-term interactive relationships', *Long Range Planning*, 20, 4, 10–20.
Gummesson, E. (1989) 'The part-time marketer', Department of Business Administration Working Paper, University of Stockholm.
Krauss, C.G. (1988) 'Customer satisfaction: a bottom line performance indicator',

in Surprenant, C. (ed.) *Add Value to Your Service*. Chicago, Ill.: American Marketing Association.

Lehtinen, J.R. (1985) 'Improving service quality by analyzing the service production process', in Grönroos, C. and Gummesson, E. (eds) 'Service marketing: Nordic School perspectives' Research Report R 1985: 2, Department of Business Administration, University of Stockholm.

McKenna, R. (1985) *The Regis Touch*. Reading, Mass.: Addison-Wesley.

Myles, D. (1988) 'Think customer: the IBM-Canada way', Presentation made at the American Marketing Association's 7th Annual Services Marketing Conference, Arlington, Va., October.

Pauli, G.A. (1987) *Services: The Driving Force of the Economy*. London: Waterlow.

Petersen, K. (1988) *The Strategic Approach to Quality Service in Health Care*. Rockville, Md.: Aspen.

Piercy, N. (1985) *Marketing Organisation*. London: George Allen and Unwin.

Shostack, L.G. (1981) 'How to design a service', in Donnelly, J.H. and George, W.R. (eds) *Marketing of Services*. Chicago, Ill.: American Marketing Association.

Chapter 4

Retailer marketing organizations: strategic development for the 1990s

Nigel Piercy and Neil Morgan

Overview

Less than two decades ago 'marketing' was deemed by organizational analysts to be a function not relevant to the analysis of retailing organizations (Pugh, 1970) since it was seen as a manufacturer's activity. However, in the course of the intervening years there have been a number of significant environmental and competitive changes which largely invalidate that earlier conclusion. It is clear that in the late 1980s 'marketing' has emerged as a dynamic activity in retailing organizations in the UK, and one which is increasingly organized as a formal function. It is the implications of this change with which we are concerned in this chapter.

However, before proceeding to evaluate the pressures which have led to increased attention to marketing issues in marketing, there is some need to lay down an initial framework of definition for the meaning of marketing as a management area. Although this is far from straightforward, a conceptual framework we have used before to describe marketing issues (Piercy, 1986) is one which distinguishes between:

- *marketing strategy*, concerned with issues of market definition and positioning, market segmentation, competitive differentiation and the mission or strategic direction;
- *marketing programmes*, concerned with integrating around market targets decisions in the areas of product policy, pricing, communications (advertising, personal selling, sales promotion, public relations), with a goal of achieving consistency in the customer's terms;
- *marketing information*, concerned with evaluation for planning and control.

If this is accepted as a description of the marketing issues facing an organization, then it follows that the marketing management task is that of managing such issues, i.e. marketing strategy or positioning, the resulting marketing programmes and marketing informational resources. It is then frequently assumed that the logical way to administer the marketing process is to create a formal organizational structure for this purpose. In fact, there are many who would challenge the validity of this assumption (see Piercy (1985) for a review of this question). However, it will be seen that large UK retailing organizations do seem to have gone through a process of establishing formal marketing organizations in recent years. This development has a number of managerial implications both for retailers and for the manufacturers who supply them.

Before considering these organizational phenomena and their managerial consequences, it is worth discussing some of the external changes in the retailing environment and situation in the UK which underpin the emergence of marketing as a formal activity.

Trade channels in the UK, in common with most of the developed countries (Hollander, 1970; Waldman, 1968), have manifested a growing and often extreme degree of concentration (see, for example, Bamfield, 1980; Davies *et al.*, 1984; Hawes and Crittenden, 1984). While this concentration has mainly been tracked as a determinant of buying and negotiating power for retailers, the implicit corollary is that of greater end-market control.

The indicators of this development are various. We may note first the intensification of competition between major retailers, and the growth in retailer own-brands and generic brands (Rushton, 1982; Knee and Walters, 1985). Similarly, it has been suggested that retailers have in recent years placed much greater emphasis on the proactive use of pricing and advertising as marketing weapons (Richards and Smeddy, 1985). This has been associated with the development of formal marketing strategies and marketing programmes, by the multiple retailers in particular, emphasizing retailer-led marketing based on such strategies as selective price reductions, retailer-orientated advertising campaigns and value-added forms of competitiveness (Davies *et al.*, 1984).

The result is that, while traditionally retail organizations in the UK have been found to be largely reactive at the level of marketing strategy (Walters, 1979), and to be preoccupied with tactical issues of merchandising and selling (Moyer, 1983), more recent observations suggest the growth in formalized strategic planning by retail firms (Davies and Gilligan, 1985).

Indeed, a recent study of the problems confronting UK retailers, as those problems are perceived by senior retailing executives, identified the major perceived problem areas as: the competitive environment; the customer environment; other aspects of the external environment; the labour force; general management and marketing strategy; and manufacturer relationships (Greenley and Shipley, 1987). This last study highlighted the need to improve the 'fit' achieved between retailers' offerings and consumers' requirements, and the power and leverage in achieving this 'fit' provided by the type of sophisticated, marketing-led competitive differentiation and specialized market positioning achieved by companies like Body Shop, Habitat and Mothercare.

One implication of such findings is the anticipation that such activities as strategic planning and marketing would be likely to become formally organized in retailing organizations as a result of such pressures from the competitive environment and the consequent need to develop increasingly sophisticated marketing strategies.

In this context, three further points should be made by way of overview. First, it should be noted that the formalization of marketing in retailing has historically proved problematic for retailing organizations because of the very nature of retailing as a services activity (Fram, 1965; Arnold *et al.*, 1983; Berman and Evans,

1986). Indeed, it may well be that we should avoid the temptation of assuming that the manufacturer model of marketing is appropriate for adoption by services companies anyway (Grönroos, 1989).

Certainly, a recent study of the way in which marketing is formally utilized by UK retailers was somewhat equivocal in its findings (Greenley and Shipley, 1988). This study found that, while many of the large retailers investigated claimed to attach a high importance to marketing, this rating was apparently neither high enough nor widespread enough to amount to a formal, systematic implementation of the marketing concept in the UK retailing sector. For instance, the study findings suggested that, although executives considered corporate and store image to be of primary importance to their companies' success, the promotional mix variables relevant to creating and maintaining such images were seen as relatively unimportant. Similarly, while executives stressed the importance of the retail 'product', there was scant evidence of the existence of any systematic marketing approach to making consistent product policy decisions.

To some extent these last findings may reflect the inertia and resistance to organizational change which might be anticipated in established companies with extant cultures and traditional 'ways of doing things'. None the less, there is probably also merit in avoiding the trap of assuming that marketing is likely to operate in retailing and other service organizations in ways directly similar to how it is presumed to operate in the manufacturing sector. Indeed, our empirical knowledge of the operation of marketing in manufacturing is anyway relatively scant, and there are suggestions that this may, in any case, be a wholly inappropriate bench-mark for marketing in services (Grönroos, 1989).

Secondly, it should be noted that many have suggested that the real issues in implementing marketing in organizations are concerned more with the 'organizational software' of managerial 'philosophy', culture, values and attitudes than with the formal organizational and administrative arrangements for marketing: the 'substance' versus 'trappings' argument (Ames, 1970; Pearson and Wilson, 1967).

To some extent this point has merit. It is possible, for instance, to point to notably successful retailing organizations in the UK where little or no formalization of marketing has taken place. However, the existence of a chief marketing executive and the verification of marketing functions have frequently been taken as an indicator of the implementation of the marketing concept (Weigand, 1961; Hise, 1965; Carson, 1968; Hayhurst and Wills, 1972; Piercy, 1986). In fact, these precedents enjoy some greater merit than might be thought. For instance, we have recently been able to uncover empirically links in financial services organizations between the formalization of marketing and variables like corporate values and marketing effectiveness, to suggest to executives an agenda of 'hard' variables (formalization of marketing) to be managed to shape and change the 'soft' variables of key corporate values and cultural attributes (Piercy and Morgan, 1989).

Thirdly, it follows from the last point that the formal organization of marketing may be associated with and indicative of much more than simply administrative convenience in managing these customer-related activities. We have suggested elsewhere (Piercy, 1985) that the implicit significance of the organization of marketing lies in three dimensions:

- structures ultimately reflect the strategies adopted by an organization, and signify to participants the strategic values given high priority by the company (Corey and Star, 1971) and the identity of the powerful forces in the organization (Pfeffer, 1981);
- structure may actually *be* strategy, in the sense that the way a company organizes its customer-related activities can be a potent source of competitive differentiation (Levitt, 1980);
- the organization structures adopted reflect a company's enactment or understanding of its markets, and hence the structure of its information processing system and flows of intelligence (Piercy, 1985; Piercy and Evans, 1983).

Such dimensions of organization suggest that the way a company organizes for marketing is indicative of far more than simple administrative arrangements.

In particular, the agenda suggested by this chapter includes the issues of how retailers may organize marketing to reflect their growing involvement in creating and managing proactive marketing strategies in the channel of distribution, the 'internal marketing' problems of acting on manager and operative behaviour to implement strategies successfully, and the information management problem of sensitizing executives to new sources and types of information about their markets and customers.

The organization of marketing in retailing

This part of the chapter presents some analysis of the results of a relatively simple enquiry into the status and functioning of marketing as a formalized function in major retailing organizations in the UK. We examine the way in which marketing departments have been formed, and the diversity in their functioning. We have attempted to put our findings into the context of retailer control of marketing strategy in the channel of distribution, although to achieve this we have only perceptual data from the retailers, with all the limitations that this implies. The study is relatively novel, in that we are not aware of any directly comparable works, but that said it is no more than exploratory in nature. We present essentially the insights gleaned from a first view of a set of emerging phenomena, and the further hypotheses we wish to test, rather than conclusive findings.

A number of recent theoretical contributions (Weitz and Anderson, 1981; Ruekert *et al.*, 1985; Piercy, 1985) have pursued the early view that the formal organizational unification of marketing functions under a chief marketing executive (CME) is a valid test of the implementation of the marketing concept (Weigand, 1961; Hise, 1965; Carson, 1968; Hayhurst and Wills, 1972). As noted earlier, however, this is not incompatible with the suggestion that the implementation of marketing requires change in organizational 'substance' not 'trappings' (Ames, 1970; Pearson and Wilson, 1967), i.e. managerial philosophy and attitude towards marketing rather than simply organizational structure.

The focus of the present study is none the less on the formal organization of marketing in large UK retailing firms and, in spite of the last comment above, this remains to some extent a conceptual and methodological limitation which has some practical significance: for example, retail firms widely perceived as successful at 'marketing' in the UK have until very recently not commonly had formal organizational structures for marketing (Piercy, 1984).

The major source of this present enquiry lies in the argument, advanced elsewhere (Piercy, 1984), that one aspect of the development of large-scale retailing and high levels of concentration in the retail sector is that, in addition to changes in other power characteristics of the channel (Anand and Stern, 1985), the power to make strategic marketing decisions is in the process of moving down the channel of distribution from the manufacturer to the retailer, and that this is reflected in the development of specialized marketing organizations in retailing companies.

In fact, the role of the formal marketing function in retailing has been the focus of very little empirical analysis in the UK, or indeed more generally in other countries. While there have been a number of studies of the status of marketing in particular service industries, for example in banking (Stall, 1978), postal services (Barnhill, 1974), public utilities (Warshaw, 1976) and public transport (Hovell, 1974), and there have also been more general surveys of marketing in the service industries, both in the USA (George and Barksdale, 1974; Upah, 1980) and in the UK (Hooley and Cowell, 1985), there has been almost no explicit attention to retailing. Indeed, in these service industry studies, especially in the former group and implicitly in the latter group, the retailing of consumer products has been excluded from consideration.

The approach in this present study was adapted from earlier studies of manufacturer marketing organizations (Piercy, 1986), but it was extended to attempt to evaluate the perception by retailers of relative control of critical marketing issues in the channel of distribution by the retailer as opposed to the manufacturer. It is here also that the present study is relatively unconventional.

There is a broad literature relating to power relationships and the emergence of conflict in the channel of distribution and the participation of distributive firms in the strategic management of the channel of distribution, for example as recently reviewed in Cron and Levy (1986). However, the approach in this present study was not to attempt to evaluate the sources of retailer power, or the direct effects of perceptions of conflict, but to attempt to relate the organizational characteristics of retailer marketing to perceived retailer control of the elements of marketing strategy in the channel. Implicity, the frame of reference is closer in source to the 'structure follows strategy' thesis (Chandler, 1962; Corey and Star, 1971) than to the traditional analysis of channel relationships, in the sense that we are hypothesizing a relationship between the formal organization of marketing in retailing and the marketing strategies pursued by retailers.

The specific hypotheses we sought to test were essentially two. First, we anticipated that on the basis of their responsibilities, size and maturity there would be a number of different types of marketing department in retailing:

> H1 – There are a variety of forms of marketing departmentation in retailing organizations.

Secondly, we anticipated that the form of marketing departmentation would reflect the marketing strategy adopted by retailers, in terms of their view of their own role in channel marketing compared to that of manufacturers:

> H2 – The strength of marketing departmentation in retailing is related to the perceived control by the retailer of marketing strategy in the channel of distribution.

The research study

Methodology

This study examined the areas of responsibility of chief marketing executives (CMEs) and marketing departments in retailing companies, and their perceived control over marketing strategies in the channel of distribution. The descriptive results of the survey are reported in Piercy and Alexander (1988) and are briefly summarized below.

The methodological background of the survey is discussed further in the appendix to this chapter, but broadly the data were collected in 1986 in a postal questionnaire of CMEs in seventy of the largest retail organizations in the UK. The seventy companies included represent in sales turnover some 15 per cent of the total UK retail market. The survey was, it should be noted, restricted to companies with a marketing organization of some kind already in place.

The research design is limited in a number of ways which should be made explicit. First, we have argued elsewhere (Piercy, 1985) that the organization of marketing is contingent on both environmental and organizational factors, and here we consider only the former. Secondly, it is likely that each of the major retailers in this study will deal with a mix of significantly differentiated suppliers – large and small, UK and foreign, heavy and light branders, and so on. We have made an assumption that the supplier mix is approximately the same for all the firms in the study. To the extent that this assumption is invalid then the results regarding channel strategies may be undermined. Thirdly, our study is restricted to the perceptions of retail managers, rather than attempting less subjective measurements or taking measurements throughout the channel system. These assumptions are to be validated in the later stages of the research, and are noted at this point as limitations to the generality and possibly to the validity of our present findings.

The operationalization of the responsibility variables used a checklist adapted from earlier studies (Hayhurst and Wills, 1972; Piercy, 1986). The question items and the scales are shown in Table 4.1. The variables display an acceptable degree of variance to permit further analysis. The channel strategy variable items and scale are shown in Table 4.2.

Reliability and validity

Before examining the results of the study, we should consider the value of the measuring instruments which were used to capture marketing department responsibilities and channel strategy, since these involved the construction of index scores to reduce the raw data.

To derive measures of retailer marketing department responsibilities, the variables scores were factor analysed, as shown in Table 4.3. Those variables loading on to the factors with a coefficient greater than 0.5 were used to construct additive scales: product and pricing policy (R1), marketing services (R2), corporate strategy (R3), and marketing communications (R4).

Adopting the Sellitz *et al.* (1976) argument that the reliability of a measurement procedure requires the estimation of the amount of variation attributable to random errors, the Cronbach alpha coefficient was used to evaluate reliability (Cronbach, 1951). Taking Nunnally's threshold of acceptable reliability as an alpha coefficient of 0.5 or greater, these scales satisfy the reliability criterion as shown in Table 4.5. To evaluate the validity of the operationalization, each scale item was correlated with the index itself. The correlation coefficients were in the expected direction, were significant at the 0.001 level and were high enough to overcome the autocorrelation objection. This suggests a strong measure of validity, in the sense of the scale items contributing to the concept that the total index was designed to measure.

The same evaluation procedure was taken towards the channel strategy variables, which were factor analysed as shown in Table 4.4 to identify factors of product strategy (CS1), promotional strategy (CS2), pricing/merchandising strategy (CS3), and logistics/market research (CS4).

These tests of reliability and validity are shown in Table 4.5, and they suggest that the measures are reasonably robust.

Results

The descriptive findings of the summary have been reported elsewhere (Piercy and Alexander, 1988), but they may be summarized as follows:

- In the sample studied, virtually *all* the firms had formal marketing departments. This limits the representativeness of the findings to large retailers with marketing departments, but given the nature of the sample it does also suggest a fairly high penetration of formalized marketing into large-scale retailers in the UK.
- Most of the retailer marketing departments are small (fewer than ten employees), but in the majority of companies marketing department size is increasing.
- Most of the marketing departments are relatively new: more than half had been established for less than five years at the time of the survey.
- In spite of this recency, retailer marketing departments were typically seen as enjoying status equal to or higher than more traditional departments.

Table 4.1 *Variable response frequencies: chief marketing executive responsibilities*

	Level of CME responsibilities						
	Sole (%)	Major (%)	Equal (%)	Some (%)	None (%)	N/A (%)	
V11 Advertising	51	38	3	8	–	–	(N = 65)
V12 Sales promotion	47	38	6	9	–	–	(N = 64)
V13 Price setting	19	19	14	22	26	–	(N = 64)
V14 Selling operations	10	8	21	34	27	–	(N = 62)
V15 Negotiations with suppliers	21	11	3	30	29	6	(N = 63)
V16 Sales forecasting	10	22	21	35	11	1	(N = 63)
V17 Marketing research	66	21	5	6	2	–	(N = 65)
V18 Marketing planning	49	40	6	5	–	–	(N = 65)
V19 Product selection and buying	15	22	11	22	27	3	(N = 64)
V20 Own-brand decisions	19	28	17	6	14	16	(N = 64)
V21 Selection of store sites	2	11	22	22	33	10	(N = 63)
V22 Stock levels	4	14	8	25	47	2	(N = 64)
V23 In-store merchandising	17	32	21	17	5	8	(N = 63)
V24 New product launches	22	42	9	8	10	9	(N = 64)
V25 Investment appraisal	3	9	30	28	24	6	(N = 64)
V26 Diversification studies	9	23	33	11	16	8	(N = 64)
V27 Marketing staff selection	62	34	2	1	1	–	(N = 65)
V28 Marketing training	46	34	11	5	2	2	(N = 65)
V29 Corporate/strategic planning	5	47	28	11	9	–	(N = 64)

Table 4.2 *Variable response frequencies: channel strategy*

	Channel strategy					
	Supplier's decision (%)	Supplier's decision in consultation with retailer (%)	Joint decision between manufacturer and retailer (%)	Retailer's decision in consultation with supplier (%)	Retailer's decision (%)	
V108 Advertising products to consumers	17	7	7	20	49	(N = 59)
V109 Sales promotions	–	5	23	38	34	(N = 60)
V110 Price levels	2	–	5	30	63	(N = 62)
V111 Price cutting	–	–	7	32	61	(N = 62)
V112 Merchandising in-store	–	–	3	30	67	(N = 61)
V113 Launch of new products	10	7	13	38	32	(N = 60)
V114 Development of new products	27	14	26	21	12	(N = 58)
V115 Branding and brand images	36	14	5	17	28	(N = 58)
V116 Packaging design	39	9	7	16	29	(N = 56)
V117 Transport and stockholding	3	3	15	21	58	(N = 62)
V118 Market research	7	5	19	9	60	(N = 58)

Table 4.3 *Factor analysis[1] of chief marketing executive responsibilities*

CME responsibility factor labels	CME responsibility variables	Factor loadings[2]			
		1	2	3	4
Product and pricing policy (R1)	V19 Product selection and buying	0.91			
	V13 Price setting	0.83			
	V15 Negotiations with suppliers	0.79			
	V20 Own-brand decisions	0.77			
	V22 Stock levels	0.63		0.31	
	V16 Sales forecasting	0.55	0.49		
	V24 New product launches	0.55	0.43		
	V23 In-store merchandising	0.47	0.31		
Marketing services (R2)	V17 Marketing research		0.82		
	V28 Marketing training		0.74		
	V27 Marketing staff selection		0.70		
	V18 Marketing planning		0.70		
Corporate strategy (R3)	V29 Corporate/strategic planning		0.30	0.76	
	V25 Investment appraisal			0.75	
	V26 Diversification studies			0.66	
	V21 Selection of store sites			0.59	
Marketing communications (R4)	V11 Advertising				0.84
	V12 Sales promotion				0.81
	V14 Selling operations				0.51
Eigenvalues		5.76	2.84	2.08	1.46
% of variance		29	14	10	7

1 Principal components analysis with varimax rotation, converging in 8 iterations.
2 Loadings of less than 0.3 are suppressed.

Table 4.4 *Factor analysis[1] of channel strategy variables*

Channel strategy factor labels	Channel strategy variables	Factor loadings[2]			
		1	2	3	4
Product strategy (CS1)	V116 Packaging design	0.86			
	V114 Development of new products	0.84			
	V115 Branding and brand images	0.78			0.31
Promotional strategy (CS2)	V109 Sales promotions		0.82		
	V108 Advertising products to consumers		0.77		
	V113 Launch of new products		0.58		0.40
Pricing merchandising strategy (CS3)	V111 Price cutting			0.87	
	V110 Price levels		0.43	0.74	
	V112 Merchandising in-store			0.34	
Logistics/ market research (CS4)	V117 Transport and stockholding				0.83
	V118 Market research				0.67
Eigenvalues		3.91	1.57	1.08	1.00
% of variance		35.5	14.3	9.8	8.9

[1] Principal components analysis with varimax rotation, converging in 6 iterations.
[2] Loadings of less than 0.3 are suppressed.

Table 4.5 *Scale statistics*

Scale	No. of items	Mean	Cronbach alpha	Inter-item correlating							
				1	2	3	4	5	6	7	8
R1	8	2.76	0.75	0.90	0.86	0.78	0.82	0.67	0.66	0.71	0.49
R2	4	4.35	0.74	0.73	0.84	0.72	0.71				
R3	4	2.56	0.86	0.75	0.82	0.72	0.66				
R4	3	3.66	0.59	0.67	0.81	0.75					
CS1	3	2.81	0.88	0.90	0.86	0.88					
CS2	3	3.84	0.70	0.79	0.86	0.74					
CS3	3	4.56	0.60	0.79	0.83	0.54					
CS4	2	4.21	0.50	0.82	0.86						

Table 4.6 *Cluster analysis*[1]

Variables/scales	Clusters				Total sample (N = 55)	Kruskal-Wallis one-way analysis of variance	
	1 (N = 21)	2 (N = 9)	3 (N = 17)	4 (N = 8)		Chi-square	Significance
CME responsibilities							
R1 Product and pricing policy	3.73	2.22	1.85	1.67	2.76	44.63	0.0000
R2 Marketing services	4.60	4.48	4.59	2.81	4.35	22.23	0.0001
R3 Corporate strategy	2.98	3.44	1.84	1.50	2.56	36.99	0.0000
R4 Marketing communications	4.00	2.74	3.73	3.66	3.66	17.33	0.0006
Cluster labels	Integrated/full-service marketing departments	Strategy/planning marketing departments	Communications/services marketing departments	Limited staff role marketing departments			
Marketing department size							
Marketing employees/no. of stores(%)	15.29	4.38	13.02	4.66	12.57	5.24	0.1551
Marketing employees/total employees(%)	0.88	0.40	0.53	0.34	0.65	3.11	0.3744
Marketing employees/sales space (000 ft²)(%)	0.032	0.001	0.002	0.001	0.02	8.31	0.0401
V8 *Marketing department growth*[2]	2.70	3.00	2.41	2.13	2.58	13.15	0.0043
V3 *Marketing department age* (years)	8.9	2.9	7.3	7.8	7.8	7.53	0.0555
V6 *CME status*[3]	2.40	2.38	2.06	2.13	2.26	5.45	0.1414
V54 *Marketing orientation*[4]	2.70	2.78	2.29	2.63	2.59	6.17	0.1034
Channel strategy							
CS1 Product strategy	2.65	3.20	2.71	3.10	2.81	0.77	0.8578
CS2 Promotional strategy	3.58	3.94	4.27	4.05	3.84	7.59	0.0552
CS3 Pricing/merchandising strategy	4.49	4.76	4.58	4.57	4.56	2.53	0.4704
CS4 Logistics market research	4.19	4.14	4.31	4.36	4.21	0.57	0.9044

1 Clustered using Ward's Method.
2 Scored as 1 = decreasing in size; 2 = stable; 3 = increasing in size.
3 Scored as 1 = CME has lower status; 2 = CME is equal in status; 3 = CME is higher in status; than other functional heads.
4 Scored as 1 = We buy from what is available and sell to whoever will buy; 2 = We place a major emphasis on advertising and promotion to ensure sales; 3 = We place a major emphasis on prior analysis of markets and consumer needs and adapting our product mix to meet them, if necessary.

Turning to our analysis of the survey data, to evaluate the first hypothesis the CME responsibility factors were used to cluster the companies into four groups, as shown in Table 4.6. The non-parametric Kruskal–Wallis one-way analysis of variance was used to evaluate the significance of the cluster differences. The responsibility factor scores suggest that the sample shows evidence of four significantly different types of retailer marketing organization.

The first group was labelled 'integrated/full-service marketing departments'. These departments scored highest on three of the four responsibility factors (product and pricing policy, marketing services and marketing communications), as well as scoring relatively high on the fourth (corporate strategy). The profile data in Table 4.6 suggest that these departments were the oldest in the sample, that their CMEs had higher status than in other companies and that these marketing departments were the largest in staffing terms.

The second group was the 'strategy/planning marketing departments'. This group had the highest level of responsibility for corporate strategy (R3) and also scored relatively high on marketing services (R2), but it scored relatively low on product and pricing policy (R1) and marketing communications (R4) responsibilities. These were the newest of the marketing departments in the study, and the smallest – although still growing. The CMEs in this group had high status and marketing orientation was at its highest.

The third group was labelled 'communications/services marketing departments', reflecting their high scores on R2 and R4, and relatively low scores on product and pricing policy and corporate strategy. These departments were, however, large in staffing terms. The fourth group was 'limited/staff role marketing departments', with low scores on all factors except marketing communications (R4), and these were small in staff numbers.

Combining the responsibility factor scores and departmental size data, it is possible to produce the type of stereotypical model shown in Figure 4.1.

On the basis of these exploratory analyses, it is suggested that the first hypothesis – that there are a number of forms of marketing departmentation in retailing – should be accepted.

However, the link between the marketing department types and the perceived control of channel marketing strategy by retailers is less clear. The mean scores for the channel strategy factors shown in Table 4.5 generally do not display significant differences between the clusters or department types. The only exception is promotional strategy (CS2) where there is some difference at a low significance level. It is perhaps notable that the integrated/full-service marketing departments have the lowest score on each channel strategy factor, while the strategy/planning marketing departments have the highest scores for product strategy (CS1) and pricing/merchandising strategy (CS3). Similarly, it may be noted that the communications/services departments have the highest score for promotional strategy in the channel.

Such a qualitative analysis of cluster differences leads to the hypothetical model in Figure 4.2. Far from supporting the notion that the greater the integration of the retailer marketing department the greater the retailer's control of channel strategy, the model suggests that the most integrated departments are *least* in control of channel marketing strategy.

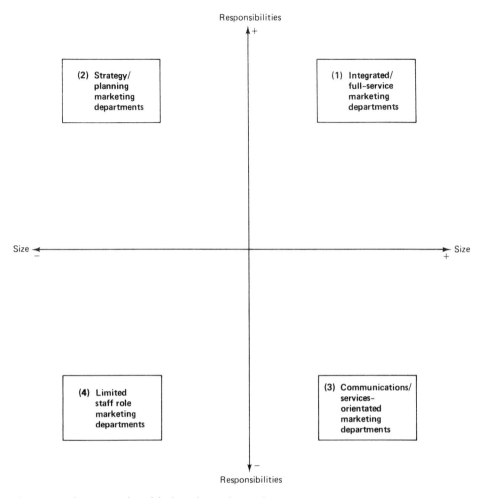

Figure 4.1   Stereotypical model of retailer marketing department types

There are a number of alternative hypotheses which could explain this phenomenon. First, it may be that the formation of the integrated retailer marketing department is a response to manufacturer marketing dominance and thus departmentation lags behind channel control. Secondly, it may be that, where the retailer takes a proactive role in channel marketing, this decision making is absorbed by another part of the organization – possibly general management – rather than the marketing department. Indeed, it may simply be that for a number of reasons executives in the integrated retailer marketing departments are unwilling to concede the reality that they control channel marketing. Such issues are the subject for further investigation, but for the present we do not find in these particular data even weak support for our second hypothesis in this study.

The closest support we did find for the hypothesis is that the communications/

Retailer marketing departments

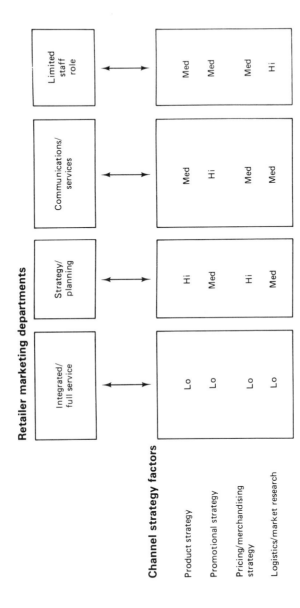

Channel strategy factors	Integrated/ full service	Strategy/ planning	Communications/ services	Limited staff role
Product strategy	Lo	Hi	Med	Med
Promotional strategy	Lo	Med	Hi	Med
Pricing/merchandising strategy	Lo	Hi	Med	Med
Logistics/market research	Lo	Med	Med	Hi

Figure 4.2 Hypothetical model of retailer marketing department types and control of channel strategy

services-orientated departments perceive themselves as controlling promotional strategy in the channel, and the strategy/planning departments see product strategy and pricing/merchandising strategy as retailer dominated. However, this support is self-evidently relatively weak.

The other evidence available is presented in Table 4.7, showing a significant correlation, for the whole sample, between R1 (CME product and pricing responsibilities) and CS2 (promotional strategy in the channel), and between product strategy in the channel and the size of the retailer marketing department in terms of employee numbers (V7). This promotes some partial support for the hypothesis, in the sense that a higher perceived control by retailers of these dimensions of channel strategy is associated with one key retailer marketing department responsibility and the size of that marketing department.

Table 4.7 *Correlations*[1]

	CME responsibilities				Channel strategy factors			
	R1	R2	R3	R4	CS1	CS2	CS3	CS4
R2	0.19							
R3	0.45**	0.20						
R4	0.28	0.24	0.15					
CS1	− 0.09	0.07	0.05	0.03				
CS2	0.45**	0.05	− 0.14	0.04	0.54**			
CS3	− 0.11	0.04	0.00	− 0.24	0.18	0.21		
CS4	− 0.21	0.17	0.06	− 0.06	0.44**	0.46**	0.15	
V7[2]	0.10	0.09	0.13	0.17	0.36*	0.15	− 0.11	0.23

[1] Spearman rank correlation coefficients.
[2] V7 = Marketing department size (no. of employees).
*Significant at 0.01 level.
**Significant at 0.001 level.

Conclusions

While the research reported above is essentially exploratory and permits only tentative conclusions, we have demonstrated the existence of formal marketing departmentation in a significant number of large retailing organizations in the UK, and incidentally that this a relatively recent phenomenon. However, the simple existence of departmentation is insufficient to uncover the real role of the marketing department in retailing. Adopting the approach developed in our earlier marketing organization studies, we used the responsibilities of the chief marketing executive as a mechanism for differentiating the operations of a number of types of marketing department. It was thus possible to identify marketing departments as 'integrated/full service', 'strategy/planning', 'communications/services orientated' and 'limited staff role' and to associate these organizational forms with different corporate characteristics like department size, status and so on. This led to the proposal of a stereotypical model of retailer marketing departments. The first hypothesis that there are a number of forms of marketing departmentation in retailing was supported.

What proved more problematic was the testing of our second hypothesis that the strength of the formalized marketing developed in the retail firm can be associated with retailer dominance of marketing strategy in the channel of distribution. The data showed only weak relationships between the forms of marketing departmentation adopted and the channel strategy factors identified. The hypothetical model suggested by the exploratory data available would suggest rejection of the hypothesis. The only significant support came from the relationship between the marketing department's product and pricing responsibility and departmentation size, the perceived retailer control of promotional and product strategy in the channel.

At best we have only limited support for the second hypothesis, and it seems that the organizational response by retailers to a proactive role in channel marketing is more complex than that hypothesized.

Emerging issues for the 1990s

The marketing issues partially uncovered can be grouped into two broad categories: first, those issues which are primarily concerned with external relationships for retail firms, in the sense of how changing relationships with manufacturers and competitors may be reflected in internal marketing structures; and secondly, a related set of issues concerned with the internal organizational changes faced by retailers in adopting and developing retailer marketing.

External relationships

At one level, the work has a number of implications for the management and development of retailing organizations, through the description of the way in which marketing has been departmentalized in large-scale retailing in the UK. In this sense the findings offer a bench-mark both for retail management in the UK and for those in other countries who may be interested in comparative studies of the issues raised.

While the data discussed here do not provide a valid base for a prescriptive model of the departmentation of marketing, they do offer some new insights. Certainly the stereotypical model in Figure 4.1 provides an interesting diagnostic instrument for retail executives to use in evaluating the present role of marketing in their companies and how this may be developed. The notion that retailer strategies of controlling marketing in the channel of distribution are reflected in the formal organization of marketing in these companies is only weakly supported by the present study, but it is certainly not abandoned.

If we follow the Chandler (1962) argument that structure follows strategy only in the event of some organizational trauma – i.e. when there is effectively no choice – or the Greiner (1972) notion of a succession of 'revolutions' in the process of organizational evolution, then the uncertainty and complexity identified is reasonable and worthy of further study.

While the diagnostic value of the summary findings has practical application, it is clear that some considerable uncertainty surrounds the formation of formal marketing organizations in retailing. It seems likely that the way to removing this uncertainty will lie in clarifying the catalysts to the departmentation of marketing: the changing marketing environment, the impact of new information technology, the resolution mechanisms for the conflict in the channel and the marketing strategies adopted by retailers and manufacturers in the channel.

It is hoped that this present study may contribute to the process of making explicit some of the alternative scenarios which exist for manufacturer–retailer marketing relationships, and thus the types of choice which are faced in developing marketing strategy and structure. For example, a preliminary framework for analysis is suggested in Figure 4.3.

This framework suggests a distinction between three possible scenarios for channel relationships, along the lines of the model provided here: manufacturer marketing dominance, joint decision making and retailer marketing dominance. The hypothesis is that it is this scenario which links together the form of organization of marketing at the retailer and manufacturer levels of the channel of distribution. For example, in the manufacturer-dominated channel environment, the existence of a limited degree of marketing by the retailer (focusing on the traditional merchandising approach) is associated with limited retailer marketing departmentation but high integration of marketing in manufacturing. Alternatively in this channel environment, a high degree of marketing structure at both ends of the channel is associated with confrontation and conflict for control.

On the other hand, we hypothesize that in the retailer-dominated channel, the low-integration marketing department in manufacturing will either be required to service retailer needs for marketing services, or may even disappear entirely and be replaced by the integrated marketing department at the retail level.

It is these hypotheses that we now seek to test in the next stages of the research, involving a more complex research design taking measurements at both ends of the same channel and controlling for environmental variables.

For the present, the major interest lies in these further hypotheses which have been generated and which provide the foundation for further studies in this area, extending the approach outlined in this chapter where we have sought to explore the relationship and to legitimatize the variables before proceeding further.

Internal organizational issues

Related to the developments above is set of issues concerned with the degree to which the successful implementation of marketing in retailing companies may require more than the formation of formal organizational units. It was argued earlier that organizational structures may have symbolic as well as substantive or task-orientated implications. However, the services literature shows many cases where this has proved insufficient to change executive and operational behaviour in the direction suggested by marketing strategies.

A number of those working in the services marketing field have arrived at the concept of 'internal marketing' as a necessary addition to the creation of formal, externally orientated marketing (Berry, 1981; Grönroos, 1985; Gummesson, 1987;

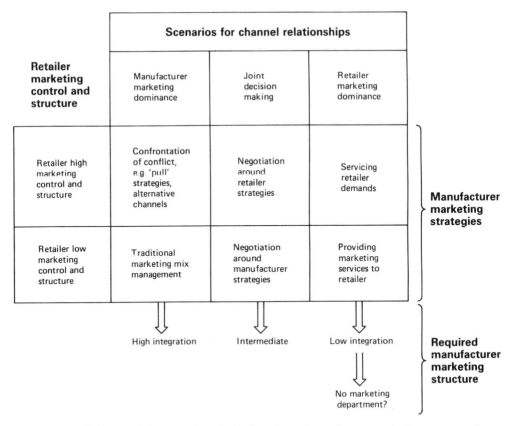

Figure 4.3   A framework for strategic analysis of retailer and manufacturer marketing strategy and structure interactions

Piercy and Morgan, 1990). The goal here is to apply the same tools and techniques to the internal market-place of employees and managers as we do to the external customer market-place. This internal marketing effort should directly parallel and reinforce the conventional marketing strategy, but is concerned with influencing those who actually create value at the point-of-sale.

We have summarized this approach in the framework shown in Figure 4.4, as a basis for discussion with executives (Piercy and Morgan, 1990). The model has attracted interest both for its application in developing appropriate staff development programmes to reinforce the direction of marketing strategies and also as a framework for empowering marketing 'change agents' in those companies essentially paying no more than lip service to marketing. The adoption of the internal marketing model seems likely to be a key issue for retailers, as it is proving to be in other service sectors.

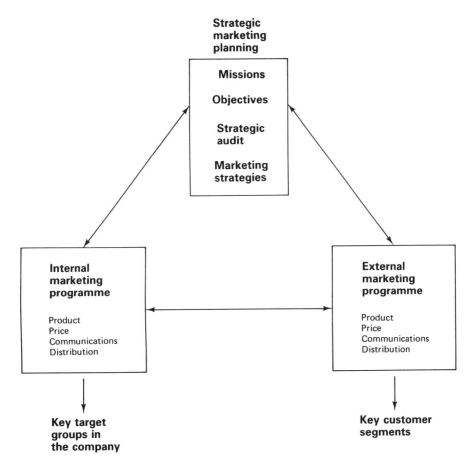

Strategic
marketing
planning

Missions

Objectives

**Strategic
audit**

**Marketing
strategies**

**Internal
marketing
programme**

Product
Price
Communications
Distribution

**External
marketing
programme**

Product
Price
Communications
Distribution

**Key target
groups in
the company**

**Key customer
segments**

Figure 4.4   Internal marketing

Discussion

We have attempted initially in this chapter to review some of the pressures on retail companies to adapt to new and growing demands from the environment, which together imply the need for the development of more formal approaches to marketing than have traditionally been required by retailers. However, we also saw that there were certain barriers and obstacles to the adoption of marketing structures drawn from the manufacturer model. Certainly, there seems some reason to suppose that the form of marketing structure most useful to retailers might be rather different from that adopted by manufacturers. Accepting that formal retailer marketing in the UK is very much a phenomenon of the 1980s, it is a job for the executive to decide the most appropriate time at which to respond to the pressure described, and the form that responses should take.

Our research study uncovered four stereotypical models of structural response, as a basis for analysing the current position of marketing in a retail company and for tracking at least some of the possibilities for evolving marketing in retailing. We were less successful in demonstrating that the development of formalized marketing structures in retailing was a response to retailer control of marketing strategy in the channel of distribution, although some supporting evidence was found.

The broad issues which emerged from the study were twofold. An urgent issue is to address the implications of retailer–manufacturer relationships for the location and structuring of marketing. It is certainly apparent that this is the key contingency faced in designing marketing organizations for the future both for manufacturers and for retailers. We have attempted to track some of the possible scenarios as a basis for discussion by channel participants.

Finally, we turned away from the 'trappings' to the 'substance' of marketing, and highlighted the growing interest in internal marketing in services firms, as a model to be addressed by retailers. This issue is of interest both to those facing the task of achieving effectiveness for new marketing organizations in retailing and to those lacking formal structure position and resource control. The internal marketing model offers the prospect of acting on the values, attitudes and cultures to bring them more closely into line with strategic goals.

If we believe in the importance of service quality in retailing, and in the significance of product market positioning to attach key market segments, then we must address the interrelated issues of tracking structure and culture in retailing.

Appendix: survey methodology

This first stage of the study consisted of some six depth interviews around the issue of the development of the marketing function in UK retail firms. These interviews were with the chief marketing executive where a marketing department existed, and with the chief executive in the other cases.

From these qualitative results a postal questionnaire was generated and tested. The model for the operationalization of the variables was the earlier studies of manufacturer marketing organization, and these instruments and their validation are discussed elsewhere (Piercy, 1986).

The postal survey was carried out in the period of January–April 1986 with the initial mail-out followed by a postal reminder and then a telephone reminder. In a small number of cases the questionnaire was completed through a telephone interview rather than respondent self-completion.[1]

The main sampling units were chief marketing executives in those cases where a marketing department existed. In other cases the approach was to the chief executive. In fact, the vast majority of responses (more than 80 per cent) were from CMEs, and none of the responses was from a retailer without a formal marketing department. The survey was limited to one response from each organization.

The sample was made up of the 277 largest retailing organizations in the UK, identified using a number of directory sources. A total of seventy usable responses were collected, giving a response rate of 25.3 per cent. It is believed that retailers without formal marketing departmentation chose not to reply.

The product market classification of the sampling frame and the sample is shown in Table A.1, and the differences are not considered significant. The sample is regarded in this respect as reasonably representative of large-scale retailers in the UK with marketing departmentation. The seventy companies included in the sample in total represent 15 per cent of total retail sales and 16 per cent of total retail employment in the UK.

The questionnaire is available from the authors to those who may be interested in the possibility of collaborating in replicative or comparative studies.

Table A.1 *Product market classification*

	Sampling frame (%)	Sample (%)
Grocery	26	32
Clothing	18	20
Others	59	48
	(N = 277)	(N = 70)

Chi-square = 5.6 with 5 d.f.

[1]Grateful acknowledgement should be made of the help of Nicholas Alexander in this stage of the work. He was then Research Assistant in Marketing and Strategy at Cardiff Business School.

References

Ames, B.C. (1970) 'Trappings versus substance in industrial marketing', *Harvard Business Review*, July/August, 93–102.

Anand, P. and Stern, L.W. (1985) 'A sociopsychological explanation for why marketing channel members relinquish control', *Journal of Marketing Research*, 2 November, 365–76.

Arnold, D.R., Capella, L.M. and Smith, G.D. (1983) *Strategic Retail Management*. London: Addison–Wesley.

Bamfield, J.A.N. (1980) 'The changing face of British retailing', *National Westminster Bank Quarterly Review*, May, 33–45.

Barnhill, J.A. (1974) 'Developing marketing orientation in a postal service', *Optimum*, 3, 36–47.

Berman, B. and Evans, J.R. (1986) *Retail Management: A Strategic Approach*. New York: Macmillan.

Berry, L.L. (1981) 'The employee as customer', *Journal of Retail Banking*, 3, 1, 271–8.

Carson, D. (1968) 'Marketing organization in British manufacturing firms', *Journal of Marketing*, 32, April, 34–9.

Chandler, A.D. (1962) *Strategy and Structure*. Cambridge, Mass.: MIT Press.

Corey, E.R. and Star, S. (1971) *Organization Strategy: A Marketing Approach*, Boston, Mass.: Harvard University Press.

Cron, W.L. and Levy, M. (1986) 'Participation in marketing channel function and economic performance', *International Journal of Physical Distribution*, 14, 6, 17–55.

Cronbach, L.J. (1951) 'Coefficient alpha and the internal structure of tests', *Psychometrika*, 16, 297–334.

Davies, K. and Gilligan, C. (1985) 'Changing retailing structures: the implications for marketing education', *Business Education*, 6, 1, 22–9.

Davies, K., Gilligan, C. and Sutton, C. (1984) 'The changing competitive structures of British grocery retailing', *Quarterly Review of Marketing*, 9, Autumn, 1–9.

Fram, E.H. (1965) 'Application of the marketing concept to retailing', *Journal of Retailing*, Summer, 19–26.

George, W.R. and Barksdale, H. C. (1974) 'Marketing activities in the service industries', *Journal of Marketing*, 35, Fall, 65–70.

Greenley, G. and Shipley, D. (1987) 'Problems confronting UK retailing organisations', *Service Industries Journal*, 7, 3, 353–64.

Greenley, G. and Shipley, D. (1988) 'An empirical overview of marketing by retailing organisations', *Service Industries Journal*, 8, 1, 49–66.

Greiner, L.E. (1972) 'Evolution and revolution as organizations grow', *Harvard Business Review*, July/August, 97–105.

Grönroos, C. (1985) 'Internal marketing: theory and practice', in T.M. Bloch, G.D. Upah and V.A. Zeithaml (eds) *Services Marketing in a Changing Environment*. Chicago, Ill.: American Marketing Association.

Grönroos, C. (1989) 'A relationship approach to marketing of services: some implications in Proceedings: European Marketing Academy Conference, Athens.

Gummesson, E. (1987) 'Using internal marketing to develop a new culture', *Journal of Business and Industrial Marketing*, 2, 3, 23–28.

Hawes, J.M. and Crittenden, W.F. (1984) 'A taxonomy of competitive retailing strategies', *Strategic Management Journal*, 5, 275–87.

Hayhurst, R. and Wills, G.S.C. (1972) *Organizational Design for Marketing Future*. London: Allen and Unwin.

Hise, R.T. (1965) 'Have manufacturing firms adopted the marketing concept?', *Journal of Marketing*, 29, July, 9–12.

Hollander, S. (1970) *Multinational Retailing*. Michigan: Michigan State University Press.

Hooley, G. and Cowell, D. (1985) 'The status of marketing in the UK service industries', *Service Industries Journal*, 5, 3, 261–72.

Hovell, P.J. (1974) 'Some organizational problems facing the marketing function in metropolitan passenger transport executives', in R.J. Lawrence (ed.), 'Marketing as a Non-American Activity', Proceedings: Marketing Education Group Conference.

Knee, D. and Walters, D. (1985) *Strategy in Retailing: Theory and Application*. Oxford: Philip Allan.

Levitt, T. (1980) 'Marketing services through differentiation – of anything', *Harvard Business Review*, 58, 1, 83–91.

Moyer, M.S. (1983) 'Marketing planning in retailing: making the basics work', in Proceedings: Marketing Education Group Conference, Cranfield, Beds.

Pearson, A.E. and Wilson, T.W. (1967) *Making Your Marketing Organization Work*. New York: National Association of Advertisers.

Pfeffer, J. (1981) *Power in Organizations*. Marshfield, Mass.: Pitman.

Piercy, N. (1984) 'Retailer marketing: informational strategies', *European Journal of Marketing*, 17, 6, 5–15.

Piercy, N. (1985) *Marketing Organization: An Analysis of Information Processing, Power and Politics*. London: Allen and Unwin.

Piercy, N. (1986) 'The role and function of the chief marketing executive and the marketing department', *Journal of Marketing Management*, 1, 3, 265–90.

Piercy, N. and Alexander, N. (1988) 'The status quo of marketing in UK retailing organizations: a neglected phenomenon of the 1980s'. *Service Industries Journal*, 8, 2, 155–75.

Piercy, N. and Evans, M. (1983) *Managing Marketing Information*, Beckenham: Croom Helm.

Piercy, N. and Morgan, N. (1989) 'Corporate culture, the formalization of marketing and marketing effectiveness', in Moutinho, L. (ed) *Marketing Audit of the 1980s*.

Proceedings: Marketing Education Group Conference, Glasgow.

Piercy, N. and Morgan, N. (1990) 'Internal marketing: strategies for implementation and change', *Long Range Planning* (forthcoming).

Pugh, D. (1970) 'The structure of marketing specializations in their context', *British Journal of Marketing*, Summer, 98–105.

Richards, J. and Smeddy, P. (1985) 'The retail market: the non-property view', *Retail Report 1985*. London: Healey and Baker.

Ruekert, R.W., Walker O.C. and Roering, K.J. (1985) 'The organization of marketing activities: a contingency theory of structure and performance', *Journal of Marketing*, 49, Winter, 15–25.

Rushton, A. (1982) 'The balance of power in a marketing channel: profitable cooperation of manufacturers and retailers', in Proceedings: ESOMAR Conference, Brussels.

Sellitz, C., Wrightman, L.S. and Cook, S.W. (1976) *Research Methods in Social Relations*. New York: Holt Rinehart and Winston.

Skinner, S.J. and Guiltinan, J.P. (1985) 'Perceptions of channel control', *Journal of Retailing*, 61, Winter, 65–88.

Stall, R.B. (1978) 'Marketing in a service industry', *Atlanta Economic Review*, 28, 3, 15–18.

Upah, G.D. (1980) 'Mass marketing in service retailing: a review and synthesis of major methods', *Journal of Retailing*, 56, Fall, 59–76.

Waldman, C. (1968) *Strategies of International Mass Retailers*. New York: Praeger.

Walters, D. (1979) 'Plotting retail strategies', in Proceedings: PTRC Summer Meeting, University of Warwick.

Warshaw, M.R. (1976), 'Re-appraising public utility marketing', *University of Michigan Business Review*, May, 18–22.

Weigand, R.E. (1961) 'Changes in the marketing organization in selected industries, 1950–1959', unpublished PhD thesis, University of Illinois.

Weitz, B. and Anderson, E. (1981) 'Organizing the marketing function', in *AMA Review of Marketing*. Chicago, Ill.: American Marketing Association.

Chapter 5

Services and information technology: emerging patterns

Ian Miles[1]

Overview

Despite the traditional view of services as labour-intensive, unindustrialized sectors of the economy, certain service sectors of the economy are in fact the main users of information technology (IT). Indeed, such services may often be the most advanced users, in terms of pioneering the use of computer networks and related systems to achieve new or more intensive information flows within and between organizations.

This is not a phenomenon restricted to the specialized IT-based services, such as those actually devoted to supplying software and new telecommunications services (VANS, etc.), although these services certainly are important in furthering the development of IT. There are good reasons to believe that other service users of IT are also often major IT producers. They may not manufacture physical IT hardware, but these services undertake a great deal of their own in-house software and system development. What is more, they are frequently involved in the upstream hardware design process (as in the case of banks seeking to define their requirements for automated teller machines and electronic funds transfer systems).

The use of IT by services has major implications, then, both for the future development of services and for the speed and direction of the 'IT revolution' itself. But research has so far focused overwhelmingly on manufacturing industry's use of IT, and the services' role remains neglected. This chapter discusses the problems researchers confront in gaining purchase on these developments, and on the host of issues associated with them. Drawing on an extensive critical review of data sources that bear on IT activities, it outlines some data sources and identifies methods of analysis that are proving useful in this effort. The chapter illustrates this work with results that lead on to the the development of some conclusions for services sector researchers and practitioners.

Black boxes in black bags

It has long been recognized that services are a Cinderella sector. Their growing social and economic importance has not met with commensurate attention on the part of official statisticians or social scientists, nor with much effort from policy makers. (Much industrial and regional policy has explicitly excluded services from its scope, although this position has become increasingly untenable.) While research interest in services took off in the 1980s – as this volume indicates – statistical sources covering services remain impoverished. While we are waiting for the deliberations of the United Nations Statistical Office – and, closer to home, the Business Statistics Office – to result in service statistics approaching the levels of disaggregation available for manufacturing sectors of the economy, researchers (and any policy makers wishing data on which to base or evaluate their programmes) remain in some difficulty.

Services are still very much a 'residual' category in economic analysis and official statistics. Less politely, the service category has been described as a 'dustbin' into which awkward products and sectors are thrown. This has become increasingly embarrassing not only because of the growth in share of output and employment accounted for by services, but also since many of the most buoyant, and possibly the most strategic, branches of the economy find themselves hidden away within catch-all categories with names like 'miscellaneous business services n.e.s.'. Data on services are frequently simply not produced – the invaluable Census of Production, for instance, fails to cover them – and often, when service firms are surveyed, the detailed information is obscured within the post-industrial dustbin: a black bag.

The use of new technology by services is a topic that poses an additional statistical dilemma. Not only are services relatively underresearched, but also new IT challenges established statistical categories. If services are bundled away into a black bag, IT is a set of black boxes as far as statistics are concerned. First, there is no consensual definition of IT: it is common to find all sorts of electronic equipment lumped together as IT, whether or not these are really 'new'. Sometimes traditional optical technologies (e.g. photography – not fibre optics!) and even print technology are included within the IT category. Many data sources indiscriminately merge data on valve and transistorized equipment together with the latest generations of IT.

But the widespread diffusion of new computer and communications technologies reflects the dramatic reductions in cost and size, and the increases in power, applicability and reliability, that have been associated with new IT. This had hinged on the development of integrated circuits and microelectronics. The miniaturization of these 'heartland components' has made low-cost, robust, efficient, fast and highly powered information processing available for a wide variety of economic applications. No longer are all computers vast room-filling devices, requiring special cooling systems and needing to be tended by legions of specialized professionals. No longer are they tools whose huge expense and unwieldly operations mean that they are reserved for huge number-crunching exercises in large-scale administration and process control. Computers have become personal, and, indeed, portable; they are cheap and user friendly enough to be used in front offices and in occasional applications. New IT has the potential of being applied to all sectors and all types of work since information processing of one type or another is constitutive of economic activity. As many services feature information processing very prominently, they may be expected to be major IT users. The first services to use computers may well have been those in which large-scale and repetitive arithmetical operations were necessary – for example, banking and insurance – but they can be expected to have diffused to many more services in recent years. How far can available data sources be used to throw light on the use of IT?

There are several shortcomings that characterize most data. In parallel with the emphasis of industrial data sources on manufacturing, when it comes to IT products we find that computer and telecommunications equipment are better documented than computer and telecommunications services. Likewise the production and diffusion of hardware is better reported than that of software. Official data tend to deal with value (expenditure) data, which neglect the increase in IT power. And where data are in volume rather than value terms, they tend to focus on items of hardware (i.e. 'stand-alone' systems) rather than on the networks and linkages between them. However, despite these problems, there are useful things that can be done with existing data – and it is surprising that application of these data has been attempted so rarely.

This chapter presents some results from my attempt to see just how much the available data can tell us about services and IT, which is part of a wider effort undertaken at the Science Policy Research Unit (SPRU) under the rubric 'Mapping and Measuring the Information Economy'. (Fuller details are provided in Miles *et al.* (1990).) Available data are sadly limited. However, they do provide some indications for further analysis, and accordingly this research is now leading to the production of new statistics. As we shall see, they do also throw light on the important role of service sectors as users of most types of new IT, and as producers of some types of IT. (For a study of new IT-based telecommunications services, see Thomas and Miles (1989).)

Mapping the diffusion of IT

Cross-sectoral survey research

Where a phenomenon is relatively rare and unfamiliar, as in the early years of computer use (and even now where we are concerned with relatively uncommon applications of IT), there is little to be gained from surveying a large population in which the phenomenon occurs in very few instances. Thus, in some cases it is justifiable to study the relevant IT users only, rather than seeking to study the whole population (in which non-users may predominate massively). In the mid-1960s and early 1970s, for example, the Department of Employment (1965, 1972) was carrying out surveys of users of computers in offices. These are interesting studies, not least for the demonstration that banking and financial services were the dominant users of office computers over twenty years ago. Indeed, in 1972 the top three user sectors were all services (public administration and defence, distributive trades, and financial services). The forecasts of computer usage for coming years contained in these reports, and the details of the establishment of data processing (DP) installations, and of the working conditions in them, also make fascinating reading.

Lists of major users (large computer installations, often mainframe computer based and thus atypical of the large number of microcomputer-using establishments) are currently generated by several organizations, more as a resource for computer and software suppliers than for academic researchers! Analyses of samples of such major IT users are presented by, for instance, the National Computing Centre in its *Information Technology Trends*, which depicts a range of important developments in the organization of IT use among such large users. Another useful source here is Price Waterhouse's annual Information Technology Survey. In part this user-based approach reflects the fact that the widespread diffusion of computer technology is relatively recent; in part it signifies also that for many research purposes a focus on the (relatively rare – perhaps only around 10,000 in the UK) large computer installations is appropriate. Research at SPRU pursues this sort of approach in some recent studies of IT in the UK: for instance, in a survey of software activities (production and use of software, and employment of related staff) among large computer users in all sectors (Brady, 1989) and a survey of private videotex systems (Jagger, 1989). In these studies, services again emerge as important in IT activities, but the statistics do not tell us directly about how important IT is within these sectors, for we are not dealing with the whole membership of the sectors.

With the wider diffusion of IT, many cross-sectoral surveys now cover users and non-users alike. But service sectors are unfortunately not included in most of the detailed studies of IT use. The Census of Production in 1986 obtained data on computer-related expenditure and employment, and the same questions are intended to be asked every few years, but, as noted above, services are excluded from this survey to date. (One interesting result of an analysis of these 1986 data is confirmation of the expected high correlation between levels of IT investment and levels of professional IT employment: high levels of use of computers require high levels of skilled staff, and we can expect this to be mirrored in services.) Turning to non-official sources, the surveys that the Policy Studies Institute has conducted over the past decade – whose results were recently published as *The Impact of Microelectronics* (Northcott and Walling, 1988) – cover only manufacturing. (Even within this, they effectively exclude the use of most office IT in manufacturing the British Industrial Computing Surveys, whose results are published in *Industrial Computing*, do pay much more attention to office-type applications, while being similarly orientated to manufacturing.)

Input–output tables and IT accounting

One official source does, however, allow for comparison of investment and consumption across all sectors of the economy. This is the set of input–output tables, currently produced on a five-yearly basis. The 1984 tables were published in spring 1988.[2]

As might be feared from earlier comments, input–output data in the UK present services in far less disaggregated detail than manufacturing. This reflects the history of national accounts statistics, which were established before services had attained their current dominant role in the economy. It limits the usefulness of the input–output tables as a basis for comparing services to other sectors, for analysing service activities in any detail and for assessing trends in these sectors. In the 1979 tables, of 100 branches of the economy, only twelve are services – and within these transport is disaggregated into four varieties while importantly different activities like 'post and telecommunications' and 'banking, finance, insurance, professional and business services, hiring' are treated as bedfellows. The 1984 tables do distinguish post from telecommunications, and other improvements give us some fourteen services (out of about 100 economic sectors): distribution, etc.; hotels, catering, etc.; railways, road transport, etc.; sea transport; air transport; transport services; postal services; telecommunications; banking and finance; insurance; business services, etc.; other services; public administration, etc.

Input–output tables can provide a picture of IT-related purchases by the various sectors of the economy – if we can define IT-related purchases as being purchases of the output of certain IT-producing sectors of the economy. Bearing in mind the caveats that (especially for earlier periods) the data are liable to contain some non-IT output under what is largely an IT sectoral heading, and that some areas omitted below may well produce new IT products and components within their products (e.g. aerospace), three branches seem to be most relevant: 43 – office machinery and computer equipment; 47 – telecommunications, etc., equipment, electronic capital goods; 48 – electronic components and subassemblies. For this study, sectors 43 and 47 will be considered the IT-producing sectors. These are the sectors whose products are devices for manipulating and communicating information. This definition of the IT-producing sector and its products will be labelled 'IT(def. 1)', in recognition of the fact that other definitions of these sectors may be desirable for some purposes, and that this indicator is inherently limited.[3]

Let us consider some results of an analysis of these figures. First, IT(def. 1) fixed capital investment was approximately 8.5 per cent of total fixed capital formation for 1984. Total investment in plant and machinery amounted to £20,348 million in 1984, and IT(def. 1) amounted to some 23 per cent of total investment in plant and machinery – a high figure, especially given our restrictive definition of IT! The computer and telecommunications equipment components of IT(def. 1) were roughly equal in value in 1984. I am currently engaged in analyses that contrast computer and telecommunications expenditure on a cross-sectoral and time-series basis. Different types of industrial activity may utilize different IT inputs as signified by these branches. For example, the purchase of telecommunications equipment or services may not parallel the purchase of computer equipment; nor need the latter coincide with the use of electronic components for, say, process control. (The 'convergence' of computers and communications may mean that expenditures will tend to converge too; this is a question for empirical analysis.)

It is important to examine trends since it may be that the 1984 data are anomalous. Input–output tables are telling us only about expenditure during a particular period. It is quite plausible that there are considerable fluctuations over time in IT spending and – more problematic in many ways – that these fluctuations are not consistent across branches of the economy. For example, it is likely that financial firms were engaged in particularly high levels of expenditure immediately prior to 'Big Bang'. (To examine how far these are posing real problems, I am seeking to use Census of Production and other data to see how consistent the newer data are with the 'snapshot' input–output IT measures.) Likewise, the tables are effectively flow rather than stock data, and they do not tell us how far there are amassed IT capabilities within sectors – unless we are prepared to impute stock data from flow statistics.

Purchases for leasing constitute a large (10.39 per cent) share of total IT(def. 1) investment: the data suggest that much computer, but very little telecommunications, equipment is leased. Unfortunately, the tables do not provide sufficient data to determine whether statistics on investment and current expenditure on IT are affected to different extents across different sectors. Again, I am seeking to use other data sources to cope with this problem in input–output tables. The Census of Production data for 1986, which also demonstrate a high proportion of leasing and hire of computer equipment, seem to indicate that in manufacturing and utilities, at least, there are different trade-offs between leasing and purchasing of computers for heavy users on the one hand, and average and light users on the other.

Tables 5.1 and 5.2 home in on investment data. The point that services are extremely important users of IT could not be made more clearly. As these tables demonstrate, around 80 per cent of all IT(def. 1) investment came from service branches. For similar estimates for the USA, see Roach (1988); Roach's lines of analysis may be worth pursuing further with UK data.

The most IT-intensive branches, in order of the share taken by IT in their plant and machinery investment, are: communications; banking, electrical and electronics engineering and instruments; gas supply; wholesale trade; retail and repairs trades; miscellaneous services; fishing; business services; and oil processing (Table 5.1). Not all of these are actually big spenders, with over £100 million IT(def. 1) investment. But they include all of these big spenders but one – electricity supply. Six of the ten most IT-intensive branches are services, as are six of the nine biggest spenders (and, indeed, the top five spenders). With some slight variations, a similar picture emerges from 1979 data.

Dominance in IT investment is more than just a reflection of the dominance of services in the UK economy. Services are even more important for IT investment than for investment in general. Table 5.2 displays the research results in terms of indices which represent this comparative dominance, confirming the importance of services as IT-using sectors. Not only are they dominant users: a greater share of their investment is in IT than is the case for goods-producing sectors. (As we can see, however, the telecommunications service sector is responsible for the high consumption of telecommunications equipment by services.) If we consider sectoral data disaggregated as in Table 5.1, and use an overall IT investment index combining computers and telecommunications equipment, the point is underlined. Of eleven branches where this comparative investment intensity index is greater than unity (i.e. more dominant in IT than general investment), six are services (and services are five of the top seven on this indicator). This is despite the poor representation of services in the input–output tables.

The discussion above merely indicates a few of the analyses that may be undertaken with input–output data. It is my intention to use these data as the core of an IT accounting framework, in which different types of (mainly official) statistic are rendered compatible and can thus be interrogated jointly. For

Table 5.1   *IT investment intensity by industry, 1984*

		IT(def. 1) (£m)	Total (£m)	% IT
1	Agriculture	5.3	1,092.5	0.49
2	Forestry	1.6	103.6	1.54
3	Fishing	1.6	11.1	14.41
4	Coal and coke	5.2	339.8	1.53
5	Extract of oil and gas	76.9	3,068.1	2.51
6	Oil processing	22.3	186.7	11.94
7	Electric etc	100.6	2,015.6	4.99
8	Gas supply	130.7	628.8	20.79
9	Water supply	3.8	413.1	0.92
10	Metals	21.1	381.6	5.53
11	Other minerals and products	28.7	497.6	5.77
12	Chemical and fibres	29.6	1,003.3	2.95
13	Metal goods n.e.s.	20.1	320.4	6.27
14	Mechanical engineering	24.2	618.1	3.92
15	Electric and instruments	269.8	950.4	28.39
16	Vehicles and parts	45.8	622.9	7.35
17	Other transport equipment	25.8	283.9	9.09
18	Food	49.8	921.6	5.40
19	Drink and tobacco	28.5	343.9	8.29
20	Textiles	0.0	208.6	0.00
21	Clothing and footwear	11.0	148.5	7.41
22	Timber	5.4	170.2	3.17
23	Paper	24.5	706.7	3.47
24	Rubber	10.9	330.5	3.30
25	Other manufactures	2.7	59.6	4.53
26	Construction	10.2	545.2	1.87
27	Wholesale	260.9	1,470.4	17.74
28	Retail and repair	407.1	2,498.4	16.29
29	Hotels and catering	13.4	761.7	1.76
30	Railways	2.4	281.4	0.85
31	Other inland transport	62.2	1,118.4	5.56
32	Sea transport	8.0	577.0	1.39
33	Air transport	6.8	419.5	1.62
34	Other transport	24.9	560.9	4.44
35	Communications	1,126.8	1,825.1	61.74
36	Banking leased	490.6	3,719.8	13.19
37	Banking other	601.0	2,401.1	25.03
38	Business services	400.5	3,062.4	13.08
39	Public administration	63.1	1,325.5	4.76
40	Roads	5.2	1,504.0	0.35
41	Education	39.6	952.2	4.16
42	Health services	23.8	1,112.7	2.14
43	Sanitary services	1.1	641.4	0.17
44	Miscellaneous services	231.0	1,543.3	14.97
45	Dwellings	0.0	11,036.0	0.00
46	Transfer costs	0.0	2,604.0	0.00
47	Total	4,724.5	55,387.5	8.53

Source: Calculated from input–output data, 1984, by Mark Matthews; for further definitional details, see Miles and Matthews (1989).

instance, labour force data can also be brought to bear on sectoral patterns of IT activity; I am currently seeking to integrate these into the IT accounting framework.

Table 5.2 *Comparative IT investment intensity ratios, 1984*

Sectors (aggregations of Table 5.1 classes)		Indicators			
		PCINVCOM	PCINVTEL	CITIIRCOM	CITIRTEL
1–3	Agriculture, forestry, fishing	0.6	0.1	0.13	0.02
4–11	Extractive sector	1.7	3.5	0.37	0.87
12–25	Manufacturing	4.1	4.0	0.92	1.00
26	Construction	0.5	1.4	0.10	0.35
27–45 (less 36)	Services	5.7	4.6	1.26	1.15
27–45 (less 36 and 37)	Services other than telecommunications	5.8	1.8	1.28	0.45

Source: Calculated from input–output data, 1984.

Note:
PCINVCOM = % of sectoral investment in computers
PCINVTEL = % of sectoral investment in telecommunications equipment
CITIIRCOM = comparative IT investment intensity ratio for computers
CITIRTEL = comparative IT investment intensity ratio for telecommunications equipment

As noted earlier, analysis of 1986 Census of Production data suggests that for manufacturing branches there is a high correlation between computer professional employment and computer investment on a sectoral level. (Analysis of the Yap survey (see below) suggests a similar high correlation on an establishment level between IT stock and employment across private services.) This suggests that at least some forms of IT employment are good indicators of IT activity, and we might hope that these are less volatile than investment data may be. If suitable volumes were available, occupation-by-industry data might be used to produce cross-sectoral maps of IT activity (although there may be sectoral differences in the use of IT producer services like computer bureaux and software houses: Brady's data, also mentioned earlier, may be informative as to this point).

I have been investigating the applicability to such ends of two regular series that provide such data: the New Earnings Survey and the Labour Force Survey. (The latter offers the possibility of intra-EEC comparisons.) Unfortunately, the sample sizes involved in these surveys are rather limited for detailed sectoral comparisons of IT employment to be made (given that such employees are only a few per cent of the labour force), and fuller census data are available only on a decennial basis. Based on Labour Force Survey data for 1984, my initial estimates are that around 50 per cent of systems analysts and programmers are based in service sectors. While less than the proportion of IT investment coming from these sectors, this figure does suggest that considerable amounts of IT activity – including the writing of software and related IT production – are under way in services sectors of the economy.

IT in services: survey studies

Official statistics are biased away from services, and most non-official studies have focused either on manufacturing or on one or other specific branch of services. There are some exceptions, however, which repay further analysis – and replication and elaboration. They can shed light upon organizational forms associated with IT use, and understanding the patterns of change here is not only an important research topic in its own right (Miles, 1988), but also has important implications for services. For instance, the growth of producer services in part reflects efforts to restructure organizations in more flexible ways by 'externalizing' some of their internal service operations.

One of the exceptional studies that does cover services is Daniels' (1987) analysis of the 1984 Workplace Industrial Relations Survey (WIRS). This draws on interviews conducted with a sample of 2,019 workplaces in Great Britain; unfortunately only workplaces with over two dozen workers were covered (which will mean missing many service establishments). As suggested by the title of the survey, much attention is focused on industrial relations, but there is also interest in technical change. Changes having occurred in the previous three years are categorized as involving 'advanced technical change' (new plant, machinery or equipment including microelectronics), 'conventional technical change' (not incorporating microelectronics) or 'organizational change' (not involving plant, machinery or equipment). In addition to the concern with change, there are other questions dealing with the 'technical stock': the computer facilities of the establishment (in-house mainframe, link to computer elsewhere in organization, link to computer outside organization, in-house minicomputer, in-house microcomputer, use of computer bureau service) and the use of word processing equipment.

Daniels presents results disaggregated by size (reporting that larger establishments are more liable to use IT, for instance). In terms of a sectoral breakdown the published study is rather disappointing. Several sets of data are disaggregated into private manufacturing, private services, nationalized industries and public services, but this makes for very restricted possibilities for comparison. Work under way at CURDS[4] suggests that, since the raw data – available from the ESRC Data Archive – are coded to the 4-digit SIC level, rather more detail can be meaningfully extracted: some ten-branch analyses have been prepared. These show that, while Daniels' tables suggest a low service sector use of IT, when examined in detail we can find that some services are exceptionally high users, others exceptionally low. Given that this survey is to be replicated and extended in the future – hopefully including more elaborate questions of technological change – it should be worth exploring the data set further.

A second survey study was explicitly orientated towards analysing services use of IT; it is a remarkable achievement since it is the basis of a doctoral dissertation (Yap, 1986).[5] Yap presents the results of a mail survey of *private* services: some 3,000 establishments were approached, yielding 638 usable service sector responses, presenting data on their circumstances in late 1984. The actual response rate was 716, since 78 manufacturing establishments also responded: thus some service–manufacturing comparisons are possible (though this sample is not pursued in the studies cited, and I do not know whether they fall only in specific subsectors of manufacturing). Yap reports analyses in terms of five sectors: wholesale distribution; retail distribution; transport and communication; business and financial services; and miscellaneous services. However, the raw data allow us not only to identify some manufacturing establishments, as noted, but also to differentiate between business services on the one hand and banking and financial services on the other.

Yap elicited a great deal of information on computer usage by the responding establishments: he requested information from respondents as to the numbers of units of offsite and onsite mainframes, and of minicomputers and microcomputers in use at the site, and he also asked whether use was made of computer bureaux. The study was concerned with predicting the extent of IT use: the published reports present useful information on, for example, the occupational profiles of users and non-users of computers in different services. The sample size is well below that of Daniels' study, let alone official surveys, the low response rate may involve some bias (towards IT users?), and a rather gross aggregation of economic sectors is restrictive. But the data do cover a wide set of features of IT use in services, they can be exploited further and replications of the study would yield useful trend data.

The survey finds considerable variation in whether or not computers are used in the establishments: over 90 per cent of banking and business service establishments use them, as opposed at the other extreme to 60 per cent of transport and 54 per cent of retail establishments. The variation is actually more marked than this since computer users range from the owner of a single microcomputer to establishments equipped with several mainframes together with other systems. Many new computer users are equipped only with one microcomputer. The sectors which are most computer intensive are more likely to be using larger computers and more elaborate computer systems.

The data set allows us to assess the use of different types and combinations of computer and, since there are questions concerning when computers were first used, to plot diffusion curves. Table 5.3 shows the more advanced sectors apparently nearing saturation in computer use, with use still accelerating in laggard sectors in the early 1980s. (All sectors are probably far from saturation in terms of computers per employee.) In terms of the different generations of computers, we see a set of overlapping diffusion curves, with mainframes being overhauled by minicomputers and then more recently by microcomputers – which are now by far the most prevalent systems, of course. Minicomputers fall in prevalence between micros and mainframes.

The sectors with highest use of mainframes (manufacturing, banking/ financial and business services) repeatedly emerge as the most computer-intensive and advanced users. These sectors tend to be highest users of mini- and microcomputers. Among the users of mainframes they have the highest ratio of microcomputers to mainframes, suggesting further movement down the path of 'distributed computing', which seems to be the wave of the future.[6] But all sectors have some establishments that are wholly reliant on mainframes, some wholly on minis and some wholly on micros.

Yap's data also cover word processor (WP) usage: the year of introduction of WPs, and the numbers of general purpose, and of dedicated, WPs in use. Fourteen

Table 5.3   *Diffusion of computers in UK establishments*

(a) Diffusion in different sectors by period (cumulative percentages)

	Year of first use of computers					
Sector	1950s	1961–4	1965–9	1970–4	1975–9	1980–4
Retail	0	1	7	15	30	54
Transport	0	2	8	15	40	60
Miscellaneous services	0	3	8	17	39	64
Wholesale	0	2	5	16	38	71
Manufacturing	0	5	10	25	44	78
Business services	1	4	8	28	57	91
Banking	4	9	17	42	73	96

(b) Diffusion of different computer systems by period (number of establishments)

	Year of first use of computers				
User types	1950–64	1965–9	1970–4	1975–9	1980–4
Users only of:					
Mainframes	3	2	5	14	10
Minicomputers	1	5	18	40	54
Microcomputers	0	1	3	30	93
All users of:					
Mainframes	14	21	33	43	21
Minicomputers	11	21	54	91	78
Microcomputers	12	23	57	90	122

Source: Data from Yap (1986).

other information technologies are studied, roughly in order of prevalence: photocopier, electronic typewriter, computer, telex, audioconferencing, radio paging, microfiche/microfilm, viewdata, facsimile, automatic telex system, group 3 facsimile, electronic mail, local area network and optical characters recognition equipment. The presence or absence, and the extent of use, of these items – and also of such telephone equipment facilities as call logging, stored numbers, automatic redial and audioconference – were also assessed. In terms of sectoral variations, finance and business services were the highest users of all ITs in 1984; manufacturing tends to be a relatively low user of technologies that are orientated to office work, so it does not resemble these services in this respect as it does in computer usage. As in Daniels' studies, establishment size (measured by turnover or by overall employment) was positively associated with the use of computers and most of the other ITs.

One way of handling the diversity of computer types is to form an aggregate indicator that takes this diversity into account. Even if this can be done only crudely, such an indicator should be more useful than treating all computers as equivalent. Yap and Walsham (1986) use such a measure of computer capacity, weighting computer use by assigning 5 points to each mainframe, 3.5 to each minicomputer and 1 to each microcomputer. We find that, for the whole sample, the sectoral ranking in terms of this computer capacity indicator actually turns out to be practically identical with that based on the incidence of computer use; thus financial and business sectors had higher capacity than other sectors.

Yap and Walsham (1986) use this indicator to relate organization size to IT usage. They find (for the whole sample and for individual sectors) a strong relationship between the computer capacity measure and the number of employees.

Overall, computer capacity increased approximately with the square root of the number of employees. The researchers contrast these results with those of a more 'mature' technology, the telephone: here the number of extensions increased roughly in line with the number of employees. It is interesting to speculate that this may be the future for computers too, as they become cheaper and more user friendly. If we examine the pattern of computer use across establishments of different sizes in more detail, however, the picture appears rather more complicated than a gradual increase in computer capacity. We find a shift from the dominance of microcomputers, through various types of minicomputer and mini plus micro system, to configurations in the larger establishments in which combinations of mainframes with other computers predominate. It will be interesting to examine how far similar computer configurations in different sectors resemble each other and how far they resemble other computer users in their own sectors. This will, for example, have implications for the transfer of computer-related skills across sectors.

Other statistics in this survey concern computer-related employment, classified into five groups (computer managers, systems analysts, programmers, operators and other computer staff); some data on the overall employment in the establishments by broad occupational categories are also provided, which makes it possible to relate computer use to the structure of the establishment.[7] Together with information on different configurations of computers installed at establishments, these data demonstrate that within sectors – even among users with similar scores on the computer capacity indicator – there are actually several significantly distinct patterns of computer use. For instance, a high-capacity user in business services may use a few mainframes – with or without other systems – or be reliant on a large number of networked microcomputers.

The composition of IT employment varies among computer users in different sectors. Banking and business services emerge as quite similar, employing relatively high proportions of programmers and systems analysts among their computer staff, and correspondingly low proportions of operatives. (Manufacturing also employs relatively high proportions of systems analysts.) The presence of systems analysts and programmers would seem to indicate that computer use is continuing to be developed, with new or modified applications taking a higher proportion of the overall effort; in contrast, large numbers of operatives would seem to indicate emphasis on relatively routine applications and large-scale data entry. We are thus in a position to speculate about IT (software) production among supposedly 'user' service sectors. Considerable activity seems to be under way in leading sectors, which are not merely using hardware in routine ways, but are actually contributing to the further development of IT.

But what are computers actually being used for? Yap asked whether or not computers were used for each of fourteen applications. There are significant variations in the pattern of computer applications in different sectors, but some applications are very widely popular – notably credit checking, sales analysis and billing. As might be expected, applications such as stock control are used to a far greater extent in services handling material products (wholesale and retail) and in manufacturing; financial applications are used mainly in banking and business services; CAD (computer-aided design) is, perhaps surprisingly, used mainly in business services (but it is not used at all frequently in the sample).

The applications data form a rich but inevitably limited data source. Many of the most common service applications are covered, such as financial planning, payroll, project control and sales analysis, together with some applications that are more manufacturing orientated, such as CAD and production planning. But there are also notable omissions, such as transactions processing, and we do not have much idea of the types of software used – it would have been valuable to have information on the use of databases, spreadsheets, etc. The data do not cover either the extent of use for these applications or the type of system on which they run.

While the overall number of applications applied in a sector is related to the computerization of the sector, once we take this latter fact into account – i.e. look at the applications of computer users only – we find that wholesale, not a heavy IT user, is likely to apply computers to a fairly wide range of purposes once actually computerized, while banking, a heavy user, is not. This feature of banking is rather surprising given the high proportions of software workers in the sector: it suggests that the list of applications fails to distinguish between diverse applications within broad classes, and perhaps between applications of very different levels of sophistication. The Yap data do not tell us whether the applications are developed and maintained in-house; Brady's current work at SPRU should help to clarify these issues since it addresses the use of in-house programmers versus external computer services as sources for software of various types.

How far is the use of IT by establishments a function of the types of activity which are their core tasks – in other words, tasks determined by the economic sector to which they belong? How far are they defined by tasks which are more a function of the type of organization which they are, such as the administrative problems associated with large scale? Several of these statistics can be brought to bear on these questions.[8] I have used for this purpose the statistical technique known as analysis of variance, which enables us to examine the differential contribution of several factors to an outcome. We can apply this method to see if there are still variations in computer use associated with sectoral membership *after* we have taken into account organizational factors (size of establishment as measured by number of full-time equivalent (FTE) employees, and organization type – whether the establishment is the whole organization, the main site or a branch).

The results of these analyses are fairly complex, but the overall picture that emerges confirms the idea that the use of computers reflects the tasks in which sectors are involved, that it is not just a reflection of there being larger organizations or different types of organization in different sectors. Of course, these latter factors are important: for instance, analysis of variance confirms the trend for larger establishments to have access to more computer power, although organizational type does not seem to be associated with this (we do note that single-site organizations are relatively unlikely to use offsite mainframes, while branches are more likely to do so). But even when these variables are taken into account, sectoral membership still emerges as an important determinant of computer capacity, and in particular of the use of microcomputers. For 1984, at any rate, the distinction between micro-intensive sectors (manufacturing, banking and business services) and the others remains striking even when organizational determinants of micro use have been factored out.

Similar analyses in respect of computer applications, employment and other IT facilities (Miles, forthcoming) confirm the inherent interest of the Yap data. Sectoral membership continues to be associated with the structure and level of computer employment, and with the types of application pursued, even when organizational variations have been taken into account.

This pattern of results confirms the idea that the use of IT reflects the informational activities of economic actors. As IT has become cheaper, more user friendly and so on, its use has spread across a wider range of sectors and applications. It is applied to administrative activities which are common to all sectors (and most marked in large organizations), but it is also applied to the core tasks of the organization. Initially, it was most easy and cost-effective to apply IT to core activities that involved fairly routine information processing on a large scale: as in regular financial activities like banking and insurance, and process control in manufacturing. More recently, increased computer power makes it possible to respond flexibly to large volumes of idiosyncratic data, such as that with which many other services deal – including, perhaps, the personal and social services which are not represented in Yap's study. We are thus witnessing a diffusion of IT in all service sectors, a process which has a lot further to run (as more powerful IT becomes available, and as the integration of 'islands of automation, is accomplished through networking IT systems) and which is liable, in turn, to have substantial implications for the future development of IT itself.

Emerging issues for the 1990s

The data I have been discussing deal mainly with 1984. Why this year was one where IT attracted such attention is a matter of conjecture, but it is clear that the pace of change in computers and telecommunications is such that the trends depicted in the data are likely to have developed to a considerable extent. More uncomfortably, it is likely that they have been joined by new trends, as new technologies have emerged (e.g. cellular telephony); as a critical mass has been reached in some other technologies (e.g. fax); and as the scope for linking up computer systems, the rationale for doing so, and pressures to do so from suppliers, clients and competitors (consider the case of the travel industry's use of videotex/viewdata) have grown.

This means that, while it would be valuable to have more up-to-date information along the lines discussed earlier, new statistics need to encompass an even wider range of ITs and related activities. Official statisticians are almost inevitably going to be tardy in meeting demands for new data, so hopes must rest on consultants, academic researchers and the relevant industries themselves. While industry has sometimes been slow in funding empirical surveys, and while those large firms that do sponsor much consultancy research tend to want to keep the results confidential, there are some reasons for hoping that common concerns will stimulate more industrial 'clubs' and trade associations to support data production exercises. Among these reasons are: the need for data to make a case to policy makers for support of training or other initiatives; the need to understand one's own sector better, so as to determine the position of leading members, the degree of reliance on particular suppliers and the situation *vis-à-vis* competitor countries; and the need to investigate some of the areas where IT implies a degree of co-operation among competing firms (for example, networking standards *can be* innovations from which all parties benefit, while a free-for-all might restrict the growth of markets).

It seems likely that the 1990s will be characterized by *integration* of various kinds. There is the market integration of 1992 in Europe, which has stimulated activity from US service firms wishing to establish themselves within a feared 'Fortress Europe', and is reflected in a wave of mergers and joint ventures among IT-related services in Europe. There is the closer integration of (groups of) suppliers and users of products in networks organized around electronic data interchange and related systems. And the latter reflects the integration of computer and communications technologies, which some commentators see as the defining feature, and the most important future trajectory, of IT. For researchers, this integration will break down many established boundaries, and make the task of analysis more difficult – but also more exciting! For practitioners, considerable challenges will be raised as previously separate parts of organizations are brought together (the past 'wars' between data processing departments, telecommunications managers and PC users are likely to seem like warming-up exercises), as new entrants and new products appear in service markets and as the scope of one's own marketing widens. The 1990s will be the decade in which Britain's service sectors face the stark choice between innovating to meet the new global economy or following the decline of manufacturing as a force to be reckoned with.

Discussion

This chapter has outlined my approaches to research on IT and services, and illustrated them with results of analyses of the (admittedly limited) data that are already available. While the detailed results raise many issues, what emerges most clearly from the studies is the mutual importance of IT for services and of services for IT.

Service sectors of the economy are being reshaped through the application of IT. In many ways, it seems that the 'new industrial revolution' associated with IT might be better thought of as the industrial revolution finally being applied to services. Services are being transformed through the application of new technology that is as relevant to their core tasks as energy and motor technologies were to the core of tasks of manufacturing industry. While it is too early to form definitive conclusions about the implications of this for the future organization of services, it does suggest that services will decreasingly find themselves shielded by the types of (not necessarily protectionist) barrier to trade and scale economy that have typically differentiated them from manufacturing. And it should not be assumed that the industrialization of services will result in twenty-first-century services resembling nineteenth-century manufacturing.

Manufacturing firms (and advanced services) find that effective use of IT may result in a change in the industrial paradigm – in new styles of organization which allow for greater flexibility, shorter production cycles and closer links with markets, and which base themselves on worker skills and commitment rather than on deskilling and casualizing work. There is considerable debate about these new paradigms, but it could well be disastrous for services to build IT into styles of organizations that are becoming unwieldy in the new global economy. Service practitioners in all service sectors need to keep abreast of the discussions about 'flexible specialization', 'just-in-time', 'economies of scope' and 'supplier–user networks' that are raised in advanced sectors.

Finally, this chapter has underlined the importance of services as consumers of IT, and as forces for the development of IT software and systems. Apart from strengthening the case for more research and statistics on services and their use of technology, this implies a rethinking of policies that tend to prioritize manufacturing industry. Indeed, it may well be that an efficient and innovative manufacturing economy in the future will need to have a forward-looking, IT-using set of producer services to complement and support it. We can expect to see services continuing to extend their role in facilitating the use of IT in all sectors of the economy, to enhance their contribution to economic activity through improved responsiveness based on their own use of IT, and to make more use of IT as user–supplier relationships intensify through the use of electronic data inter-change and related systems.

This will call for a more technically skilled workforce, and will pose challenges to firms (and to training bodies) around how to bring together and integrate the traditional 'people' skills of services with computer, communications and media skills. It will be necessary for new training and recruitment policies to be developed, and, unless there is to be a free-for-all of headhunting skilled staff (with the inflated salaries this is likely to bring), this will require co-operation within (and often between) service sectors. This co-operation may take the form of joint training programmes, new professional qualifications and new initiatives in respect of public education and training bodies.

Notes

1. This paper is an output of the project 'Mapping and Measuring the Information Economy', undertaken as part of the Economic and Social Research Council's PICT (Programme on Information and Communication Technologies) network. I would like to thank the ESRC for financial support and encouragement, and my PICT colleagues within and beyond SPRU for intellectual stimulation and practical assistance.
2. My work using the input–output tables is being carried out jointly with Mark Matthews, and the results discussed below draw heavily on his efforts and insights. Mary Newsom has contributed to the related analysis of employment data, notably data from the Labour Force Survey.
3. Data on software and services are hidden in the 'black bags' of the input–output tables. Instrument engineering, and telecommunications services may, in contrast, be identi-fied from the tables: for specific analyses they too may be included in the definition of IT-producing sectors. Telecommunications services and electronic components tend not to feature heavily as investment goods, so their exclusion is not of any great signifi-cance to the data presented below.

4. The Centre for Urban and Regional Development Studies at Newcastle University. Steve Johnson is thanked for this account of his CURDS work, and for making working papers on this research available. For a first report of the CURDS analyses, focusing on regional aspects of diffusion, see Goddard (1988).
5. The study is also reported in part in Walsham and Yap (1985) and Yap and Walsham (1986).
6. While the input–output analyses discussed above show communication services to be high IT users, the mixture of transport with telecommunication and other communication services presumably obscures this trend in the Yap data.
7. See Yap (1986) for such analyses. My own studies of manufacturing industry as documented in the 1986 Census of Production, demonstrate a positive correlation between the proportion of investment going on computers and the proportion of the workforce that is 'non-production workers'.
8. This follows the impressionistic analysis presented in Miles (1987), and the forecasts of Miles *et al.* (1988).

References

Brady, T. (1989) *Users as Producers: Software's Silent Majority*. Falmer, Brighton: Science Policy Research Unit (Centre for Information and Communication Technologies Working Paper no. 3).

Daniels, W.W. (1987) *Workplace Industrial Relations and Technical Change*. London: Frances Pinter.

Department of Employment (1965) *Computers in Offices*. London: HMSO. (Manpower Studies no. 4).

Department of Employment (1972) *Computers in Offices 1972*. London: HMSO. (Manpower Studies no. 12).

Goddard, J. (1988) 'Mapping and measuring the geography of the information economy', paper presented at Royal Institute of International Affairs, 30 March (mimeo, Centre for Urban and Regional Development Studies, University of Newcastle).

Jagger, N. (1989) *Prestel's Alter Egos: The Diffusion of Private Videotex Systems in the UK*. Falmer, Brighton: Science Policy Research Unit (Centre for Information and Communication Technologies Working Paper no. 6).

Miles, I. (1987) 'Information technology and the services economy', in Zorkoczy, P. (ed.) *Oxford Surveys in Information Technology No. 4*. Oxford: Oxford University Press.

Miles, I. (1988) 'Information technology and information society: options for the future', PICT Policy Research Papers, No. 2 Economic and Social Research Council, London (now available from the ESRC in Swindon).

Miles, I. (forthcoming) *Sectoral and Organisational Patterns of Use of Information Technology*. Falmer, Brighton: Science Policy Research Unit (Centre for Information and Communication Technologies Working Papers Series).

Miles, I. and Matthews, M. (1989) 'The statistical analysis of the information economy: why an accounting framework is needed'. Report to the ICCP Committee, OECD, Paris (mimeo). Falmer, Brighton: Science Policy Research Unit.

Miles, I., Rush, H., Turner, K. and Bessant, J. (1988) *Information Horizons*. Aldershot: Edward Elgar.

Miles, I., Brady, T., Davies, A., Haddon, L., Jagger, N., Matthews, M., Rush, H. and Wyatt, S. (1990). *Mapping and Measuring the Information Economy*. Boston Spa: British Library. LIR Report No. 77.

Northcott, J. and Walling, A. (1988) *The Impact of Microelectronics: Diffusion, Benefits and Problems in British Industry*. London: Policy Studies Institute.

Roach, S.S. (1988) 'Technology and the services sector: America's hidden competitive challenge', in White, R.M. and Guile, B.R. (eds) *Technology in Services*. Washington, DC: National Academy Press.

Thomas, G. and Miles, I. (1989) *Telematics in Transition: The Emergence of New Interactive Services in the UK.* Harlow: Longman.

Walsham, G. and Yap, C.S. (1986) *Information Technology and Your Business.* Cambridge: Cambridge University Engineering Department, Management Studies Group, Information Engineering Division.

Yap, C.S. (1986) 'Information technology in organisations in the service sector', unpublished PhD thesis, University of Cambridge.

Yap, C.S. and Walsham, G. (1986) 'A survey of information technology in the UK service sector', *Information and Management,* 10, 267–74.

Chapter 6

Productivity and Quality in Service Operations

Colin Armistead

Overview

Service organizations have been increasingly concerned with improving the quality of customer service and have used quality as a strategic dimension to gain market share or to increase profitability; examples abound in all sectors of services from air transport and retailing to financial service and after-sales services. However, increasingly many service organizations are being forced by market pressures in their sectors to improve their productivity while at the same time maintaining or improving quality levels. This is likely to be an increasing trend because at present the improvements in productivity which have been made in service industries are fewer than the improvements made in manufacturing organizations. In the period 1980 to 1986 labour productivity in services in the UK increased by 4 per cent against a 42 per cent gain in manufacturing industries (Armistead *et al.*, 1988; Johnston, 1988), although one must be careful of comparisons between the two sectors because of the difficulties associated with services productivity and the differences in the methods of measurement (Millward, 1988).

The continuing increase in the numbers of people that work in services rather than manufacturing businesses will undoubtedly focus attention on issues of productivity in services. Indicators of change come from the level of interest shown by productivity professionals discussing productivity in services at the 6th World Productivity Congress in 1988 and from the realization by many service organizations that the competitive strategies being developed around improvements in customer service have a cost which can be addressed only by simultaneously considering quality and productivity.

Technology is seen often as a major contributor to the improvement of productivity, but it is necessary to consider the context for the use of technology. In back room environments productivity gains without loss of quality are as accessible as in manufacturing. However, for front office activities the picture is less clear and productivity gains may interfere with customer contact and affect the quality of customer service. Whether or not this happens can be something of a paradox: would the use of scanning systems operated by the customers in food retailing increase or decrease the quality of that service, and would the overall productivity of the operation be increased?

Resolving these issues depends somewhat on the approaches to measurement. Service productivity presents special problems in measurement both at the level of the economy as already indicated and at the level of the business or part of the business. In back room activities the traditional approaches to productivity using work study have a place in productivity schemes, and measurements have the same level of difficulty as in manufacturing: hence perhaps the focus on office productivity in services. Difficulties in measurement intensify in those areas where there is customer involvement in the service process.

Here the main issue concerns the nature of the output, which is a mixture of physical, tangible items and other, intangible items like friendliness, atmosphere and security. Just what should be taken as the output for the purpose of measurement? It is relatively easy to measure physical aspects (such as the number of meals served in a restaurant and the number of sales made in a shop). However, these measures miss most of the less tangible features of the service package because the latter are less easily captured.

Likewise when measuring inputs to the service process things are not as clear cut as might at first appear, even when labour is taken as the partial input measurement. Consider the case of the customer performing part of the service process: should that contribution be included in the labour content for productivity purposes? If it is included, are the productivity gains frequently claimed from the use of customers as workers illusory because there is no real change of resources of the service organization? Perhaps the way to resolve some of the dilemmas over measurement is to make the link between productivity and quality.

Service operations managers need to understand the relationship between quality and productivity and to recognize the effect the use of technology may have on the relationship. This chapter looks at the strategic influences on productivity and quality, and attempts to provide some guidelines for examining operating systems and identifying those areas of quality and productivity in services which are in need of further investigation.

Strategic aspects of service operations

Approaches to the development of service business strategy build on general models of the Porter type (Porter, 1980) and have been refined for service operations (Heskett, 1986; Johnston, 1988; Sasser *et al.*, 1978; Voss *et al.*, 1985). The derived service strategies present the service business in the context of its market environment and in relation to perturbating forces which include competitors, customers, suppliers and substitute product services. Such analyses allow the development of broad strategies which are classified in three groups: differentiation, cost focus and market focus.

The business strategy provides a starting point for developing the definition of the task to be undertaken by the service production and delivery system. Irrespective of the general direction of the business strategy, the operations managers require statements which define boundaries for the operations task. It is these boundary setters who transpose the service concept and the market demand into terms which can be worked on by the operations.

The definition of the operations task results from knowledge in three areas: the volume and nature of the demand, the variety of the services, and the variation in the level and the nature of the demand (Armistead *et al.*, 1988). The nature of the demand includes statements on how the service products gain and retain customers at the expense of competitive products. The criteria derived are similar in essence to the 'order winning' and 'order qualifying criteria' for manufacturing companies (Hill, 1985). However, to reflect the softer nature of the service encounter and to recognize the place of the customer in them, the terms 'customer catching criteria' and 'competitive status criteria' are perhaps more suitable.

Taken together with information on the three dimensions of volume, variety and variation, the customer catching criteria permit the establishment of a service operations directive. Developing from this is the creation of the means to produce and to deliver the service product, entailing decisions on the use of technology and the operational factors involved in running the operation and controlling the service output. The control aspects contain the quality and productivity measurement elements, although many aspects of quality and productivity are determined by the design of the service production and delivery system.

Operations management theories have in the past tended to pronounce a trade-off between quality and productivity: however, the manufacturing experience has shown that such a trade-off is not inevitable and there may be reasons to question the trade-off theory in the context of the service encounter. Furthermore, evaluation of the relationship between quality and productivity requires an understanding of the elements of productivity and of quality relative to the operations strategy.

A framework for service quality and productivity

Service productivity comprises three elements: the input costs to the production system, the utilization of the production system and the efficiency of the product system. The strategic dimensions of volume, variety and variation affect the productivity in a variety of ways and these are summarized in Figure 6.1 (Armistead *et al.*, 1988).

Performance in an operating system includes not only a productivity but also a quality dimension, and the relationship between the two requires examination. A further understanding of the operating boundaries can be gained from an examination of the elements of productivity and quality of customer service and their relationship in different service operations. The focus of attention in the following discussion is on the front office activities.

Input costs vs quality

The influence of input costs on the quality of the service package is not as easy to predict as might at first be thought. There might in many instances be a direct relation between the two through expenditure on technology or on more service contact personnel. Examples exist from banking and insurance of the use of technology to give quality of service delivery for front-line service people. However, for many operations it is unlikely always to be the case that higher

	Productivity elements		
	Input costs	Efficiency of resources	Utilization of resources
Volume	Quantity factors; specialization	Learning; specialization	Accommodation of service mix
Variety	Reduces volume; range of skills	Learning; general purpose technology	Time to manage variety; change costs
Variation	Overtime; subcontract	Regularity of pacing; standards; predictability	Capacity more fixed than demand

Figure 6.1

resource spending means improved service quality, because improvements in the delivery of the intangible attributes of service quality are not necessarily achieved by increased costs. Consequently, even though the front-line service person is supported by increased information technology, the service quality may still be perceived as poor because intangible aspects of the service package are not being addressed. Retail banks have found themselves in this position with many of their customers.

Perhaps more insight for the operations manager can be gained from considering extremes of quality and input costs (Figure 6.2). The goal of operations managers is high-quality delivery at low cost, although what may be achieved in many cases is a low quality of service. The danger is shown by the experience of British Telecom: attempts to reduce input costs by cutting the number of service staff led to a fall in service quality and was followed by a subsequent increase in labour numbers in an attempt to improve service quality.

High input costs (relative to competitors) and low quality are a dangerous combination for service operations, just as high quality with high input costs are if company profitability is threatened. British Airways is an example of a service operation which has moved between these two positions. Poor quality with high input costs threatened the future of the company a few years ago before the start of 'customer care' programmes. In the future, with increased competition in the airline industry, the danger is that the company will remain in the high-quality, high-input-cost segment while not being able to maintain profitability at levels acceptable to shareholders, particularly with any restraint on prices.

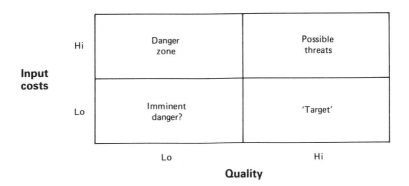

Figure 6.2

Utilization vs quality

Operations management concepts predict an inverse relationship between the utilization of the resources of the service delivery system and the quality of the service package, i.e. a trend towards reduction in quality of service with increasing utilization.

Considering the matrix of extremes for utilization and quality shown in Figure 6.3, the segment for low utilization and low quality is clearly an indicator of the incipient failure of the operation.

Low utilization may of itself be acceptable as for an emergency service like a fire brigade. However, if when there is an emergency the fire brigade fails to respond, the quality of the service is clearly inadequate. The most likely position

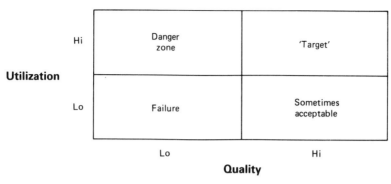

Figure 6.3

achieved by service operations is high utilization and low quality, or low utilization and high quality. Service operations which find themselves in the high-utilization, low-quality segment are in danger from competition, particularly if their sector of business is currently being influenced by competitors who differentiate on quality rather than being undifferentiated and relying on low prices. There are indications of this occurring within food retailing in recent years, with the market leaders aiming to differentiate themselves on quality. Those businesses which are in the high-quality, low-utilization segment either rely on a low dependence on utilization productivity where the costs are low or where sufficiently high prices can be charged, or they form part of the emergency services sector.

The goal is for a positioning in the upper-right segment where high utilization and high quality of service is achieved. Can this be achieved from a theoretical standpoint? High utilization in service operations is usually only achieved consistently either in low-contact back room operations or through customers being prepared to wait for service, resulting in queueing. Unless any waiting period can be seen as part of the acceptable quality of the service product, this type of service delivery cannot be placed in this segment of the matrix.

It is not uncommon, however, to find service activities where the waiting period is included in the main service package. Many restaurant operations seek to maintain high utilization of the main eating area by providing additional services for the waiting period. One of the best examples of this is in the Chicago Pizza Pie Factory (Voss *et al.*, 1985) where people in the queue to the restaurant are at times served garlic bread and then provided with a bar area adjacent to the restaurant; these features and the behaviour of the service personnel lead to the delivery having an overall high-quality service whilst at the same time maintaining high utilization of resources.

An alternative strategy for maintaining high utilization and high quality is to manage the capacity of the delivery system to keep in line with demand. This can be achieved by workforce scheduling and by the use of part-time staff. The latter requires careful handling for quality standards to be consistently maintained. Also short-term peaks may frustrate the objectives of this strategy.

Efficiency vs quality

The efficiency of the service delivery system is most likely to be in a direct relationship with the quality of the service package. Efficiency is characterized by lack of
waste of resources and time, and optimization of efficiency elements is in line with
high quality so long as they correspond to the quality attributes and variables of
the service package.

In a matrix of efficiency and quality (Figure 6.4), the most common outcome is
low efficiency and low quality, typified by the service organization which is late
with the delivery of the service and which at the same time makes many mistakes.
A common example is of jobbing builders who start late and then fail to do all that
has been requested. Service operations in this segment are the source of many of
the anecdotes of poor service which we all have and which abound from service
operations such as British Telecom, British Rail and the Post Office.

Service operations which lie in the high-efficiency, low-quality segment are
those for which there are aspects of efficiency which might affect quality, as they
do not correspond to the customers' expectation of the service. This is often seen
when customers feel that they are being unduly hurried through a service
encounter, for example patients who are discharged from hospital when they feel
unready to leave.

The low-efficiency, high-quality segment seems an improbable position for
any service operation, and any service business which finds itself in that fortunate
position has an opportunity to improve efficiency and make savings so long as this
does not influence the quality achieved.

The goal is for high efficiency and quality commensurate with the requirements set for the customer service. This might be demonstrated by speed of
response in a field service operation and speed of repair in an after-sales service.

Figure 6.4

The role of technology

The introduction of new technology into a service operation has the potential
for improving both productivity and quality. The productivity gain is usually
through a reduction in labour costs which compensates for the additional capital

costs, and increased efficiency by way of faster processing and higher utilization (particularly in back room operations but also in some front office environments e.g. with automatic cash dispensers and ticketing machines). Quality gains may come through factors like faster processing, availability of information or access to service personnel.

However, there are dangers as illustrated by the share dealing service offered to small investors in the wake of 'Big Bang'. One large City firm increased its number of small investors from 2,000 to 12,000, but the firm was unable to handle all the paperwork and enquiries. The technology introduced at the time did not help and the costs of the operation increased due to capital charges and labour costs. The result has been an increase of 70 to 100 per cent in minimum commission for small transactions, along with a diminution in other service factors. Improvements in technology are now to be introduced which will improve the efficiency of this type of transaction and make possible a better service.

If technology is introduced, its likely effect must be viewed against all the services that the service organization offers and an appraisal made of the quality factors and the elements of productivity.

Case studies

People Transport Reservation Service

A passenger transport company has a large reservation centre which provides a range of services to both the travel trade and the travelling public. What began as an order taking function has developed with time into an order making operation with staff being responsible for selling.

The operation has to deal with a high volume of demand, a high variety of services and a high variation in the level of demand.

Current activity

The centre receives over 200,000 calls a month, split into three units: calls from small travel agents, calls from large multiple travel agents and calls from the public. The calls are taken by reservation agents who give a range of travel information and make or change bookings in response to the calls. The skills required in the three units differ. Also the performance attributes for the centre reflect a combination of aims:

- to be 'the best' at meeting the market needs: this includes response time to answer calls, correctness of information and attitude of the staff to the customers;
- to handle the volume of calls as cheaply as possible and maintain the highest volume of booked revenue for journeys.

Some of the main operational measures are:

- the number of calls/offered/answered/lost from each unit;
- the transaction time for each call;
- the response time for a call to be answered.

Capacity and demand

Demand for the three units is variable on a monthly basis, and there is also variation through a day. At times the system cannot cope with demand and calls are lost with the consequential loss of potential revenue and customer goodwill. It is not practice to staff according to peak demand, and it takes several months to train new staff. Also there is a loss of staff into other positions in the company.

Aspects of quality and productivity

The main issues are balancing demand and capacity and increasing revenue. Policies to reduce input costs lead to increasing lost calls and a poorer quality of service, either by customers not being able to get through or by inexperienced staff making errors. High utilization at times of peak demand has a similar effect on quality.

Technology assists in the assembly of information, and without it the reservation centre could not operate. The efficiency measured by the time for a transaction has been increased. Also there is the capability to redirect calls from one unit to another at times of overload.

Productivity could be raised by reducing input costs if units were staffed at the appropriate skill level. While not reducing staff numbers, this would reduce costs because of differential grade payments and the quality should not suffer. However, there would be loss of the flexibility to move staff between units. Performance as measured by revenue could be increased by capturing lost calls, and this could also have the effect of raising quality standards as fewer customers would be frustrated at not being able to get through.

The issue is whether a strategy to chase demand can be managed without raising input costs too much and without reducing the flexibility of skills and experience.

Data Information Services plc

Data Information Services is a company which provides information on companies for purposes of company appraisal and creditworthiness. Included in the product package is an up-to-date balance sheet, trade information, a list of directors, numbers of employees and market creditworthiness. Customers can choose to access information online or by teleprinter, fax line, telex or mail.

The operations have to deal with medium levels of volume of demand and variation in the level of demand, and with medium to high variety of services.

Current activity

There are about 10,000 customers for the service, although up to 300 could be within one company for which a contract has been negotiated. At the present time, demand is greater than available capacity and it takes four to six months for a new analyst to be fully effective.

The operation consists of company analysis carried out by analysts, who gain information about a company from Companies House, bankers and trade referees. The information which is gathered is first prepared manually on paper and then subsequently fed into the central database by data entry personnel. The database maintenance aims to keep information current, but it could be several years old if there has not been a direct enquiry about a particular company.

Performance standards relate to the accuracy of data and to the speed of delivery. Current standards are 60 per cent of enquiries met within five days and 100 per cent within nine days. A constraining factor is the time taken to obtain data and information about a company which does not exist on the database. The analysts' tasks are regulated by standards times, and part of the reward system is linked to the meeting of standards.

Information accuracy is very important because the use of incorrect information by a customer could result in Data Information Services being sued if it causes commercial loss to the customer.

Aspects of quality and productivity

The service delivery process leads itself to standardization even though there is a fairly high level of skill required by the business analyst. Productivity issues focus on the lowering of costs while dealing with the constraints of high utilization due to shortage of capacity.

The ability to reduce costs is limited because of the high labour cost of the operation. If staff numbers were reduced, the quality of service would decrease by lowering the speed of response for a larger proportion of the customers and by increasing the likelihood of errors occurring. Efficiency tends to increase with the experience of the analysts, although it is difficult to maintain at a constant level as there is a high turnover of staff.

Installation of new technology to enable analysts to work on PCs and input their own data could assist with productivity by reducing labour costs (data entry personnel would no longer be needed) and by improving efficiency through the ability to build in quality checks for the integrity of the data. Examples exist from other companies of improvements in throughput time which can be gained in this way: by the use of a PC network the actuarial department of a life assurance company reduced from two weeks to 1–2 hours the time staff needed to enter and check all the rates for policies (*Financial Times*, 1988).

Reduction in delivery time to the customer would be restricted to some extent by the time taken to deliver on the part of information suppliers. Further improvements in technology to allow a wider use of tape-to-tape transfer of information from, say, Companies House to Data Information Services would overcome this shortcoming. However, such developments are some way off.

The issue is to reduce input costs in order to raise productivity through the use of technology. As the operation has a high back room element, this is likely not to lower quality but rather to bring about improvements.

Comex Motor Services

Comex is a bus company operating in the South Midlands area, where it runs services in a town and between the town and London. The company owns nearly 200 buses, the majority of which are double-deckers and coaches (for the London service); the rest are minibuses. The double-deckers hold seventy people and the minibuses twenty or twenty-seven people. The main quality factors for the service are a function of the speed of the journey, the frequency of the service and the comfort of the passengers.

The operation has to handle medium to high levels of demand, with high variation in the demand over time but a low variety in the services offered.

Current activity

On the town service Comex operates between 6 a.m. and 12 midnight. During peak demand on a weekday 13,000 passengers per hour are carried; this figure drops to 5,000 passengers per hour during the day, with a further reduction to 1,000 passengers per hour in the evenings. The travellers are categorized as making journeys for educational, social, work or shopping purposes.

The costs are due to the cost of buses, fuel, drivers, other staff and maintenance. These are influenced by the length of routes and the type of bus used. The performance of the operation is measured in terms of cost and revenue per bus, cost and revenue per bus mile, cost and revenue per employee, and cost and revenue per passenger.

Aspects of quality and productivity

Input costs could most easily be influenced by labour costs. Reducing numbers of drivers would put the availability of the service at risk for Comex as the absentee rate is currently high; likewise reduction in maintenance could have a similar effect by reducing the availability of buses. Reduction of these costs would have to be carried out alongside measures to improve labour availability and the efficiency of the maintenance activity.

Utilization is of great importance. Two devices are used: interlinking where two or more services have part of their route in common, and interworking where two or more services are operated by one bus or a group of buses. While these practices have operational advantages both for recovering costs and for satisfying peak demand, they could affect quality adversely through overcrowding or reduction in frequency of service.

Efficiency of operation can be heavily influenced by external factors of traffic density and road conditions. Improvements in fare collection and boarding operations could clearly assist efficiency, although there could be a reduction in quality if these did not match customer expectations.

The newer technology used in the operation is in the form of electronic ticket machines which give more information about performance on a daily basis. This company does not use a bus tracking system which would allow the position of buses to be known so that alterations to the services could be made to cope with unforeseen events.

The main issue for the operations management is maintaining an adequate frequency of service to foster demand and to cope with peak demand. Measures to improve productivity must be handled carefully if these quality elements are not to be eroded in the process.

Discussion

The strategy dimensions of volume, variation and variety have a great effect on the ability of operations managers to change productivity through the elements of input costs, utilization and efficiency. Any alteration in these productivity elements can lead to adverse changes in the quality of the service package.

In the three systems in the case studies above there are factors which make the attainment of high productivity difficult. The current positions of the service systems on the dimensions of quality against the elements of productivity are shown in Figure 6.5. In the cases of People Transport Reservation Service and Data Information Services, low input costs are frustrated by the need to deliver a variety of services. This makes it difficult to achieve economies of scale. Comex finds it hard to lower input costs through the variation effect and the consequent recourse to overtime payments.

High efficiency is also made difficult for People Transport Reservation Service and Data Information Services to attain because of the variety of the services delivered, which reduces the ability to gain learning advantages. Variation in the level of demand affects the People Transport Reservation Service and Comex, making high efficiency difficult because of the different pacing created in the work as the system tries to adjust to changes in demand.

High utilization is made difficult to achieve in People Transport Reservation Service and Comex because of variation effects. Consequently, as the capacity of the operations is more fixed than demand, it is not possible to alter capacity in line with demand. Data Information Services is able to maintain high utilization, but at the cost of customers waiting.

It is important for operations managers to understand the possible movements in the quality with the productivity elements. This is particularly true if new technology is being introduced, when it is important to understand the effect the new process might have on the main dimensions of quality and also on the elements of productivity.

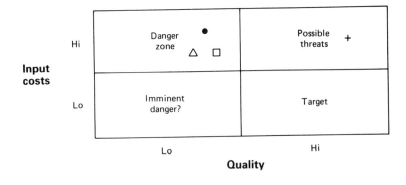

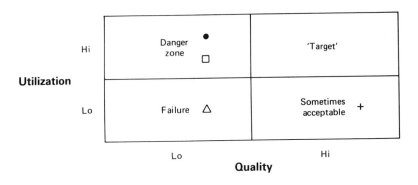

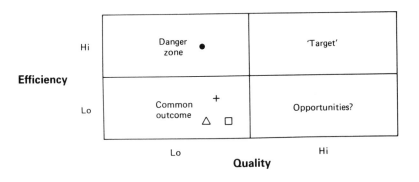

● People Transport Reservation Service (peak)

+ People Transport Reservation Service (trough)

☐ Data Information Services plc

△ Comex Motor Services

Figure 6.5

Issues for further research and development

Further research work on productivity and quality in part needs to subsume the two under the term 'performance improvement'. This title recognizes that there is often congruence between quality and productivity improvements. However, there would seem to be a case also for a better understanding of productivity in services businesses and for acknowledging that this will be dependent on aspects of quality in ways which have been highlighted in the preceding sections.

So there are a number of areas which are in need of further research, namely:

- what service organizations are currently doing to improve productivity;
- the relationship between service operations strategy and productivity;
- the measurement of productivity in services;
- the application of approaches to productivity improvement from manufacturing environments and the usefulness of traditional tools of Organization and Methods and work study.

The area of productivity in service businesses is not extensively researched. There have been some notable attempts to establish the formal approaches made by companies to productivity improvement in public sector organizations and the activities which are engaged in to this end by productivity managers (Shaw, 1988). These are useful in providing a glimpse of the state of companies. This type of research needs to be extended in order to further the understanding of how various service industries view productivity and the techniques and tools they use to bring about improvements.

The standpoint taken in the preceding sections has been that productivity improvements come only through a strategic understanding of the service business and of the service production and delivery system in relation to meeting strategically defined objectives in customer service and financial terms. Support for this hyphothesis comes from case research which suggests that the capability for productivity improvement, and the concomitant provision of customer service quality to meet customer expectations, emanates from the design of the service production and delivery system. The successful design provides a system which is focused on the needs of the market and the corporate financial objectives, and is robust in the provision of quality and productivity. This hyphothesis would appear to be true for high back room manufacturing environments, and further work is needed to establish the extent to which it also holds true for service delivery systems with a high front office content.

The question of measurements of productivity which give a true reflection of the way in which resources are used, and which can be the subject of comparison between service delivery systems, is one which needs exploration on a number of levels. First, there is the more theoretical aspect of the measurement of service productivity given problems of measuring output because of the nature of a service package and of measuring inputs because of the presence of customers in part of the delivery process and their effect and treatment as resources. Secondly, there is the examination of pragmatic measures of productivity, and here the framework of the elements of productivity of input costs, efficiency and utilization form an appropriate starting point.

The final area for research suggested above is the appropriateness of the tools for productivity improvement which have been successfully used in some sectors of manufacturing. These include just-in-time and total quality management approaches, which give a focus to continuous problem solving, the elimination of waste and the removal of bottlenecks in production systems in order to increase the throughput rate and deliver high quality. The application of total quality management is being applied in service businesses, and there is research evidence of improvements in quality of customer service. However, the link with productivity is not always clear.

The question of resource productivity in service businesses is obviously an important issue which must be examined along with quality of customer service. However, it has a separateness which suggests a research approach that aims to identify those aspects of designing and managing service production and delivery systems, and that focuses on productivity improvement while holding or improving customer service quality.

Implications for practitioners in the service sector

Practitioners in service businesses are in many cases aware of the need to maintain low costs and of the growing importance of customer service. A recent survey (Humble, 1989) among European managers in a range of organizations showed that they think that improved customer service is the key to competitive success. However, the achievement of improved customer service requires an investment in time and money, and the same survey revealed that organizations were not always willing to give this commitment. The reasons for this are not absolute; however, the lack of priority given to customer service may be important in many cases and this suggests concentration on aspects of cost, i.e. internal productivity priorities. If service managers are to implement strategies to improve quality of customer service and also improve productivity, an understanding of the interplay between the two in their own businesses is necessary.

There is another trend taking place in a number of service industries which will force managers to confront the issue of productivity and quality of customer service. For service companies in sectors where the level of competition is very high, overcapacity results in companies reducing prices and hence there are pressures to reduce resource operating costs. Examples can be seen in tour operators and increasingly in banking in the retail sector.

So how can service managers both meet a criterion for customer service at the required levels and also continue to improve resource productivity? There are two fundamental approaches:

- understand the service strategy and the implications for the service delivery system in terms of productivity and quality;
- understand some of the common barriers to improving quality of customer service and productivity, and the approaches to overcoming them.

There are a series of questions to be considered by service managers which cover the two complementary approaches.

Service strategy and quality and productivity

- What is the nature of service concept?
- What do competitors offer?
- What are the demand dimensions on the service delivery system, expressed in terms of the variety of services, volume of demand and variation in the nature and the level of demand?
- What are the customer catching and the competitive status criteria for people using the service?
- What are the business objectives and financial constraints?
- What measurements are made of quality and of productivity?
- Are the measurements directly linked to the customer catching criteria for customer service and the productivity objectives?
- Is the service delivery system capable of meeting the customer service quality criteria and the productivity objectives?
- What are the standards which are met by the main competitors?

Barriers to quality and productivity improvement

Quality

There are three main factors which act as barriers to quality improvement (Johnston, 1988), namely:

- specification of quality standards which causes difficulties due to the intangible nature of part of a service package and the management of the customer expectations;
- control systems which do not include statements defining
  what is to be measured
  what are the targets
  how measurements are to be made and by whom;
- staff development which fails to make staff aware of quality objectives and fails to give them the capability to meet targets.

In seeking ways to improve productivity and quality service, managers should be aware of some of the actions which can help in the specific areas of productivity. Input costs can be reduced overall through increased training of high-contact service personnel and the use of technology to support high-contact personnel and to automate the service delivery process. Care must be taken in the assessment if concentration is only on labour costs.

Efficiency aspects of productivity are essentially concerned with throughput time in a service and how well the service is delivered from a customer's viewpoint.

Consequently, it is closely linked to aspects of quality and there is often a reinforcement of the quality and productivity improvement. However, care must be taken in cases when the speed of throughput is at variance with the needs and expectations of the customers.

Utilization elements of productivity are helped if it is possible to maintain a match between the capacity of the service delivery system and the demand load. The capability to achieve this will depend very much on the nature of the service and on the effect of variation in the demand and the variety of services.

Productivity

There are a number of factors in three areas which act to provide barriers to productivity improvement, namely:

- not understanding the needs of the customer (note the link with service operations strategy);
- not understanding what really happens in the service delivery process;
- confusion in the flow of information, materials and people in the service process;
- lack of understanding between different stages in a service delivery system;
- unplanned changes in the way the service is produced and delivered;
- poor quality of service;
- failure to measure productivity;
- failure to measure the right things, i.e. those which are directly linked to the aspect of productivity that is most important: input costs, efficiency or utilization;
- reliance on a single productivity measurement;
- use of too complicated measurements and discrete values rather than trends.

In conclusion there are a number of main points which managers should address if they wish to understand and improve quality and resource productivity in service delivery systems:

- quality and productivity should be linked to customer needs and expectations;
- quality and productivity should be linked to corporate objectives, i.e. decisions on service levels should take account of cost implications;
- productivity and quality have no absolute measures and so measurements should
    reinforce directly critical aspects of customer service
    be compared against bench-marks of competitors over time;
- productivity and quality improvement require the support and understanding of all staff.

References

Armistead, C.G., Johnston, R. and Slack, N. (1988) 'The strategic determinants of productivity', *International Journal of Production and Operations Management, 8, 3,* 109–15.

Financial Times (1988) 16 September.

Heskett, J.L. (1986) *Managing in the Service Economy.* Boston: Harvard Business School Press.

Hill, T. (1985) *Manufacturing Strategy.* London: Macmillan.

Humble, J. (1989) *Service: The New Competitive Edge.* Brussels: Management Centre Europe.

Johnston, R. (1988) 'Service industries: improving competitive performance', *Service Industries Journal, 8, 2,* 202–11.

Johnston, R. (1988) personal communication.

Johnston, R. (1989) 'The management of service operations', in Wild, R. (ed.) *The International Handbook of Production and Operations Management.* London: Cassell.

Millward, R. (1988) 'The UK services sector, productivity change and the recession in long-term perspective', *Service Industries Journal, 8, 3,* 263–76.

Porter, M.E. (1980) *Competitive Strategy: Techniques for Analysing Industries and Competitors.* New York: Free Press.

Sasser, F.W., Olsen, P.R. and Wyckoff, D.D. (1978) *Management of Service Operations.* Boston: Allyn and Bacon.

Shaw, W.N. (1988) 'Productivity improvement: an important issue for private and public sector organisations', *International Journal of Operations and Production Management, 8, 7,* 42–53.

Voss, C.A., Armistead, C.G., Johnston, R. and Morris B. (eds) (1985) *Operations Management in Service Industries and the Public Sector.* Chichester: John Wiley.

Chapter 7

Patterns of measurement of service performance: empirical results

Christopher Voss, Robert Johnston, Lin Fitzgerald and *Rhian Sylvestro*

Overview

In an influential article 'Measuring manufacturing performance: a new challenge for accounting research', Robert Kaplan (1983) argued that, whilst manufacturing industry was competing in areas such as quality, innovation and flexibility, the measures of performance in these areas were inadequate, inappropriate or unavailable, and new measures needed to be developed. This was accentuated by the advent of new production technologies such as flexible manufacturing systems, which make the traditional standard cost model inappropriate. Firms seem to measure only what is easy to measure, such as productivity and cost, and neglect measurement and control of other factors that are vital to the firms' competitive success. Such arguments have also been put forward in service industries. Voss and Nicol (1985) for example, have examined performance measures in contract repair and maintenance services, and have identified that 'the traditional view of . . . service is . . . to provide adequate service at minimum cost'. They argue that there are two issues in measuring service performance:

- service industries compete not just on cost but on the level of service offered;
- much of the service is intangible and difficult to measure, and thus tends not to be measured.

Voss and Nicol propose three sets of measures for service performance: cost, 'hard' performance (measures of performance that are easily quantified) and 'soft' performance (performance measures that are not easily quantified). Examples of soft measures quoted include the attitude and appearance of the service representative and the quality of service documentation.

This work by Voss and Nicol, and work by others such as Sasser *et al.* (1982), highlights three important issues:

- Kaplan's propositions on manufacturing, namely that companies are competing on dimensions beyond cost and productivity, apply equally to service industries;
- many of the important measures of service operation performance are intangible and present measurement difficulties;

- the work being conducted on measures of performance in companies and by academics is often being undertaken in the operations and quality areas, as well as in accounting.

The latter point presents a strong argument that research would benefit through co-operation of the operation management and accounting areas as prescribed by Scapens (1979).

The research in this chapter addresses the issues identified by Voss and Nicol, listed above, using a team comprising both financial and operations management researchers.

Objectives

The objectives were to identify and develop good practice in performance measurement through the provision of:

- case studies that document the nature of service industries and in particular the nature of operational and financial control in service businesses;
- the development and appraisal of a conceptual base for assessing the nature, varieties and types of control in service organizations;
- guidelines for the implementation of operational and financial control systems.

Specific objectives within this included:

- to identify best practice and state of the art in measurement of financial and operational performance;
- to evaluate critically the control systems and the identified performance measures of both tangible and intangible activities;
- to develop an understanding of the relationship between financial and operational control in services;
- to identify the major characteristics and requirements for operational information and the control systems to support financial, market and other corporate goals;
- to develop an understanding of how performance measurement and control varies between different service organizations.

Method

The study was based on case research in a number of sites. Information was collected through in-company documentation and by means of structured interviews with a sample of key personnel in each company, including senior management, financial management, systems management and operations management. The data collected included:

- position audit – documentation of the company background and its competitive position;
- description of the service system, including the flow of control information through the system, in both the formal and informal networks;
- identification and description of the operational and financial control systems;
- description of the goals of each system and how they support corporate goals.

This chapter describes one set of the data collected and reviews this data in the context of a model of the performance measurement process.

A process-based model

Any service can be considered as a series of processes. The core of the model is the service process. The performance of a process can be measured in five areas: process, productivity, process inputs and outputs, service output (service level) and cost/profit. In addition the market impact can be measured.

- *Process.* The first stage in delivering a service is the design and specification of the process(es). The first opportunity for measurement and control is therefore to measure whether the process has been designed to specification, and whether it is being operated as specified.

- *Productivity.* Any process can be seen as a transformation, with inputs and outputs. The productivity of any process is the ratio of outputs to inputs. The major inputs are labour and capital (plant and facilities). Standards of labour and plant/facilities productivity can be set and measured.

- *Process inputs.* It is possible to measure the quality of inputs to the process such as people and material. Given the importance of contact personnel, it might be expected that measures of the quality of staff (or related measures of the recruitment and training processes) are more important in services than in manufacturing.

- *Process outputs.* The output of the process is service, and measurement of outputs is therefore measurement of the service level. These service levels can be specified and measured in terms of either hard or soft (intangible) measures (Voss and Nicol, 1985), and can be measured either by the company or by its customers. Company measurement will normally take place *during* the service process, as service is delivered and consumed simultaneously. There can be many mechanisms for measuring, ranging from 'mystery shoppers' to routine measurement by managers. Customer measurement can take place during the delivery of the service. More commonly customers are asked about their views after the service has been delivered. There is a range in the nature of customer measurement. They can be asked to rate service against pre-specified service levels (hard or soft). They can just be asked about their general satisfaction with the service, and/or they can have their complaints recorded.

- *Financial control*. The above measures are related to operational control; the other main area of measurement is financial control. Financial control can be considered in three main areas: cost, profit or margins, and prices. In each of these areas companies may choose to measure at the company level, the unit or branch level and/or the level of the individual service.

- *Market measures*. The final area where managerial measurement and control occurs is in the service's impact in the market-place. A wide variety of measures can be used, from market share to level of sales.

Any measurement and control model must have feedback loops. This model has two. The one in the upper half of Figure 7.1 feeds back to the design and specification of the process; the one in the bottom half feeds back to the operating management.

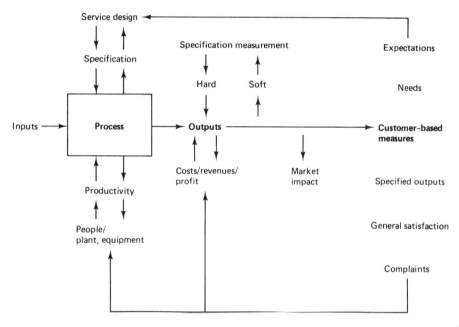

Figure 7.1   Service processes measurement and control

Results

Each of the nine companies in the sample was examined to identify the patterns of measurement and control with reference to the model outlined above. The measures used and the results are outlined in Table 7.1. These results should be treated with some care. Although a yes/no classification was used, when a yes is given there were differences between companies as to the number of measures used and the frequency with which they were used. The results in Table 7.1 are discussed more fully below.

Table 7.1   *Measures of service: empirical results*

Measure	Company								
	1	2	3	4	5	6	7	8	9
Specification of:									
Service process	Yes (full)	Yes (some)	No	Yes	Yes (design)	Yes	Yes (layout)	No	Yes (layout)
Process outputs (service level)									
Hard	No	Yes	No	Yes	No	Yes	Yes	Yes	Yes
Soft	No	No	No	Yes	No	Yes	No	Yes	No
Measurement by company of:									
Service process	Yes	No	No	No	Yes	Yes	Yes	No	Yes
Process outputs (service level)									
Hard	No	Yes	No	Yes	No	Yes	Yes	Yes	Yes
Soft	No	No	No	Yes	No	Yes	Yes	Yes	Yes
Standards set for:									
Plant productivity	No	No	No	No	Yes	Yes	No	No	No
People productivity	Yes	No	Yes	Yes	No	Yes	No	Yes	No
Measurement of:									
Plant productivity	No	No	No	No	Yes	Yes	No	No	No
People productivity	Yes	No	Yes	Yes	No	Yes	No	Yes	No
Measures sought from customers:									
General satisfaction	No	Yes	No	No	Yes	Yes	No	Yes	No
Process outputs (service level) versus specification	No	No	No	Yes	Yes	Yes	No	Yes	No
Perception of service level	No	No	No	Yes	No	Yes	No	Yes	No
Expectations	No	No	No	No	No	No	No	No	No
Needs	No	No	No	No	No	Yes	No	No	No
Complaints	No	No	No	Yes	No	Yes	Yes	Yes	No
Market measures	No	No	Yes	NR	Yes	Yes	Yes	No	Yes
Financial measures:									
Margin/prices	Yes	No	Yes	NR	Yes	Yes	Yes	No	Yes
Unit costs (by branch)	Yes	No	Yes	Yes	Yes	No	Yes	Yes	Yes
Cost per individual service	Yes	No	No[2]	No	Yes[1]	No	No[2]	No	No[2]
Profit per branch	Yes	No	Yes	NR	Yes	Yes	Yes	Yes	Yes
Profit per individual service	No	No	No	NR	No[1]	No	No	No	No

Notes: NR = Not relevant (i.e. run as a cost centre or not a traded service).
[1] Measured by department, but not by individual service.
[2] Measurement of cost of sales by item sold.

- *Process specification.* Five of the companies had some degree of central specification of the service process to be used in the service site (all companies were multi-site). However, in only two was this a detailed specification. Of the five only three had measurement of the service process (as opposed to the service output). An example of a company that did so was the management consultant. It set detailed specifications of how a particular consulting assignment was to be performed. A consulting assignment by any company in the world in any language was performed in the same way. For any assignment beyond a certain length, a partner was assigned to check that the process was being performed to specification.

- *Process outputs.* The results indicated that hard measures were far more commonly specified and measured (by six companies) than soft measures (by three companies). This may reflect the greater difficulty of specifying and measuring soft measures.

- *Productivity*. Five companies specified and measured the productivity of service personnel, and three measured the productivity of the plant and equipment. As might be expected, both companies that measured plant productivity were capital intensive.

- *Customer measures*. There was great variability in the use of customers for measuring the service that had been delivered. Three companies used no form of customer-based measurement, two used only vague satisfaction measures and one only analysed customer complaints. The other three organizations were considerably more sophisticated. Each measured perceptions of the process outputs that had been previously specified. Company 6 also used market research to measure the stated needs of customers.

- *Market measures*. Two of the organizations studied were field or support services which were not marketed *per se*. Of the remainder, all had one or more market-based measures. Such measures included market share and sales by service.

- *Financial measures*. All but two companies had financial measures of the service at the local level. Measures of margins and prices were used by five companies, as were measures of cost. Measures of profit were used by only three companies.

Patterns of measurement and control

Qualitative analysis of the data leads to the identification of a number of possible patterns of measurement and control in the companies observed. The first group is companies 1, 5 and 6. The common factor linking all three organizations was the central specification of process *and* control of the process against this specification. The logic behind this is clear. If the process has been properly designed and specified, then if the process is in control good service will be delivered and no further measurement is necessary. This approach is consistent with the 'total quality' approach put forward by Deming and developed in Japan. Company 1 was the most true to this approach. The opposite extreme would be reflected by company 3 (and to a lesser extent by company 9). This company had no specification or measurement of service process or output, and was controlled almost entirely by a tight financial control system.

The third main approach was to focus on measurement of service level or output (either as the main focus or in support of other measures). Companies 4, 6 and 8 were the best examples of this. The 'best practice' was probably exhibited by company 6. It displayed sophisticated use of market research and operations research to determine customer needs, and to specify appropriate service levels and design systems to deliver these service levels. This was accompanied by careful measurement of service at points throughout the process. Both hard and soft measures were used. In addition customers were used to cross-check that specific service levels had been delivered.

A special case was company 2. This delivered a complex systemic service of

Table 7.2 *Company description*

	Company								
	1	2	3	4	5	6	7	8	9
Industry	Management consultant	Communi-cation	Retail	Customer service	Hotel	Transport terminus	Retail	Field service	Retail
Cost structure									
Labour costs	High	Low	High	High	Low	Low	High	High	Low
Plant/equipment costs	Low	High	Low	Low	High	High	Low	Low	High
Front office/back office dominant	Mix	BO	FO	FO	FO	FO	FO	Mix	FO
Systemic/stand alone	Alone	Systemic	Alone	Alone	Alone	Alone	Alone	Alone	Alone
Span of process	Months	Mins	½ hour	Mins	Days	Hours	Mins	½ hour	½ hour
Multi-site	Yes	Yes	Yes	Yes	Yes	Yes	Yes	Yes	Yes
Visibility of process to customers	High	Low	High	Low	High	High	High	Med	High

the sort found in airlines, telecommunications, railway systems, etc. The service was being delivered by obsolete plant and equipment, and until this could be replaced, low service levels would continue to be delivered. In this situation, the service standards and measurement process had little impact as line management had no influence on the level of service offered in the short term.

The final general observation was that there was almost no measurement of customer needs or expectations.

Implications for practitioners

The following was observed and could be considered good practice:

- specification and measurement of the service process;
- specification and measurement of specific service process outputs or service levels;
- use of customers to measure specific service process outputs or service levels.

The following was observed and could be considered bad practice:

- control based solely on productivity and financial measures.

The following potentially good practice was not widely used:

- measurement of customer needs and expectations.

Emerging issues

This chapter reports just one area of analysis of the very rich sets of data collected in this research. Other areas for analysis include:

- the nature of the measures used;
- the measurement techniques;
- the level of aggregation or disaggregation of service measures at each level of the organization;
- the nature and effectiveness of the feedback loops.

In addition, with further data, it may be possible to develop propositions concerning the relationships between different organizational contexts and different measures of service.

Acknowledgements

The authors gratefully acknowledge the support of the Chartered Institute of Management Accountants who funded the research on which this chapter is based.

References

Kaplan, R.S. (1983) 'Measuring manufacturing performance: a new challenge for accounting research', *Accounting Review*, 17, 4, 686–705.

Sasser, W., Olsen, R. and Wyckoff, D.D. (1982) *Management of Service Operations*, Newton, Mass.: Allyn and Bacon.

Scapens, R.W. (1979) 'Profit measurement in divisionalised companies', *Journal of Business Finance and Accounting*, Autumn.

Voss, C.A. and Nicol, R. (1985) 'Field service management', in Voss, C.A., Armistead, C., Johnston, R and Morris, B. (eds) *Operations Management in Service Industries and the Public Sector*, pp. 149–56. Chichester: John Wiley.

Part 3

Managing financial services

Introduction

Neil Morgan

One of the fastest-growing service industries in the 1980s has been financial services. It is also one of the few areas in the service sector with a long history.

The content of Part 3 of this volume reflects the recent emphasis on marketing as a management function in financial service organizations, and this is explored on a number of levels. A central theme is the relationship between the very competitive business environment and the emergence of marketing as a management function and business philosophy.

The financial services industry has, in the very recent past, begun to receive much research attention. Changes in legislation have affected the business environment, and have contributed to the current focus on strategic planning and marketing management. As a result, business theory grounded in the needs and problems of managing financial service firms has started to emerge.

The many financial service activities which involve simultaneous production and consumption mean that all customer contact staff in financial service firms are involved in marketing. This explains the emphasis in several of the contributions on issues relating to the management of organizational culture and development.

In spite of its relatively long history, the financial services industry still has a long way to go in terms of understanding the role and importance of customer service and in marketing development. Customer service is increasingly recognized as a critical success factor in the service sector because service organizations are largely 'people' businesses. Given the characteristics of service firms and their interaction with the market-places that they serve, there is clearly a degree of commonality in management and marketing methods. This is certainly an important theme in the chapters on managing financial services which follow.

Chapter 8

Marketing in financial services organization: policy and practice

Neil Morgan and *Nigel Piercy*

Overview

Historically, financial services organizations, and particularly banks, have been seemingly disinclined to adopt the marketing concept and have been criticized for being largely 'product led' (Brien and Stafford, 1967; Wasem, 1969; Lewis, 1984). The 1980s have, however, seen a number of changes in the business environment which have impacted upon the role and function of marketing within financial services organizations. Legislative changes have deregulated large parts of the financial services markets, have effectively changed the boundaries of the markets served by financial services firms and have also removed many of the barriers between different types of financial services organization (Wright and Watkins, 1986, 1987). Technological developments in terms of information technology have led to benefits in the administration costs and in the provision of services. Developments such as ATMS and EFTPOS have also not only changed the distribution patterns within the financial services market (Clark and Guscott, 1986) but have even changed the basis of competition in many aspects of money transmission services (Howcroft and Lavis, 1986; Middleton, 1987). There is also some evidence of a growth in the financial awareness of consumers in the financial services market-place, which has led to increasingly sophisticated customer demands upon financial services organizations (Lewis, 1984; Middleton, 1987).

These environmental changes have, effectively increased competitive pressure across the broad spectrum of the financial services markets (Baker, 1977; Yorke, 1982; Meidan, 1983). Several writers have linked these environmental and resulting competitive changes with a change in attitude towards marketing as both a business function and a business philosophy in the financial services sector (Crawley, 1982; Yorke, 1982; Meidan, 1983; Lewis, 1984; Majaro, 1984; Middleton, 1987). In the light of these environmental, competitive and perceived attitudinal changes in the role of marketing, the present study examines the marketing function in the context of major financial services organizations in the UK. In particular, this article focuses on the issues of organization for marketing and marketing effectiveness.

Early studies of the issue of marketing organization focused upon the role of marketing structures in the implementation of the marketing paradigm. Whilst it was argued that the implementation of marketing was primarily dependent upon organizational culture and the prevailing philosophy of top management and not upon marketing structures (Ames, 1970; Pearson and Wilson, 1967), this view was not universally accepted. Others took the view that the successful implementation of the marketing concept was essentially concerned with the integration of marketing functions under the direct control of a chief marketing executive (CME) and with the position of the CME within the management structure of the organization (Weigand, 1961; Hise, 1965; Carson, 1968; Hayhurst and Wills, 1972). The publication of some recent theoretical contributions to this area (Weitz and Anderson, 1981; Ruekert *et al.*, 1985; Piercy, 1985) has revived some general academic interest in the area of organization for marketing.

To a certain extent this chapter revives some of the early debate by examining the question of organizational structure in marketing not only as an area worthy of study in its own right but by relating the form of marketing structure to a notion of marketing effectiveness. The measures used to evaluate marketing effectiveness in this study have an obvious relationship with the measures used to examine the degree of implementation of the marketing concept in earlier studies.

A number of studies of the chief marketing executive and the marketing department have been undertaken in the context of the UK manufacturing industry (British Institute of Management, 1970; Hayhurst and Wills, 1972; Piercy, 1986; Doyle, 1987). Academic interest in services marketing, whilst increasing, has failed to grow at a rate that reflects the importance of marketing within service organizations or the importance of the service sector within the UK economy. Relatively little attention has been focused upon UK service industries in anything other than a very general sense (see, for example, Hooley and Cowell, 1985). This study focuses specifically upon marketing organization and its relationship with marketing effectiveness in UK financial services organizations, and is to some extent a continuation of earlier organizational studies in manufacturing companies (Piercy, 1985, 1986) and the retail sector (Piercy and Alexander, 1988).

In particular, the study tests two critical hypotheses. First, we hypothesized that in terms of responsibilities, size and maturity there are a number of different types of marketing department in financial services firms:

H1 – There are different forms of marketing departmentation in financial services organizations.

Secondly, we anticipated that the form of marketing departmentation adopted by financial services organizations would be related to the marketing effectiveness of the company.

H2 – The strength and form of marketing departmentation in financial services organizations is related to the marketing effectiveness of those companies.

The research study

Methodology

This chapter reports the findings of an exploratory study of the areas of responsibility of chief marketing executives (CMEs) and marketing departments in financial services organizations in the UK, together with the perceived effectiveness of marketing in the companies.

The data were collected in a postal survey, using a pre-tested questionnaire, at the end of 1987. The sample consisted of 376 of the largest financial services organizations in the UK, drawn from the banking, building society and insurance sectors. The sampling units were chief marketing executives (effectively excluding organizations without a CME), and the response rate was 35 per cent. The responses represent banks (14 per cent), building societies (39 per cent) and insurance companies (47 per cent).

The operationalization of the CME responsibility variables used a checklist adapted from earlier studies of manufacturing (Piercy, 1986) and retailing services (Piercy and Alexander, 1988). The question items and scales are shown in Table 8.1. The operationalization of the marketing effectiveness variables used measurement scales developed by Kotler (1977), which identified marketing effectiveness as a function of a company's ability to combine five activities: customer philosophy, integrated marketing organization, strategic orientation, marketing information and operational efficiency. The question items and scales are shown in Table 8.2.

The descriptive results shown in Table 8.1 demonstrate some variance in the responsibility measures, suggesting some diversity in the grouping and degree of CME responsibilities in these organizations. The descriptive results of the marketing effectiveness variables shown in Table 8.2 similarly demonstrate a degree of diversity in respondents' perceived effectiveness in component parts of overall effectiveness in marketing.

Reliability and validity

Before examining the results of the study, it is obviously necessary to discuss the operationalization of the key indices used to capture CME responsibilities and marketing effectiveness.

To derive measures of CME responsibilities the variable scores shown in Table 8.1 were factor analysed as shown in Table 8.3. These variables loading on to factors with coefficients greater than 0.3 were used to construct four additive scales: marketing services (RES1), distribution (RES2), product and pricing policy (RES3) and corporate strategy (RES4).

Similarly, measures of marketing effectiveness were derived from the factor analysis of the variable scores shown in Table 8.2. The results of the factor analysis are shown in Table 8.4. Variables loading on to factors with coefficients greater than 0.3 were used to construct three additive scales: marketing formalization (MEI), organizational effectiveness (ME2) and market sensitivity (ME3).

Table 8.1 *Variable response frequencies: chief marketing executive responsibilities*

			Level of CME responsibilities				
	Sole (%)	Major (%)	Equal (%)	Some (%)	None (%)	N/A (%)	
V11 Advertising	37	56	2	5	1	0	(N = 95)
V12 Sales promotion	33	53	6	6	2	0	(N = 94)
V13 Price setting	4	25	19	34	14	4	(N = 95)
V14 Selling operations	16	24	21	27	11	1	(N = 94)
V15 Branch management	13	11	6	25	41	4	(N = 94)
V16 Sales forecasting	7	35	30	13	12	3	(N = 94)
V17 Marketing research	51	38	8	1	1	1	(N = 95)
V18 Branch target setting	20	30	18	15	13	4	(N = 94)
V19 Marketing planning	45	41	11	1	1	1	(N = 95)
V20 Product selection and development	14	52	26	4	4	0	(N = 95)
V21 Branch site selection	5	14	16	18	41	6	(N = 93)
V22 Agency control	13	16	16	15	33	7	(N = 95)
V23 Branch design and merchandising	24	36	12	19	6	3	(N = 93)
V24 New product launches	33	55	7	5	0	0	(N = 95)
V25 Internal investment appraisal	3	14	22	24	27	10	(N = 94)
V26 Diversification studies	4	28	27	24	9	8	(N = 92)
V27 Marketing staff selection	52	35	7	2	2	2	(N = 94)
V28 Marketing training	51	28	10	7	2	2	(N = 94)
V29 Corporate/strategic planning	3	31	36	22	8	0	(N = 95)

Table 8.2 *Variable response frequencies: marketing effectiveness*

	True (%)	More true than false (%)	Difficult to say (%)	More false than true (%)	False (%)
V71 Management recognizes the importance of designing or providing products or services which serve the needs and wants of chosen markets	74	19	3	3	1
V72 Management takes into account competitors, customers and its operating environment in planning its marketing organization	64	29	6	2	2
V73 Management develops different strategies for different segments of the market	53	29	7	6	5
V74 There is marketing integration and control of major marketing functions (i.e. advertising, product development, marketing research and personal selling)	42	33	9	8	8
V75 Employees responsible for marketing activities work well with employees in other functional areas	42	37	13	3	5
V76 The process for assessing new product or service opportunities is very well organized	15	32	26	21	6
V77 The market-place is studied systematically and frequently	34	25	12	23	6
V78 Management knows the sales potential and profitability of different market segments	15	38	21	15	11
V79 A great deal of effort is expended to measure the cost-effectiveness of different marketing expenditures	16	23	16	26	19
V80 Formal marketing planning operates effectively	18	31	25	11	15
V81 Our current organization strategy is well thought-out and effective	26	42	19	9	4
V82 Marketing thinking is communicated and implemented down the line	22	46	15	12	5
V83 Management is doing an effective job with the marketing resources	18	49	20	8	5
V84 Management reacts quickly and efficiently to on-the-spot marketing changes	20	34	26	12	8

Table 8.3 *Factor analysis[1] of chief marketing executive responsibilities*

CME responsibility factor labels	CME responsibility variables	Factor loadings[2]					
		1	2	3	4	5	6
Marketing services (RES1)	V28 Marketing training	0.84					
	V27 Marketing staff selection	0.82					
	V11 Advertising	0.76					
	V19 Marketing planning	0.70					
	V17 Marketing research	0.69					
Distribution (RES2)	V15 Branch management		0.85				
	V14 Selling operations		0.80				
	V22 Agency control		0.76				
	V21 Branch site selection		0.75				
	V18 Branch target setting		0.58				
	V23 Branch design and merchandising		0.35				0.79
Product and pricing policy (RES3)	V13 Price setting			0.74			
	V20 Product selection and development			0.73			
	V24 New product launches			0.69			
	V12 Sales promotion			0.65			
Corporate strategy (RES4)	V29 Corporate planning				0.69		
	V16 Sales forecasting				0.66		
	V25 Internal investment appraisal					0.81	
	V26 Diversification studies					0.79	

[1] Principal components analysis with varimax rotation, converging in 6 iterations.
[2] Loadings of less than 0.3 are suppressed; the two variables loading on to factor 5 are included for scaling purposes in factor 4; the single variable loading on to factor 6 is included for scaling purposes in factor 2.

Adopting the Sellitz *et al.* (1976) argument that an evaluation of a measurement procedure requires the estimation of the amount of variation attributable to random errors, the Cronbach alpha coefficient was used to evaluate reliability (Cronbach, 1951). Using Nunnally's threshold of acceptable reliability of an alpha coefficient of 0.5 or greater, both the responsibility and marketing effectiveness scales satisfy the realiability criteria, as shown in Table 8.5. In order to evalute the validity of the operationalization, each scale item was correlated with the index itself. These correlation coefficients were found to be in the expected direction, were significant at the 0.001 level and were high enough to overcome the auto-correlation objection. This suggests a relatively high level of inter-item validity, in the sense of scale items contributing to the concept that the total index was designed to measure.

Results

The descriptive results for CME responsibility and marketing effectiveness are shown in Tables 8.1 and 8.2 respectively. The responsibility variables show some diversity in the areas for which CMEs in the industry have sole or major responsibility. The marketing effectiveness variables similarly show some diversity in the component areas of marketing effectiveness in which CMEs believe their organizations to be effective.

Table 8.4 *Factor analysis[1] of marketing effectiveness variables*

Marketing effectiveness factor labels	Marketing effectiveness variables		Factor loadings[2]		
			1	2	3
Marketing formalization (ME1)	V74	There is marketing integration and control of major marketing functions (i.e. advertising, product development, marketing research and personal selling)			
	V80	Formal marketing planning operates effectively	0.75	0.55	
	V79	A great deal of effort is expended to measure the cost-effectiveness of different marketing expenditures	0.64		
	V77	The market-place is studied systematically and frequently	0.63	0.33	
	V78	Management knows the sales potential and profitability of different market segments	0.62		
	V76	The process for assessing new products or service opportunities is very well organized	0.60	0.38	0.34
	V75	Employees responsible for marketing activities work well with employees in other functional areas	0.48		0.46
Organizational effectiveness (ME2)	V84	Management reacts quickly and efficiently to on-the-spot marketing changes		0.79	
	V81	Our current organization strategy is well-thought-out and effective		0.77	
	V83	Management is doing an effective job with the marketing resources		0.70	
	V82	Marketing thinking is communicated and implemented down the line		0.53	
Market sensitivity (ME3)	V71	Management recognizes the importance of designing or providing products or services which serve the needs and wants of chosen markets			0.88
	V72	Management takes into account competitors, customers and its operating environment in planning its marketing organization			0.73
	V73	Management develops different strategies for different segments of the market			0.56
Eigenvalues			6.07	1.36	1.14
% of variance			43.3	9.7	8.1

[1] Principal components analysis with varimax rotation, converging in 6 iterations.
[2] Loadings of less than 0.3 are suppressed.

Table 8.5 *Scale statistics*

Scales	No. of items	Mean[1]	SD	Cronbach alpha	Inter-item correlations[2]						
					1	2	3	4	5	6	7
RES1	5	4.24	0.77	4.85	0.83	0.77	0.70	0.62	0.72		
RES2	6	2.71	1.06	0.83	0.80	0.75	0.66	0.74	0.77	0.61	
RES3	4	3.63	0.73	0.76	0.80	0.77	0.73	0.62			
RES4	4	2.73	0.88	0.68	0.65	0.65	0.75	0.81			
ME1	7	3.48	0.90	0.85	0.66	0.85	0.72	0.67	0.70	0.78	0.53
ME2	4	3.65	0.85	0.79	0.72	0.78	0.77	0.77			
ME3	3	4.43	0.74	0.71	0.63	0.69	0.79				

[1] Derived as arithmetic mean scores from Tables 8.3 and 8.4.
[2] Spearman rank correlation coefficients, all significant at the 0.001 level.

The descriptive data were tested for differences between the three sectors making up the sample (banks, building societies and insurance companies). Table 8.6 indicates that there were no significant differences between either the CME responsibility factor mean scores or the marketing effectiveness factor mean scores in the three sectors, i.e. the data suggest that there is little difference in CME responsibilities and marketing effectiveness between the banks, building societies and insurance companies surveyed. Although this may seem surprising, we hypothesize that this may be explained by the growing 'financial services' orientation of all sectors of the industry, as opposed to the traditional sectoral specialization in banking, insurance and so on. In terms of marketing department characteristics, there are significant differences in absolute and relative department size, although not in the age of the departments.

Thus, for the purposes of this exploratory work, it seems reasonable for the analysis to be carried out for the sample as a whole rather than for each sectoral segment.

Marketing departments

In order to evalute the first of our hypotheses, the companies were clustered into four groups on the basis of their CME responsibility factors, as shown in Table 8.7. This procedure identified four distinct forms of marketing departmentation in the financial services industry.

The first group was labelled 'integrated full-service marketing departments'. This group had the highest level of responsibility for distribution (RES2) and relatively high scores for all the other responsibility factors. These were the largest departments in terms of staff and were relatively long established, with a median age of five years.

The second group was labelled 'limited staff-role marketing departments'. In these companies, marketing departments scored lowest on each of the responsibility factors, particularly in the key areas of distribution (RES2) and corporate strategy (RES4). These are relatively small departments in terms of marketing employees and are the youngest in the sample with a median age of $2\frac{1}{2}$ years. This group was small in the total sample and the departments were found mainly in building societies.

The third group was labelled 'centralized/strategic marketing departments'. These departments had the highest scores in the sample for marketing services (RES1) and product and pricing policy (RES3), and relatively high scores for corporate strategy (RES4). They are distinguished from the integrated full-service departments mainly by their low scores on distribution factors (RES2). The picture is of a relatively powerful department heavily involved in product and corporate strategy, but not linked to the branch or office network. These were relatively small departments in terms of staff and had a median age of four years.

The final group was labelled 'centralized services-orientated marketing departments'. These departments score highly on marketing services (RES1) and are distinguished from the strategy-orientated departments by a considerably lower score for corporate strategy (RES4) and product and pricing policy (RES3).

Table 8.6 *Sector differences in CME responsibilities, marketing departments and marketing effectiveness*

		Mean scores			Kruskal-Wallis one-way analysis of variance	
	Banks (N = 18)	Building societies (N = 48)	Insurance companies (N = 60)	Total sample (N = 126)	Chi-square	Significance
CME responsibilities [1]						
RES1 Marketing services	4.12	4.04	4.41	4.24	3.64	0.16
RES2 Distribution	2.59	2.79	2.71	2.71	0.38	0.83
RES3 Product and pricing policy	3.79	3.57	3.62	3.63	0.40	0.82
RES4 Corporate strategy	2.86	2.88	2.57	2.73	3.87	0.15
Marketing departments						
V7 No. of marketing employees	38.6	13.7	31.1	26.1	8.74	0.01
V7 Marketing employees/total employees(%)	1.3	1.7	3.7	2.7	8.12	0.01
V3 Marketing department age (years)	6.9	5.8	6.6	6.3	0.03	0.99
Marketing effectiveness [2]						
ME1 Marketing formalization	3.70	3.52	3.37	3.47	3.48	0.18
ME2 Organizational effectiveness	3.61	3.82	3.52	3.65	3.39	0.18
ME3 Market sensitivity	4.55	4.36	4.46	4.43	1.46	0.48

1 5-point scale as in Table 8.1.
2 5-point scale as in Table 8.2.

These departments also received a very low score on distribution (RES2). These were relatively large departments in staff terms and were the oldest in the sample.

Taking the responsibility and size data, it is possible to construct the stereotypical model in Figure 8.1.

On the basis of the exploratory analyses, it is suggested that the first hypothesis – that there are a number of different forms of marketing departmentation in the financial services industry – should be accepted.

The first step in the evaluation of the second of our hypotheses was to establish the relationship between CME responsibilities and marketing effectiveness. The sample was therefore analysed for correlations between the variable mean scores on the CME marketing responsibility and marketing effectiveness scales. The correlation matrix shown in Table 8.8 shows a relationship between CME responsibilities and marketing effectiveness which is in the expected direction. A

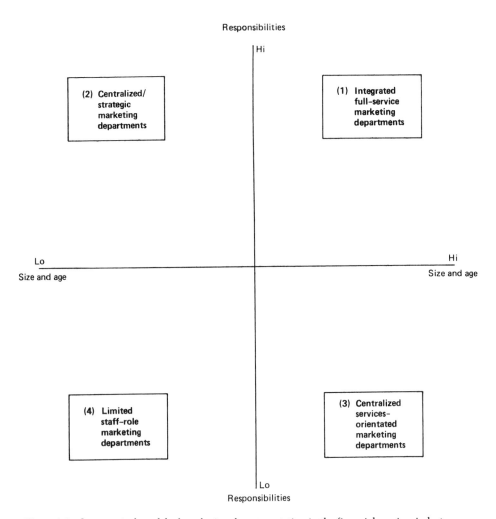

Figure 8.1 Stereotypical model of marketing departmentation in the financial services industry

Table 8.7 *Cluster analysis*

Variables/scales	Clusters				
CME responsibilities	1 (N = 19)	2 (N = 7)	3 (N = 41)	4 (N = 27)	Total sample (N = 94)
RES1 Marketing services	4.25	2.49	4.60	4.10	4.24
RES2 Distribution	4.32	1.69	2.71	1.84	2.71
RES3 Product and pricing policy	3.76	2.25	4.02	3.28	3.63
RES4 Corporate strategy	3.20	1.32	3.10	2.14	2.73
Cluster labels	Integrated full-service marketing departments	Limited staff-role marketing department	Centralized strategic marketing departments	Centralized services-orientated marketing departments	
Marketing department size Marketing employees/total employees (%)	1.51	1.16	1.16	1.25	
Marketing department age (years)	5.00	2.50	4.00	7.00	
Sectors Banks (%)	5	–	17	22	
Building societies (%)	42	71	39	19	
Insurance companies (%)	53	29	44	59	

Table 8.8 *Correlations*[1]

	ME1 Marketing formalization	ME2 Organizational effectiveness	ME3 Market sensitivity
CME responsibilities			
RES1 Marketing services	0.25*	0.25*	0.07
RES2 Distribution	0.19	0.34**	0.08
RES3 Product and price policy	0.27*	0.28*	0.26*
RES4 Corporate strategy	0.41**	0.48**	0.22

[1] Spearman rank correlation coefficients.
*Significant at 0.01 level.
**Significant at 0.001 level.

Table 8.9 *Clusters by marketing effectiveness factors*

	Cluster 1 (N = 75)	Cluster 2 (N = 53)	Analysis of variance	
			F-value	Significance
Cluster variable				
ME1	2.93	4.27	149.5	0.00
ME2	3.17	4.34	107.8	0.00
ME3	4.15	4.83	33.0	0.00
	Low marketing effectiveness	High marketing effectiveness		
RES1	4.07	4.45	5.74	0.02
RES2	2.43	3.06	9.24	0.00
RES3	3.41	3.88	5.01	0.00
RES4	2.40	3.14	18.91	0.00

large number of the component relationships in the correlation matrix are highly significant.

The correlation between CME responsibilities and marketing effectiveness is sufficient to establish that there is a relationship between marketing effectiveness and CME responsibilities.

In order to establish further the existence and significance of this relationship, the marketing effectiveness factors were used to cluster the companies into two groups. This procedure identified two distinctly different levels of marketing effectiveness, as shown in Table 8.9.

The first, and largest, group in the sample was labelled 'low marketing effectiveness' and scored lowest on marketing formalization (ME1), organizational effectiveness (ME2) and market sensitivity (ME3). The second group of companies was labelled 'high marketing effectiveness' and scored highly on all three of the marketing effectiveness additive scales. These high and low marketing effectiveness companies were found to exhibit significant differences in their factor scores in the CME responsibility scales, as shown in Table 8.9. The high marketing effectiveness companies in the sample exhibit significantly higher CME marketing responsibility scores on all four scales than low marketing effectiveness companies. The data do therefore suggest that there is a significant relationship between marketing effectiveness and CME responsibility levels.

Finally, in order to evaluate the second hypothesis in terms of the marketing department types identified earlier, it was necessary to establish the relationship between the high and low marketing effectiveness companies identified in Table 8.9 and the marketing departments identified in Table 8.7. This relationship was more problematic to establish due to the small number of limited staff-role marketing departments found in the sample. It was therefore necessary to group the four marketing department types identified. As the marketing departments

		Marketing effectiveness score	
		Low	High
		(no. of cases)	(no. of cases)
Degree of CME responsibility	High	25	35
	Low	26	7

Chi-square: 10.39

DF: 1

Significance: 0.0013

Figure 8.2 Marketing effectiveness and department responsibility

were essentially identified on CME marketing responsibility scales, it was decided to group the departments into high CME marketing responsibility departments (integrated full-service marketing departments and centralized/strategic marketing departments) and low CME marketing responsibility departments (limited staff-role marketing departments and centralized services-orientated marketing departments).

The high and low marketing effectiveness companies were then tested to establish the significance of the level of marketing department CME responsibility. In order to do this, the low and high marketing effectiveness companies were cross-tabulated with the low and high degrees of marketing department CME responsibility. The cross-tabulation is shown in Figure 8.2.

On the basis of these exploratory analyses, it is suggested that the second hypothesis – that the strength and form of marketing departmentation is related to the marketing effectiveness of companies – should be provisionally accepted. Whilst the relationship between the marketing effectiveness and the strength of the marketing department in terms of CME responsibility levels is reasonably clear, further analysis of the data is necessary to establish the relationship between marketing department form and marketing effectiveness.

Emerging issues for the 1990s

For financial service organizations the 1990s will be dominated by the increasingly competitive nature of the financial services market-place. Competition is unlikely to be restricted to those organizations that have historically serviced the market for financial services: new competition is likely to emerge from the retail sector and also from post-1992 Europe. The key problem that needs to be addressed is that of achieving competitive differentiation in offering largely generic financial services. It was the emerging competitive environment of the 1980s that led to the introduction of a marketing function in many UK financial services organizations. The continuing competition of the 1990s is likely to lead to a reappraisal of the role of marketing in this sector.

Marketing is still a relatively young management function in many service industries, and the financial services sector is no exception. This is particularly the case *vis-à-vis* the manufacturing sector. It is therefore likely that the role of marketing within financial service organizations will become an important issue, particularly if the rapidly increasing size of many marketing departments continues. Any reappraisal of the role of marketing will need to address the centralization problem: is marketing primarily a staff function or a line function in the branch/office network? The resolution of this issue will obviously impact enormously upon how marketing is organized.

Given the ongoing complexity and uncertainty of the financial services market-place, coupled with the relative youth but rapidly increasing sophistication of the marketing function, it is likely that the management agenda in financial services organizations will be increasingly concerned with addressing issues of organizational culture and, more particularly, the management of change. Changing markets and environments demand new strategies that will necessitate internal organizational change if they are to be successfully implemented. This realization will lead to cultural issues becoming increasingly important in the 1990s.

Discussion

At a time when issues of marketing development are to the fore in the financial services industry, this exploratory study offers some new insights into the development of the formal marketing function and its links with overall corporate marketing effectiveness.

The data from this survey of a significant number of the largest financial services organizations in the UK demonstrates the development of formal marketing organizations in financial services companies. The analyses interestingly suggest that industry differences in the approach to organizing marketing are not related to sectoral differences (i.e. between banks, building societies and insurance companies) and are more likely to be related to the individual stage of corporate evolution.

Using a replicated methodology from studies in other sectors, the CME responsibilities measured in the survey allowed the identification of four different types of marketing organization existing in the UK financial services industry. These organizational forms for marketing were stereotyped as: integrated full-service marketing departments, with broad responsibilities for both service and line areas of the business and relatively large staffing; limited staff-role marketing departments, with low staffing and little responsibility in anything other than marketing services; centralized/strategic marketing departments, with relatively limited staffing and little involvement in the branch network but a high degree of responsibility in product and pricing policy and in corporate strategy; and centralized services-orientated marketing departments, with higher staffing levels but lower involvement in areas other than marketing services. The largest groups were the centralized departments focusing on strategy or services, which accounted for three-quarters of the companies studied. Only one in five of the departments studied fell into the integrated full-service category.

Whilst this is an exploratory study with a necessarily small sample (due to the degree of concentration in the industry), the hypotheses are sufficiently robust to provide some insight into the present evolution of the marketing function in the UK financial services industry. The stereotypical model in Figure 8.1 and the responsibility scales in Table 8.1 provide the basis for a self-diagnostic instrument with which executives in the industry can locate their own marketing departments, in order to provide a foundation for comparing their own policies with those of competitors and as a basis for planning the future of their organizational development in the marketing area. This approach to organizational analysis has proved fruitful in other sectors.

The relationship between marketing organization and marketing effectiveness modelled in this study also offers a number of useful insights.

Management at all levels and in all functional areas in financial services organizations is necessarily concerned with organizational effectiveness. This study indicates that in the marketing area there is a significant relationship between the type of marketing department formed by a financial services organization and the perceived effectiveness of its marketing function and activities.

The marketing departmentation types identified in this study were constructed upon the basis of chief marketing executive responsibilities for marketing functions. The two main discriminating areas of responsibility with which the departmentation types were identified were the degree of chief marketing executive (and hence marketing department) responsibility for marketing functions connected with distribution, and corporate strategy.

The implication of this study is that marketing departments with a high degree of responsibility for distribution, i.e. a presence in the branch/office network of financial organizations, and a high degree of responsibility for corporate strategic management, i.e. a large input into corporate planning and strategic decisions, are more likely to be marketing effective. These key areas of marketing responsibility do not, however, appear to stand alone. The survey produced no examples of marketing departments with high responsibility for distribution and corporate strategy and low responsibility for marketing services and for product and pricing policy. Thus, whilst this exploratory study identifies distribution responsibilities and strategic responsibilities as predictors of perceived organizational marketing effectiveness, it is by no means clear whether responsibilities in these areas without responsibility in marketing services and in product and pricing policy would have the same predictive value.

References

Ames, B.C. (1970) 'Trappings versus substance in industrial marketing', *Harvard Business Review*, July/August, 93–102.

Baker, M.J. (1977) 'Bank marketing', *Scottish Bankers Magazine*, July, 106–20.

Brien, R.H. and Stafford, J.E. (1967) 'The myth of marketing in banking', *Business Horizons*, 10, Spring, 71–8.

British Institute of Management (1970) *Marketing Organization in British Industry.* London: BIM.

Carson, D. (1968) 'Marketing organization in British manufacturing firms', *Journal of Marketing*, 32, April, 34–9.

Clark, R.T. and Guscott, P.E. (1986) 'Technology and marketing: which is master?', *The Banker*, April, 91–5.

Crawley, F.W. (1982) 'Competition in retail banking', *Long Range Planning*, 15, 3, 71–9.

Cronbach, L.J. (1951) 'Coefficient alpha and the internal structure of tests', *Psychometrika*, 16, 297–334.

Doyle, P. (1987) 'Marketing and the British chief executive', *Journal of Marketing Management*, 3, 2, 121–33.

George, W.R. and Barksdale, H.C. (1974) 'Marketing activities in the service industries', *Journal of Marketing*, 35, Fall, 65–70.

Hayhurst, R. and Wills, G.S.C. (1972) *Organizational Design for Marketing Futures.* London: Allen and Unwin.

Hise, R.T. (1965) 'Have manufacturing firms adopted the marketing concept?', *Journal of Marketing*, 29, Summer, 9–12.

Hooley, G, and Cowell, D. (1985) 'The status of marketing in the UK service industries', *Service Industries Journal*, 5, 3, 261–72.

Howcroft, B. and Lavis, J. (1986) 'A strategic perspective on delivery systems in UK retail banking', *Service Industries Journal*, 6, 2, 144–58.

Kotler, P. (1977) 'From sales obsession to marketing effectiveness', *Harvard Business Review*, November/December, 67 75.

Lewis, B.R. (1984) 'Marketing bank services', *Service Industries Journal*, 4, 3, 61–76.

Majaro, S. (1984) 'Marketing insurance services: the main challenge', *Service Industries Journal*, 4, 5, 77–90.

Meidan, A. (1983) 'The roles of marketing management in banking', *Quarterly Review of Marketing*, Spring, 11–18.

Middleton, P. (1987) 'Are non banks winning in retail financial services?', *International Journal of Bank Marketing*, 5, 1, 3–18.

Pearson, A.E. and Wilson, T.W. (1967) *Making Your Marketing Organization Work*. New York: National Association of Advertisers.

Piercy, N. (1985) *Marketing Organization: An Analysis of Information Processing, Power and Politics*. London: Allen and Unwin.

Piercy, N. (1986) 'The role and function of the chief marketing executive and the marketing department', *Journal of Marketing Management*, 1, 3, 265–90.

Piercy, N. and Alexander, N. (1988) 'The status quo of marketing in UK retailing organizations: a neglected phenomenon of the 1980s', *Service Industries Journal*, 8, 2, 155–75.

Ruekert, R.W., Walker, O.C. and Roering, K.J. 'The organization of marketing activities: a contingency theory of structure and performance', *Journal of Marketing*, 49, Winter, 15–25.

Sellitz, C., Wrightman, L.S. and Cook, S.W. (1976) *Research Methods in Social Relations*. New York: Holt, Rinehart and Winston.

Wasem, G.M. (1969) 'The triple dilemma of bank marketing', *Bankers Magazine* (USA), 152, 65–9.

Weigand, R.E. (1961) 'Changes in the marketing organization in selected industries, 1950–1959', unpublished PhD thesis, University of Illinois.

Weitz, B. and Anderson, E. (1981) 'Organizing the marketing function', in *AMA Review of Marketing*. Chicago, Ill.: American Marketing Association.

Wright, M. and Watkins, T. (1986) 'Banks and developments in the personal financial services market: evidence from a questionnaire survey', *International Journal of Bank Marketing*, 4, 2, 24–34.

Wright, M. and Watkins, T. (1987) 'The impact of deregulation on the strategy and structure of building societies', *Service Industries Journal*, 7, 2, 216–31.

Yorke, D.A. (ed.) (1982) *The Marketing of Bank Services*. Bradford: MCB.

Chapter 9

Personal financial services: an appraisal of recent developments and research issues

Christine Ennew, Trevor Watkins and *Mike Wright*

Overview

The personal financial services sector in the UK has recently been experiencing the effects of changes in its regulatory framework and the consequent impact upon the competitive environment. These changes have mainly stemmed from the introduction of the Financial Services Act and the Building Societies Act, although other legislative changes have also been influential. The increase in competition is also related to other factors beyond regulatory developments, particularly the internationalization of financial markets and the development of information technology (Carter *et al.*, 1986; Watkins and Wright, 1986a; Robbie and Wright, 1988).

In this chapter we seek to examine the effects of these changes on financial firms. The issues are examined in turn at three interrelated levels: corporate strategy, marketing, and internal organization and governance structures. The success of the first is closely related to how well marketing and internal organization are matched to the demands of corporate strategy. Within marketing an increasing emphasis is being placed upon market research, advertising, distribution channels and information technology. As regards internal organization, attention is focused upon whether organizational structures and management styles are equipped to deal with changing circumstances, and whether new products should be provided internally or through some form of quasi-market relationship with another supplier. The traditional nature of the sector has exacerbated the trauma normally associated with imposed changes in the competitive process. Most of the changes affect the supply side of the industry, with little evidence of significant proactive shifts in the pattern of demand.

In the early 1980s the pricing cartel of the building societies broke down and the banks made a determined push into the mortgage market. These changes led to a move into money transmission services by the largest building societies. In addition, attention in the sector focused on the retailing of insurance products and the considerable commission earnings which this activity could generate. Thus all the major types of financial institution moved into direct competition across the sector. Instead of the traditional institutions' view of the market, a customer view became a more useful way of approaching corporate strategy. Recently, competition across types of institution has focused particularly on:

- mortage provision (banks, building societies, insurance companies and specialists suppliers);

- attraction of young investors (banks and building societies);
- money transmission services (banks and building societies);
- longer-term investments (insurance companies, unit trusts and stockbrokers);
- higher-interest accounts (banks and building societies).

Through the use of survey evidence, which seeks to quantify the changes taking place, we hope to highlight the nature of the strategic and organizational problems facing managers in personal financial services institutions and to indicate potential solutions. An important theme is the need for flexibility of response and for experimentation. The chapter is intended as a case study of an industry under change, and in the concluding section we identify lessons to be learned from the experience. The approach draws on various strands in the relevant literature and new evidence from a recent survey undertaken by the Nottingham Institute of Financial Studies (NIFS) of 265 firms which provide personal financial services.

Corporate strategy

With the recent legislative and institutional changes, the market for personal financial services has undergone considerable structural changes. To maintain previously profitable positions, suppliers of personal financial services are being forced to adjust their corporate and marketing strategies in response to these changes. The precise form of these adjustments is only now becoming clear, primarily because the changes mentioned above have not yet fully worked through their impact on the market. The importance of developing a coherent corporate marketing strategy in the financial services sector has been outlined by Watkins (1986). Some indications of the changing patterns of corporate strategy as currently perceived by financial service firms can be obtained from the results of the recent survey conducted by NIFS. The survey focused attention on how firms expected their strategies to evolve over the period up to 1992. To approach used was broadly based on Porter's (1985) classification of strategies according to competitive scope (broad or narrow) and competitive advantage (cost or differentiation). In the context of the survey question, broad competitive scope was represented by strategies entailing broad market coverage, while the narrow or focus strategy was represented by the market nichers. A cost competitive advantage was represented by a narrow range of (usually standardized) products, while a differentiation competitive advantage was reflected in a wide range of products.

The results of the strategy survey are presented in Tables 9.1 and 9.2. Comparing current and future strategies, the survey results show that 64 per cent of firms currently rely on cost-based strategies (narrow product range) and the bulk of these are focus strategies. However, over the next five years we observe a significant shift in favour of differentiation strategies, with 54 per cent of respondents planning to pursue this route, thus taking advantage of the removal of restrictions on product ranges. It is interesting to note that the biggest increase appears to occur in the category representing differentiation leadership. It is

Table 9.1 *Current corporate strategy*

	All firms		Insurance companies		Insurance brokers		Banks		Unit/ investment trusts		Building societies		Stock- brokers	
	No.	%	No.	%	No.	%	No.	%	No.	%	No.	%	No.	%
Cost focus Narrow product range; small number of sectors	111	42.0	27	42.2	11	23.9	6	27.3	18	42.9	20	43.5	17	63.0
Cost lead Narrow product range; large number of sectors	59	22.3	18	28.1	7	15.2	3	13.6	12	28.6	14	30.4	4	14.8
Differential focus Broad product range; few sectors	52	19.7	11	17.2	14	30.4	5	22.7	9	21.4	8	17.4	2	7.4
Differential lead Broad product range; broad sectors	42	16.0	8	12.5	14	30.4	8	36.4	3	7.1	4	8.7	4	14.8
Total respondents	264	100.0	64	100.0	46	100.0	22	100.0	42	100.0	46	100.0	27	100.0

Table 9.2 Future corporate strategy

	All firms		Insurance companies		Insurance brokers		Banks		Unit/ investment trusts		Building societies		Stock-brokers	
	No.	%	No.	%	No.	%	No.	%	No.	%	No.	%	No.	%
Cost focus Narrow product range; small number of sectors	56	22.0	10	16.4	7	16.7	3	14.3	10	25.0	9	19.6	11	44.0
Cost lead Narrow product range; large number of sectors	61	24.0	22	36.0	7	16.7	2	9.5	13	32.5	9	19.6	5	20.0
Differential focus Broad product range; few sectors	57	22.5	12	19.7	11	26.2	5	23.8	8	20.0	11	23.9	5	20.0
Differential lead Broad product range; broad sectors	80	31.5	17	27.9	17	40.4	11	52.4	9	22.5	17	37.0	4	16.0
Total respondents	254	100.0	61	100.0	42	100.0	21	100.0	40	100.0	46	100.0	25	100.0

unlikely that the current market will support this number of leaders, and these responses may reflect some over-optimism on the part of a number of participants.

Considering patterns of change over the next five years, there is little evidence of firms opting for major strategic shifts (e.g. cost focus to differentiation leadership). The number of cost focusers declines: 44.8 per cent seek to retain their existing strategy, 23.8 per cent opt for cost leadership and 21 per cent opt for differentiation focus. Among cost leaders, the most common change in strategy is made in order to take advantage of deregulation to broader product ranges: 51.6 per cent of cost leaders retain that strategy but 31.6 per cent anticipate moving to differentiation leadership. Among those firms currently pursuing a differentiation-based strategy, there is no evidence of any significant move away from this source of competitive advantage: 55.3 per cent of differentiation focusers and 75 per cent of differentiation leaders envisage retaining their existing strategy, with the only obvious move being from differentiation focus to differentiation leadership (42.6 per cent of differentiation focusers).

If we examine patterns of strategy across sub-groups within the survey then some interesting differences arise. Insurance brokers and banks are already strongly reliant on differentiation strategies; brokers indicated the likelihood of a slight shift from differentiation focus to differentiation leadership but the change is rather small. The banks, on the other hand, envisage a more significant shift in favour of differentiation, perhaps in response to greater competition in their traditional areas of business.

By contrast, though not unsurprisingly given the nature of their work, stockbrokers see their strategy as primarily a cost focus strategy: only 22 per cent currently identify themselves as pursuing a differentiation-based strategy. However, as a group, the stockbrokers seem to envisage some developments in their traditional business which will encourage differentiation, and by 1992 some 36 per cent expect to be pursuing a differentiation-based strategy. The insurance companies, unit/investment trusts and the building societies correspond much more to the sample norm. Until now, they have perceived their role as primarily specialists in particular types of product; for these types of organization, deregulation has clearly had a major impact, making it possible for them to diversify within the market for personal financial services and to move quite strongly in the direction of differentiation strategies.

Clearly, with a large number of firms moving in the direction of greater differentiation and away from a cost-based strategy, the extent of competition within personal financial services is bound to increase. In particular, with many firms pursuing similar strategies it is unlikely that all will succeed; indeed, this extensive move towards differentiation may well create gaps in certain market segments, providing opportunities for the alert firm to develop such segments on the basis of a cost focus strategy. There is clearly scope for further research in this area to monitor the dynamics of marketing strategy.

Marketing

With the changes outlined in the previous section there are a number of important marketing issues facing the suppliers of personal financial services. In this section we select four of those issues for more detailed discussion: market research, advertising, distribution and the role of information technology.

Marketing and market research departments

With an increased emphasis upon the market, a key issue becomes the existence and roles of marketing and market research departments.

A recent survey of banks, building societies and insurance companies found that 83.6 per cent of organizations had a marketing function, the large majority of which could identify it as being a separate department (Davison, Watkins and Wright, 1989). For 27.3 per cent of the 110 respondents to the survey, the marketing function had been introduced within the past two years (Table 9.3).

Separate market research functions were identified for only 28.2 per cent of respondents. Whilst both large and small organizations had a high representation of marketing functions, market research functions were twice as likely to be present in large organizations as in small ones. The representation of these functions in financial services organizations appears less marked than in other sectors (e.g. fast-moving consumer goods), although a catching-up process may be expected to occur as a result of an increasingly competitive environment (Hooley *et al.*, 1984; Piercy, 1987). Not only is a catching-up process expected, but the nature of the function may be expected to change from one of selling to one of marketing or, as Clarke *et al.* (1988) would have it, from just 'doing' the organization's marketing to changing it into a marketing-controlled institution.

An important element in the roles of marketing and market research department is the behaviour of purchasers of personal financial services. This aspect may be relevant at several levels. At one level there may be a need to monitor general

Table 9.3 *Length of time marketing and marketing research departments established in personal financial services*

Time	Marketing function (%)	Marketing research function (%)
Function absent	16.4	71.8
Less than 1 year	8.2	3.6
1–2 years	19.1	4.5
3–5 years	20.9	8.2
6–10 years	20.9	6.4
Over 10 years	11.8	5.5
Not known	2.7	–
Total	100.0	100.0
No. of respondents	110	110

Source: Davison, Watkins and Wright (1989).

developments in personal wealth, and to analyse findings by various potential market segments. Although there is little published market research data on the personal financial services sector, commercial market research organizations occasionally publish some useful information (for example, see the chapters 'Who is there?' and 'Market analysis' in Dyer and Watkins (1988)). A second level relates to developments in consumer attitudes to financial institutions and financial products, particularly to the identification of mismatches or asymmetries in perceptions. Consumers' images of financial institutions and products may lag behind and affect changes that the institution wishes to introduce (Howcroft and Lavis, 1986). Hence there may be a need continually to examine how individuals are likely to react in general to new products and methods of distribution. For example, whilst the issues of customer convenience and sophistication may be important (Watkins and Wright, 1985), they by no means involve an either/or choice. Detailed research may be required to identify separate market segments. Customer preference for convenience may rank behind other criteria for certain specialist products, where expertise and quality of service are more important (Furlong and Brent Ritchie, 1986). In addition, it is by no means clear to what extent results from one culture or market apply directly to another (see, for example, the different results obtained for Canada and the USA reported in Furlong and Brent Ritchie (1986)).

However, a crucial issue relates to the nature and extent of new product development (NPD). Introducing a new product may be a relatively simple task if it meets the requirements of the organization's existing system and allows for the copying of competitors' innovations in a short space of time. This supply-side increase in the types of product available has to compete for a finite amount of consumer funds, which together with continuing innovation may mean that the market for a particular product is quite limited. However, it may be difficult to withdraw a product from the market, so that barriers to exit can be relatively high. A life insurance product, for example, cannot simply be deleted just because demand is low since customers will continue to be paying premiums. Firms will seek to minimize costs by ceasing to make active communication (advertising, etc.) to the market. The number of redundant products within a company's portfolio may well illustrate the importance of tracking consumer demand both at the early stages of development and during the life cycle of the product. The survey by Davison, Watkins and Wright (1989) examined institutions' NPD experience in terms of idea generation, number of NPD ideas, concept and product testing, decision to launch, criteria for launch and the extent to which products were withdrawn. A general conclusion was that there was a relatively low level of use of market research techniques in NPD. Part of the reason for this finding is the ease of copying of products and the need to introduce some product (e.g. new types of account) quickly in order to emulate competitors. Senior management was also seen to take strategic decisions to introduce a new product or type of product which overrode the NPD process. In addition, the cost of research was often considered to outweigh the costs of failure. There was also evidence that a low level of NPD research was undertaken because of customer sensitivity about revealing personal financial information and because consumers were perceived to be not very interested in financial products, buying them only on a need basis.

Moreover, product complexity was seen to cause difficulties for market research as consumers were generally unaware of the technical implications of their potential needs.

Advertising strategy

With the observed movements away from cost-based strategies, the importance of other marketing mix variables will increase. Effective promotion and, in particular, effective advertising will become increasingly important. In this market, advertising has a number of prime functions. Increasing consumer awareness of the company and its products is of particular importance for many organizations. While high street banks have been well known to the public for some years (as evidenced by scores of over 90 per cent in unprompted awareness tests), the same is not true of other personal financial services firms. Similarly, with the wider range of products likely to be offered, effective advertising and promotion will be crucial in attracting consumer attention – particularly so as the degree of product differentiation within organizations increases. Greater use of market segmentation has also prompted more extensive advertising to target specific markets and, as is illustrated below, the increased preference for direct response advertising to reduce distribution cost will expand advertising budgets.

Advertising strategies and methods used are presented according to importance, in Tables 9.4 and 9.5, based on results from the recent NIFS survey. Although significant changes were anticipated in corporate strategy (see above), this is not mirrored by substantial changes in advertising strategy. The emphasis remains on company image rather than specific products. Advertising of the company in new markets is expected to increase in the next year. The contrast between corporate and advertising strategies observed appears to reflect the time horizon in the question: a small shift away from traditional markets to new markets and new products is observed and seems likely to continue. This would be consistent with the move towards a differentiation strategy discussed above.

In terms of the media used for advertising, the questionnaire indicates little significant change in the coming year. There is slight evidence of an increase in usage of direct response advertising and computer software, but otherwise respondents are expecting to continue using broadly similar measures, directing them at newer markets.

Distribution

The provisions of the Financial Services Act, and the requirements imposed on their members by various self-regulatory organizations (SROs), are pushing financial services firms towards changes in distribution strategy. Drawing on the results of the NIFS survey, we find that the majority of those firms surveyed identify the Financial Services Act as a major influence on their distribution strategy (see Table 9.6). Similar high rankings are attached to the specific polarization requirements contained within the Act. Other legislative/institutional

Table 9.4   *Advertising strategies now and in twelve months' time*

	Very important		Important		Not important	
	No.	%	No.	%	No.	%
Advertising strategy now						
Insurance customer awareness of company in traditional markets	156	67	62	26	16	7
Increase customer awareness of traditional products	106	48	90	41	24	11
Create customer awareness of new markets	94	44	77	36	44	20
Launch new products in traditional markets	99	45	79	36	42	19
Advertising strategy in twelve months' time						
Increase customer awareness of company in traditional markets	154	67	59	26	16	7
Increase customer awareness of traditional products	110	52	82	39	20	9
Create customer awareness of new markets	117	55	74	35	23	10
Launch new products in traditional markets	114	55	72	35	22	10

Table 9.5   *Advertising methods now and in twelve months' time*

	Very important		Important		Not important	
	No.	%	No.	%	No.	%
Advertising methods now						
TV advertising	33	14	23	10	178	76
National press	70	29	73	31	96	40
Local press	59	25	74	31	105	44
Specialist financial press	53	22	101	42	86	36
Sponsorship	18	8	68	29	146	63
Direct response	60	25	96	41	81	34
Point-of-sale displays	46	20	68	30	116	50
Sales literature	119	48	107	43	21	9
Software/product illustration programmes	24	12	56	27	126	61
Advertising methods in twelve months' time						
TV advertising	36	16	42	19	146	65
National press	76	33	76	33	78	34
Local press	51	26	55	28	90	46
Specialist financial press	59	26	104	45	67	29
Sponsorship	21	10	76	34	125	56
Direct response	74	32	91	40	63	28
Point-of-sale displays	55	25	68	30	101	45
Sales literature	124	53	93	40	16	7
Software/product illustration programmes	42	21	68	33	93	46

changes are somewhat more specific in their impact: the Building Societies Act, for example, has its greatest influence on the building societies themselves and is of rather less significance to other groupings. The broad picture is one of recent changes exerting considerable influence on distribution strategies.

Some clearer indication of the nature of these developments can be obtained from an examination of patterns of usage of distribution channels now and in the future. Given the nature of the Financial Services Act, there are a number of trends which we might expect to observe: specifically, the requirements regarding sales force training might be expected to lead to a decline in the use of this particular channel. Similarly, the increased competition in indirect distribution channels (particularly broker networks) encouraged by the Act might be expected to encourage firms to make greater use of direct distribution (Watkins and Wright, 1986b).

The survey results for current and expected future distribution methods are presented in Tables 9.7 and 9.8. From these results and from the analysis of data for specific groups within the industry, it is clear that the majority of the organizations surveyed use a variety of distribution channels and that inter-organizational differences arise mainly from the relative importance of specific channels. In general, if we consider the likely changes, the most obvious one is the increase in importance of direct response advertising and direct response mail. Despite the relatively high costs of this particular channel, increased competition in indirect distribution has encouraged many firms to increase their usage of this method because of its value in getting direct access to specific customer groups. Building societies and unit/investment trusts, in particular, indicate a substantial increase in the importance of these channels.

Interestingly enough, despite the increases in the costs of training and licensing sales staff implied by the Financial Services Act, a significant number of respondents view this as an efficient method of distribution now and continue to emphasize its importance in the future. Insurance companies especially place considerable emphasis on this method, and the only significant change appears to be a slight shift over time from commission and salary sales in favour of commission-only sales.

The other major area of indirect distribution which needs consideration is the use of intermediaries and, in particular, branch networks. The polarization requirements of the Securities and Investment Board and the rules on commission led to the belief that many insurance broking networks would opt for tied company representative status. The implications of this trend for market competition were potentially adverse. However, the formation of CAMIFA (Campaign for Independent Financial Advice) has encouraged many intermediaries to retain their independent status, and a recent survey commissioned by the Office of Fair Trading indicated that 72.8 per cent of the smaller brokers and 94.4 per cent of the larger brokers had opted for independent status (Office of Fair Trading, 1987).

Bank and building society branch networks have also been required to make the decision as to whether to adopt tied or independent status in respect of their sales of insurance products. Among the banks, the National Westminster and the three Scottish banks have opted for independent status, while the rest have decided to take the status of a tied intermediary. Most of the smaller building

Table 9.6 *Influences on distribution strategy: all sectors*

	Very important		Important		Not important	
	No.	%	No.	%	No.	%
Financial Services Act	231	80	45	17	7	3
Building Societies Act	72	30	61	21	118	49
SIB rules on polarization	151	59	76	30	28	11
Branch network costs	67	28	103	43	68	29
Sales force costs	67	27	133	54	45	19
Impact of information technology	86	34	133	54	29	12
Competitors' strategies	64	26	147	61	32	13
Improved customer databases	110	44	105	43	32	13
Cross-selling products	29	14	50	25	121	61
Own-label brands to non-traditional suppliers	33	15	60	28	121	57
Joint ventures	39	18	104	48	75	34

Note: Percentages are based on number of respondents for each row. Some respondents did not answer certain questions.

Table 9.7 *Importance of current distribution methods: all sectors*

	Very important		Important		Not important	
	No.	%	No.	%	No.	%
Commission sales only	41	19	27	12	151	69
Commission/salary sales	66	28	58	24	113	48
Direct response advertising	46	18	97	39	109	43
Direct mail	40	16	110	43	103	41
Building society branches	47	20	30	13	156	67
Bank branches	28	13	30	13	166	74
Insurance company branches	37	16	59	26	129	58
Broker branches	76	32	55	23	104	44
Estate agents (owned)	15	7	10	5	192	88
Estate agents (not owned)	7	3	46	20	173	77
Franchising	2	1	9	4	206	95

Table 9.8 *Importance of distribution methods in five years' time*

	Very important		Important		Not important	
	No.	%	No.	%	No.	%
Commission sales only	48	23	36	18	122	59
Commission/salary sales	95	40	63	26	82	34
Direct response advertising	73	29	110	44	66	27
Direct mail	85	34	110	44	56	22
Building society branches	50	21	47	20	138	59
Bank branches	28	12	45	20	153	68
Insurance company branches	47	21	61	27	117	52
Broker branches	71	31	64	28	92	41
Estate agents (owned)	26	12	22	10	172	78
Estate agents (not owned)	9	4	53	25	159	72
Franchising	4	2	26	12	187	86

societies have also selected tied status, whereas the larger societies have generally taken the independent alternative (we return to the permanence of these decisions below).

Despite the relatively high cost of branch networks, and the costs associated with training staff to act as independent intermediaries, the branch network appears likely to remain an important distribution channel. For most organizations this simply represents a high level of dependence on own branch networks, but for unit and investment trusts a continued dependence on bank, building society and insurance company branch networks is envisaged. Over the next five years, they foresee a slight decline in the use of bank branch networks, but this is more than compensated for by the expected increase in the use of insurance company networks.

The Financial Services Act requirements on polarization and 'best' advice are essentially requirements to increase competition in distribution channels in order to provide improved services to the consumers of personal financial sevices. Given the importance of distribution in a mature market, and the growing trend towards a 'customer-orientated' market, the selection of appropriate marketing channels and the ability to compete effectively in those channels become of paramount importance. A priori, given the nature of the Financial Services Act, it might have been expected that a large number of firms would move towards direct distribution, in particular direct mail and direct response advertising. This expectation is confirmed in part by the NIFS survey results, with unit and investment trusts making the most obvious move in this direction. However, in overall terms the evidence suggests that, rather than switching between channels, firms are looking to increase the number and variety of channels in use in order to compete over a wider range of outlets.

Information technology (IT)

Originally, the driving force for computerization in the personal financial services sector was the need to deal more efficiently with transactions. Thus the systems which were set up were account or policy based. Recently, competitive pressure is pushing companies into the formation of customer-orientated databases as an aid to marketing effectiveness.

The use of IT in sales and marketing has been aided by technological advance, particularly in portable PCs and database systems. These developments have enabled sales presentations to make use of customized product illustrations (see Watkins, 1988). The perceived importance of IT in distribution strategy and advertising was seen in the previous section.

The financial services sector has been slow to make maximum use of available technology despite the wealth of customer information made available to companies in applications to buy services (e.g. insurance proposal forms, mortage applications). Companies are trying to gain competitive advantage by closing the gap between technological capability and actual use (see Dyer and Watkins (1988) for discussion of progress from the industry's perspective). However, there remains much to be done before IT is fully exploited. Conceptually, EFTPOS,

EPOS, EFTPOB and EFTPOL are well developed, but their penetration into the market is patchy. EFTPOB has probably developed most, but the others remain at a more experimental stage (e.g. Nottingham Building Society's Homelink; Anglia Building Society's EFTPOS). There is little published work on the success of and problems faced by these experiments (but see Robbie and Wright, 1988), and further case study analysis would seem warranted. In addition, useful insights may be gained from research into problems of acceptance of these systems by individual customers and retailers. An important aspect is the appropriate pricing structure for transactions (e.g. percentage fee vs flat rate fee). This issue has attracted attention in a wider context with the Monopolies Commission investigation of credit cards, which at the time of writing is still under way. (A previous Monopolies Commission report on credit cards in 1980 was particularly critical of pricing structures.)

Organizationally, the personal financial services sector is still some way from widespread use of marketing information systems as conceived in the literature (see Piercy and Evans, 1983; Watkins, 1985; Watkins and Wright, 1986a). This situation seems to be similar in other sectors (Johnson and Woodward, 1988). Major issues involved relate to problems in integrating information from various sources and constructing information on relevant bases. The extent to which branch officers can be encouraged and educated to make use of centrally held information for local marketing purposes may also have to be considered. The introduction of marketing information systems also raises issues about how managers react to change and the problems of how organizational cultures adapt to and influence change. These aspects are addressed further in the next section.

Internal organization and governance structures

Developments in corporate strategy which involve movements into new product areas and which entail enhancement of distribution systems raise important managerial and organizational issues which may be crucial in determining whether intentions are successful in practice.

The discussion in this section is essentially divided into two parts. First, the issues concerned with changes in management style, organization structure and organizational culture are examined. Secondly, an analysis is provided of the nature of the boundary between provision of a wider range of products internally and provision through a set of governance structures which depend upon the nature of the transactions.

Management style, organization structure and organization culture

Corporate strategic shifts occasioned by increases in competition and other changes in the environment place pressure upon the traditional skills required of management and the ways in which those skills are exercised. An important aspect of these developments is the effect upon the traditional head office–branch relationship and the differing skills required of managers in both parts of the organization (Howcroft and Lavis, 1987). Various strands in the general literature on the economies of internal organization suggest guidelines (Thompson and Wright, 1988). Increased divisionalization in more diversified organizations and more organic hierarchies may be expected. Moreover, as discussed in the previous section, a greater variety of distribution (or delivery) systems will be required. Evidence from the recent study conducted by NIFS sheds light on the extent of organizational changes taking place to deal with new product introductions and the managerial problems involved.

Respondents were asked to state which changes had occurred for products introduced in the past year, and what was expected in the coming five years (Table 9.9). Most notable in both respects is the recruitment of specialist management, a need which is expected to increase substantially in the next five years. A similar increase is expected in changes in the highest level of managers. Part of this change, of course, may be due to retirement, but the magnitude of the increase may indicate a perceived need to introduce senior management with a more strategic perspective. The actual and perceived need for a more flexible organizational structure also figures very strongly, and keys in with expected changes. Changes in head office–branch relations, however, figure relatively little. These differences may reflect an emphasis upon strategic thinking. But a key issue is the extent to which branch networks respond fully to the new directions expected of them. For example, it is not clear to what extent branch managers market and sell new products as effectively as head offices might wish, or make effective use of and inputs into new marketing information systems which may be introduced. There may be perceived managerial problems in introducing new products. The NIFS survey distinguishes between product introduced by acquisition and those developed internally (Table 9.10).

For those institutions having introduced new products by acquisition, difficulties in combining different management styles and in combining different computer systems are both seen to be important, as might be expected. For those institutions introducing products by internal development, difficulties in recruiting staff are noticeably the most important problem, followed by difficulties in reacting quickly to competition. However, whilst the issue of dealing with change in an organization is seen as quite important, relatively few respondents saw it as an important problem. This last point is perhaps a little surprising.

The manner in which change is introduced into an organization has long been recognized in the organization literature as having an important bearing on whether or not change succeeds. Moreover, there is a well-recognized need to match the process of change to the particular organizational context.

The concept of an organization's culture has an important role in analysing how change is to take place and at what speed. That organizations have well-developed codes by which they function (Arrow, 1974) and established ways in which they adapt (Srivastava, 1983) is well known. Moreover, changing those codes and learning systems, and hence the organization's culture, may be difficult. Johne and Harborne (1985), in analysing product innovation in commercial banks, drew attention to several factors which were key to the successful introduction of new products, prominent amongst which were the need for a flexible management

Table 9.9 *New products and organizational changes*

Type of change	For products introduced in last year (%)	Expected in next five years (%)
Changes in highest-level managers	16.9	30.2
More flexible organizational structure	18.0	22.7
New tier of management	9.7	15.8
Introduction of divisionalization	12.2	13.7
Removal of a tier of management	1.4	1.4
Recruitment of specialist management	19.8	35.3
Change in head office–branch relations	5.0	10.1

Source: NIFS survey.
Note: Bases for percentages: 265.

Table 9.10 *Managerial problems in introducing new products*

	Important (%)	Quite important (%)	Not important (%)	Not answered (%)
Products introduced by acquisition				
Difficulties in combining different management styles	23.4	21.2	8.6	46.8
Difficulties in combining different computer systems	26.6	19.4	9.0	45.0
Products introduced by internal product development				
Difficulties in recruiting specialist staff	35.6	32.4	11.9	20.1
Difficulties in dealing with change in the organization	20.5	38.1	19.1	22.3
Difficulties in reacting quickly to competition	30.6	27.0	19.8	22.6

Note: Bases for percentages: 265.

structure that stimulates and progresses efficient product innovation, good internal integration of all activities involved in innovation and a corporate culture receptive to innovation. Further difficulties may be raised with new products introduced by acquisition rather than internal development, as our survey evidence shows. Question marks over the realization of gains from merger are well known (Chiplin and Wright, 1987 (a general review); Barnes, 1985 (a study of building societies)). Jones (1985) has shown that key problems are caused in the integration of different cultures and management styles. Whilst there may be a need to introduce a monitoring system consistent with other parts of the organization, there is an extensive literature which strongly indicates that different management styles and organization structures may be appropriate for different circumstances (see Otley (1988) for a review of this literature). Moreover, managers and employees operating in different market sectors may need to be remunerated differently to give then the incentive to perform (Thompson and Wright, 1988). Failure to take account of these factors may provoke resistance to change and difficulties in meeting competition in the market.

Piercy and Peattie (1988) in a recent paper have argued that the process of matching strategy with culture should be viewed along a continuum. At the one extreme, an organization should seek to change its strategic choice to match a given organizational culture. At the other extreme, culture may be changed to match a given strategy. Various approaches are suggested for identifying the appropriate mix along this continuum and for securing effective implementation.

There have recently been several studies of the relationship between organizational form and performance, and between organizational form and environmental factors and strategy (see the chapters by Cable and Otley in Thompson and Wright (1988)). These studies have focused upon manufacturing industry, and it would appear that studies relating to the financial sector are required. (For some evidence in this area, prior to the recent changes, see Channon (1978).)

However, to focus solely upon changes in organizational structure as referring to the optimal decomposition of a given set of activities would seem to take too narrow a view (Wright and Thompson, 1987). A full analysis of organizational issues requires consideration of whether an activity should be carried out internally within a firm or externally, and if the latter what form the transactional relationship between firms ought to take. These issues are now examined in the context of personal financial services.

Governance structures

Recent developments in the economics of internal organization have argued that the dichotomy between carrying out transactions either within the firm or between firms is too simplistic. Rather it may be more instructive to consider the firm as a set of contractual relations and to examine which kinds of contract are suitable for which kind of activity (Klein *et al.*, 1978). Hence there is scope for internal transactions, spot market transactions and those which involve a managed market whereby the parties to the transaction co-operate in ensuring that the specific attributes of the exchange are met (Williamson, 1979). The implications for the personal financial services sector concern the need to examine appropriate governance structures for the moves into new product areas now taking place.

The relevant issues are well illustrated by several aspects of the behaviour of firms providing personal financial services. The first aspect concerns the motives and means by which some organizations have become involved in estate agency services. The second aspect relates to the polarization decision as to how investment (and particularly insurance) products will be distributed. These developments have already been referred to above and here we extend the points made. The third element relates to the degree to which experimentation in respect of transactional forms is occurring.

Entry into estate agency provision has been made in several ways: acquisitions, franchising, cold start, minority shareholdings and joint ventures. Moreover, the manner in which institutions have signalled their presence to the market has also varied, from replacing original agents' names with their own, to making little or no outward change to for-sale boards and shop fronts, via a mixture of in-between styles (Robbie *et al.*, 1987). Whilst estate agents occupy an important position in the house buying process and provide opportunities for selling mortgages and insurance, serious issue need to be considered in using them as a distribution route.

Estate agents have traditionally had a poor reputation in the eyes of the public, as surveys by the Price Commission in 1979 and regular surveys published in *Which?* magazine continue to show. Hence societies and other institutions face an important task in changing the image of estate agents in order that their own reputations are not damaged. A second major problem arises in integrating a large number of acquisitions made in a short period of time, particularly as the managerial skills required in estate agency are very different from those involved in running financial institutions. These problems may be overcome by recruiting estate agency people to undertake the task, whose skills may now be at a premium because of the increased demand for them. However, there remains a problem in motivating managers of estate agents who have just become very wealthy as a result of being bought out and whose entrepreneurial style is at variance with traditional financial institution approaches to business. The franchise route avoids the high premiums being paid on acquisitions (and hence the implications for profitability) and the internal managerial issues just noted. However, there are major issues involved in establishing a brand image, in ensuring adequate quality of management performance (especially given the recent wave of acquisitions in which a large proportion of the better estate agents have been incorporated into groups (Robbie *et al.*, 1987)) and in maintaining adequate control so that the institution's reputation is not harmed.

As yet it is a little early to form a reliable judgement on the outcome of institutions' decisions to enter estate agency. Many are still in a transitional phase, and the house price boom of 1987 and 1988 may have cushioned some of the adverse aspects. However, an important research area is the examination of performance, the problems involved in integration and the extent to which divestment subsequently occurs (Wright and Thompson, 1987), and the comparative performance of the different modes chosen for offering estate agency services.

The polarization decision involves distributors of investment products opting either to be tied representatives, or to offer independent advice or act as an introducer to someone who will provide advice (Wright and Diacon, 1988). The problem of controlling opportunism in independent sales forces, which is generally less of a problem with own sales forces, has been examined in another context by Anderson (1988). Similarly, Brickley and Dark (1987) have examined the agency cost problems involved in internalized distribution versus franchising. Institutions have now made their polarization decisions. Building societies' decisions in respect of the distribution of insurance are shown in Table 9.11. As noted earlier, the majority, mainly small and medium-sized ones, have opted for tied status, not least because of the training costs that would otherwise be involved. However, it is by no means clear how successful or permanent these arrangements will be. Evidence from other sectors indicates changing forms of relationship over time. Those insurance companies with more mediocre performance still relying on referrals by independent agents may in time need to revise further their distribution decisions. Those with tied arrangements may need to question how effective their agents have been and what effects there are on

Table 9.11 *Building societies' decisions on polarization*

	No.	%
Independent	26	23.2
Tied	70	62.5
Introducer	16	14.3
Total	112	100.0

Source: BSA.

company reputations. Agents themselves may come to compare remuneration levels between suppliers. Some evidence of switching has already occurred: for example, Cheltenham and Gloucester Building Society has switched from being independent to having a tied arrangement with Legal and General.

Whether the provision of new products means ownership or some kind of market relationship, and whether it is permanent or temporary, does not as yet seem clear. What is evident is that effectively a great deal of experimentation is currently taking place. Developments in information technology and the use of joint ventures may mean that de-integeration or vertical separation of activities is possible (Chiplin, 1986). Moreover, developments in financial instruments are also leading to an examination of products which have traditionally been provided in an integrated fashion, e.g. the securitization of mortgages. (Robbie and Wright, 1988, Ch. 3). Some of the managerial and organizational issues referred to in the first part of this section may, if they cannot be overcome, indicate that externalization is required. However, such a move would need to ensure that the monitoring costs involved in protecting a supplier's reputation did not exceed the benefits of this mode of transaction.

Failure of markets to develop as anticipated may also suggest that exit from a sector is necessary. Divestment has already been seen in respect of certain market-making activities of some of the clearing banks. Strategic 'search' for activities which 'fit' is a well-known notion in the internal organization literature (see Thompson and Wright, 1988, Ch. 10), and it would be useful to see to what extent search processes are currently occurring in the financial services sector.

Emerging issues for the 1990s

We will now restate some of the major issues which we feel are worthy of further research.

With a large number of firms moving in the direction of greater differentiation and away from a cost-based strategy, the extent of competition within personal financial services is bound to increase. In particular, with many firms pursuing similar strategies it is unlikely that all will succeed; indeed, this extensive move towards differentiation may well create gaps in certain market segments, providing opportunities for the alert firm to develop such segments on the basis of a cost focus strategy. There is clearly scope for further research in this area to monitor the dynamics of marketing strategy.

An important element in assessing the roles of marketing and market research departments is to examine various aspects of the behaviour of purchasers of personal financial services. This may be relevant at several levels. At one level there may be a need to monitor general developments in personal wealth and to analyse findings by various potential market segments. Although there are few published market research data on the personal financial services sector, commercial market research organizations occasionally publish some useful information. A second level related to developments in consumer attitudes to financial institutions and financial products, particularly the identification of mismatches or asymmetries in perceptions. Consumers' images of financing institutions and products may lag behind and affect the changes that the institution wishes to introduce. Hence there may be a need continually to examine how individuals are likely to react in general to new products and methods of distribution. Detailed research may be required to identify separate market segments. Customer preference for convenience may rank behind other criteria for certain specialist products where expertise and quality of service are more important.

The Financial Services Act provisions on polarization and 'best' advice are essentially requirements to increase competition in distribution channels in order to provide improved services to the consumers of personal financial services. Given the importance of distribution in a mature market, and the growing trend towards a 'customer-orientated' market, the selection of appropriate marketing channels and the ability to compete effectively in those channels becomes of paramount importance. In overall terms, the evidence suggests that, rather than switching between channels, firms are looking to increase the number and variety of channels in use in order to compete over a wider range of outlets.

Despite the relatively high cost of branch networks, and the costs associated with training staff to act as independent intermediaries, the branch network appears likely to continue to be an important distribution channel.

Organizationally, the personal financial services sector is still some way from widespread use of marketing information systems. Major issues involved relate to problems in integrating information from various sources and constructing information on relevant bases. The extent to which branch officers can be encouraged and educated to make use of centrally held information for local marketing purposes may also have to be considered. The introduction of marketing information systems also raises issues about how managers react to change and the problems of how organizational cultures adapt to and influence change.

Discussion

The issues raised in this chapter suggest a number of implications for practitioners. These include the need to:

- identify a diversification strategy which reflects both company aims and competitors' intentions as expressed in our survey;
- develop effective marketing and, particularly, market research operations

which continuously monitor consumer perceptions of the supply-side changes taking place;

- evaluate the NPD processes in personal financial services so as to avoid the costs of introducing products which subsequently fail to achieve their targets;
- evaluate the match and the appropriateness of advertising in conjunction with changes in corporate strategic direction;
- evaluate the effectiveness of the growing diversity of distribution channels being used;
- evaluate the relative success of information technology-driven distribution methods;
- examine the organizational problems in introducing new products by acquisition versus internal generation and how those problems might be resolved, including an evaluation of the relationships between organizational form and performance;
- analyse the appropriate governance structures for the provision of various products, including internal provision versus joint ventures versus managed market/quasi-integrated arrangements;
- evaluate the appropriate incentive mechanisms for employees providing different services within the same organization.

It is worth noting that the development of strategic options for particular financial services organizations will need to remain flexible. Further supply-side changes are likely to affect the sector in the early 1990s. Awareness of the 1992 single European market has already been responsible for a number of mergers and acquisitions as firms take up strategic distribution positions within the EEC. The North American Free Trade Area may cause similar repositioning. Many UK insurance companies have been well represented historically in Canada and their links may be exploited so as to attack the huge US market. The acquisition of Farmers, a large US insurer, by BAT is one example of a direct move by UK financial services conglomerates into the USA. The growing internationalization of financial services provision is a further supply-side change which will continue to effect the sector in the 1990s.

In this chapter we have attempted to identify and quantify, using survey data, trends which will affect the financial services sector into the 1990s. We have presented information on the strategic options which face firms in the sector, and guidelines on the governance and other organizational implications of the implementation of strategic choice.

References

Anderson, E. (1988) 'Transaction costs as determinants of opportunism in integrated and independent sales forces', *Journal of Economic Behaviour and Organisation*, 9, 247–64.

Arrow, K. (1974) *The Limits of Organization*. New York: Norton.

Barnes, P.A. (1985) 'UK building societies: a study of the gains from merger', *Journal of Business Finance and Accounting*, 12, 1, 75–92.

Brickley, J.A. and Dark, F.H. (1987) 'The choice of organisational form: the case of franchising', *Journal of Financial Economics*, 18, 401–20.

Carter, R.L., Chiplin, B. and Lewis, M.K. (eds) (1986) *Personal Financial Markets*. Oxford: Philip Allan.

Channon, D. (1978) *The Service Industries*. London: Macmillan.

Chiplin, B. (1986) 'Information technology and personal financial services', in Carter *et al.*, 1986.

Chiplin, B. and Wright, M. (1987) 'The logic of mergers: the competitive market in corporate control in theory and practice', IEA Hobart Paper 107, April.

Clarke, P.D., Gardener, E.P.M., Feeney, P. and Molyneux, P. (1988) 'The genesis of strategic marketing control in British retail banking', *International Journal of Bank Marketing*, 6, 2, 5–19.

Davison, H., Watkins, T. and Wright, M. (1989) 'Developing new personal financial products: some evidence of the role of market research', *International Journal of Bank Marketing* (forthcoming).

Dyer, N. and Watkins, T. (eds) (1988) *Marketing Insurance*, 2nd edn. London: Kluwer.

Furlong, C.B. and Brent Ritchie, J.R. (1986) 'Consumer concept testing of personal financial services', *International Journal of Bank Marketing*, 4, 1, 3–18.

Hooley, G.T., West, C.J. and Lynch, J.E. (1984) *Marketing in the UK: A Survey of Current Practice and Performance*. Cookham: Institute of Marketing.

Howcroft, J.B. and Lavis, J.C. (1986) 'Image in retail banking', *International Journal of Bank Marketing*, 4, 4, 3–13.

Howcroft, J.B. and Lavis, J.C. (1987) 'Retail banking in the UK: a change in organisational forms', *Journal of Retail Banking*, 9, 3, 35–42.

Johne, A.F. and Harborne, P. (1985) 'How large commercial banks manage product innovation', *International Journal of Bank Marketing*, 3, 1.

Johnson, S. and Woodward, S. (1988) 'Marketing management information systems: a review of current practice', *Marketing Intelligence and Planning*, 6, 2, 27–9.

Jones, C.S. (1985) 'An empirical study of the role of management accounting systems following takeover or merger', *Accounting Organisations and Society*, 10, 177–200.

Klein, B., Crawford, R.G. and Alchian, A.A. (1978) 'Vertical integration, appropriable rents and the competitive contracting process', *Journal of Law and Economics*, 21, 297–326.

Office of Fair Trading (1987) *Study of Insurance Intermediaries' Costs: Report of a Survey*. London: OFT.

Otley, D. (1988) 'The contingency theory of organisational control', in Thompson and Wright, 1988.

Piercy, N. (1987) *Marketing Organization: An Analysis of Information Processing, Power and Politics*. London: Allen and Unwin.

Piercy, N. and Evans, M. (1983) *Managing Marketing Information*. London: Croom Helm.

Piercy, N. and Peattie, K.J. (1988) 'Matching marketing strategies to corporate culture: the parcel and the wall', *Journal of General Management*, 13, 4, 33–44.

Porter, M.E. (1985) *Competitive Advantage: Creating and Sustaining Superior Performance*. New York: Free Press.

Robbie, K. and Wright, M. (1988) *Personal Financial Services*. London: Euromonitor.

Robbie, K., Wright, M. and Watkins, T. (1987) *Estate Agents and House Buying Services*. London: Euromonitor.

Srivastava, R. (1983) 'A typology of organisational learning systems', *Journal of Management Studies*, 20, 1–35.

Thompson, R.S. and Wright, M. (eds) (1988) *Internal Organisation, Efficiency and Profit*. Oxford: Philip Allan.

Watkins, T. (1985) 'Marketing information systems: theoretical and practical issues', in Sparks, L., Shaw, S. and Kaynak, K. (eds) *Marketing in the 1990s and Beyond*. University of Stirling: Proceedings of the World Marketing Congress.

Watkins, T. (1986) 'Marketing of financial services' in Carter, Chiplin and Lewis (1986).

Watkins, T. (1988) 'The use of information technology in insurance marketing', *Marketing Intelligence and Planning*, 6, 2, 21–6.

Watkins, T. and Wright, M. (1985) 'Consumer convenience or sophistication: a crucial question in bank services marketing', *Internation Journal of Bank Marketing*, 3, 1, 35–42.

Watkins, T. and Wright, M. (1986a) *Marketing Financial Services*. London: Butterworth.

Watkins, T. and Wright, M. (1986b) 'Distribution systems in insurance', *Quarterly Review of Marketing*, August, 1–6.

Williamson, O.E. (1979) 'Transaction cost economics: the governance of contractual relations', *Journal of Law and Economics*, 22, 233–62.

Wright, M. and Diacon, S.R. (1988) 'Regulation of the marketing of long term insurance', in Dyer and Watkins, 1988.

Wright, M. and Thompson, R.S. (1987) 'Divestment and the control of divisionalised firms', *Accounting and Business Research*, Summer, 259–67.

Chapter 10

Evolution of retail branch banking in the UK

Barry Howcroft

Overview

The past two decades have seen the banks' role in both the financial system and the community change rapidly (Llewellyn, 1985). In the 1960s banks operated a cartel which restricted competition. Subsequent legislation, however, introduced to encourage competition and effect better control of the financial system, slowly removed some of these barriers. The net result was that traditional banks lost a substantial proportion of their domestic business to essentially 'non-bank' competition.

Against this background, this chapter attempts to identify the main environmental, legal and economic factors which have affected retail banking. The eventual changes in corporate objectives and the emerging issues focused primarily on containing costs and improving efficiency are subsequently identified and analysed.

Past trends and evolution

Retail banks, like all financial institutions, are not passive agents. They will change in reaction to alterations in their external environment, but they will also change because they choose to behave differently. At the commencement of an analysis of the evolution of retail branch banking it is therefore imperative that the complicated interaction of external factors and internal corporate objectives is fully appreciated (Johnson and Scholes, 1988).

Externally induced changes

- *Domestic recession.* In the aftermath of the oil price increases in the 1970s, industrialized domestic economies experienced a series of prolonged and deep recessions in the period 1973–82. This was a significant contributory factor in explaining why banks focused attention towards international markets where growth rates were perceived as high. Since 1982 the international debt crisis and the phenomenon known as 'securitization of debt' have combined (along with other factors) to refocus attention back towards the domestic market.

- *Disclosure of profits.* The requirement since 1969 for a true disclosure of clearing bank profits has accentuated the trend (apparent for other reasons) towards a heightened awareness of profitability.

- *Mergers.* The eleven clearing banks that existed in the 1960s had been reduced to six by 1969. These mergers subsequently resulted in significant branch rationalization programmes throughout the following decade.

- *Deregulation.* In moving away from the cartelized oligopoly, a policy of systematic deregulation of the financial sector was introduced. The major examples were the introduction of competition and credit control in 1971; the TSB Act and the Post Office (Bank Services) Act in 1976; the abolition of exchange controls in 1979; the final abolition of the Corset in June 1980; the ending of hire-purchase controls; and the elimination of an official bias against bank lending.

  More recently, this trend has been evidenced by the agreement in 1983 between the Government and the Stock Exchange which resulted in the phenomenon known as the 'Big Bang' (27 October 1986); the Building Societies Act 1986; and the Financial Services Act 1986.

- *Inflation.* High and volatile rates of inflation increased banking risk by simultaneously inducing inflated balance sheet growth and increasing unpredictability. Attempts were made to compensate for these trends by introducing new pricing formulas based on floating rates and by devising new lending techniques that moved away from the traditional bank overdraft. Consequently, corporate customers attracted by these innovations, at a time when the traditional fixed-interest capital markets were decidedly depressed, increasingly came to regard the banking sector as their primary source of funds.

Internally induced changes

The key external catalysts of change in retail banking throughout the 1970s and early 1980s were undoubtedly a combination of increased competition (Bank of England, 1971), deregulation and at times unprecedentedly high rates of inflation. In a general sense retail banking responded (as did banking generally) by becoming more competitive and more profit conscious. Increasingly aggressive marketing policies were introduced in all areas of business, and an unprecedented level of financial innovation occurred.

Most financial innovation initially occurred in the international sector, which, in addition to the above-mentioned incentives, had to contend with the additional problems posed by the recycling of petro-dollars, the eventual international debt crisis and the securitization of debt (Bank for International Settlements, 1986). In contrast, the 1970s witnessed relatively little bank innovation in the retail sector. Domestic competition was initially perceived only in terms of competition from foreign corporate banks. This resulted in the evolution of new funding techniques (liability management) which, like the foreign banks which had no real access to retail deposits, concentrated almost exclusively on the relatively cheaper wholesale money markets.

Nevertheless, the evolution of liability management had very significant and wide-ranging implications for banking generally. In particular, it enabled banks to become asset orientated. Previously, assets had been managed (asset management) on a given level of deposits, whereas it now became possible to secure the level of deposits (liability management) to fund the desired volume of assets. In essence, banks began to fund loans rather than lend deposits.

This development facilitated competition by enabling banks to set future lending targets free from the constraints of having first to obtain deposits. It also encouraged financial innovation by enabling banks to perform 'maturity transformation' (the transformation of short-term deposits into longer-term loans). Consequently, retail banking became less restrictive in its lending technique and substantially diversified its asset portfolio. Less reliance was placed on the traditional short-term overdraft facility and greater emphasis was placed on term lending and other medium-term facilities aimed at satisfying more exactly the needs of corporate customers. Funding in the relatively less expensive wholesale money markets also introduced unprecedented flexibility in pricing. Specifically, it enabled retail banks to quote spreads above LIBOR and thereby compete far more effectively with foreign banks (Midland Bank, 1981).

Undoubtedly there was a competitive threat posed by foreign banks in the UK, but the overemphasis placed upon the corporate sector and the commensurate neglect of the personal sector was partially based upon a fallacy: namely, the belief that the perceived most competitive sector must by definition be the most profitable. Clearly, this is not necessarily true, but it certainly was a significant contributory factor in the relative absence of any bank innovation in the personal sector throughout the 1970s.

The preoccupation of retail banks with the corporate sector provided an unparalleled opportunity for competitors to improve market position in the personal sector. Building societies with the benefit of structural advantages (particularly taxation) seized the opportunity and developed an aggressive marketing strategy and a wide range of savings schemes aimed specifically at retail deposits. Consequently, they eventually became the largest holders of personal sector deposits, having overtaken the banks in 1975.

By the late 1970s banks were beginning to refocus attention on the personal sector for a variety of reasons. International banking in the aftermath of the second oil price increase and the imminent debt crisis was no longer attractive. Industrial recession in the UK had simultaneously constrained profitability and increased risks in the corporate sector. Combined with high rates of inflation, these factors began to increase concern about bank profitability and capital adequacy at a time when risks in banking were increasing.

This heightened awareness of bank profitability and risk, together with the dramatic loss of market share in retail deposits, led banks to reassess their position in the high-cost retail banking sector. Specifically, the clearing banks began to question the justification for relying increasingly on wholesale deposits while having approximately 12,000 branches (Hammond, 1981). Moreover, in contrast to the corporate sector, the personal sector was growing in terms of both sophistication and absolute size. Deregulation, particularly the abolition of the Corset in 1980, also enabled them to compete, for the first time, in the fast-growing, low-risk house mortgage market without any artificial balance sheet constraints (Bank of England, 1985).

Strategic conclusions

Several important observations can be concluded from the strategies which emanated from the post-war era of initial deregulation and competition. The clearing banks quickly discovered that competitive strategies are indiscriminate and will affect *all* players in the market. Therefore, although designed primarily to regain market share in the personal sector and aimed essentially at building societies, competitive strategies in retail banking introduced very aggressive competition between the clearing banks themselves.

In an oligopoly like the retail banking market, there is naturally a great deal of similarity between the market players, which resulted in competitors introducing similar, if not identical, competitive strategies. Financial products, too, being relatively homogeneous, resulted in financial innovations being quickly replicated, with a corresponding reduction in the innovator's reward.

These strategic considerations, compounded by a herd mentality, were responsible for the clearing banks replicating each other's services. An exceedingly wide and diverse range of identical products was offered by each bank, with the result that management in retail banking became commensurately more complicated and less cost-effective.

Current trends and future evolution

The scope for yet further deregulation in the financial sector is now limited, but competition will undoubtedly continue to be a significant factor, with emerging technology as the other major external catalyst of change. In an era when intense competition will be greatly facilitated by technology, the need to differentiate products and maintain market position will necessitate that retail banks become increasingly marketing orientated. This will result in a commensurate emphasis being placed upon the quality and efficiency of management (The Institute of Bankers, 1986).

The main catalysts of change in the future evolution of retail banking are:

- competition
- technology
- management
- marketing

These factors have already begun to cause considerable change in the organizational form of retail banking. Figure 10.1 summarizes the potentially radical changes under four distinct headings: the market, delivery systems, marketing and management.

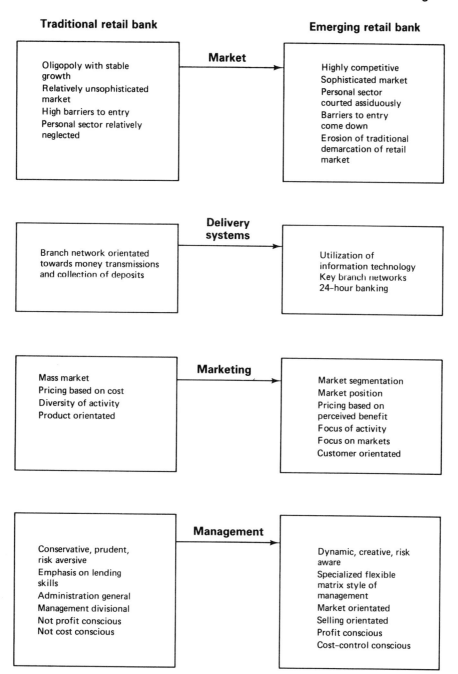

Figure 10.1 Evolution of retail banking

The market

The traditional UK retail banking market was initially a cartelized oligopoly with stable growth which catered for a fairly unsophisticated market. The personal sector was relatively neglected, and reliance upon an extremely high-cost branch infrastructure provided an extremely effective barrier to entry.

The gradual emergence of a highly competitive and increasingly sophisticated personal market, combined with the various 'catalysts of change' already discussed, has led the clearing banks to refocus attention towards this sector. However, the branch network is no longer an effective barrier to entry. An extensive branch network system is no longer a prerequisite for effective collection of deposits and money transmission. Information technology is enabling different financial institutions to provide these services more efficiently and more cost-effectively.

Consequently, the traditional demarcation between different financial institutions is being steadily eroded. Institutions are moving into each other's traditional preserves, and in the process the financial system is becoming less structured (HMSO, 1984). In essence, banking activity is no longer restricted to 'banks' and may not even be restricted to financial institutions. Some major retail chains have the infrastructure and image to provide a limited range of banking services in addition to the already prevalent in-house credit cards (Middleton, 1987).

This erosion of traditional business demarcation is probably most acute in the retail banking sector and has caused banks to question the very purpose of their branches and to introduce strategies aimed at making them more cost-effective. In a much wider sense it has also introduced the future possibility of horizontal mergers and acquisitions (Maycock, 1986).

Delivery systems

Historically, retail banks perceived delivery systems solely in terms of the high-cost branch network which was essentially orientated towards money transmission and deposit collection. Developments in technology, however, have enabled retail banks to be less reliant upon branches and to offer a quick and efficient service twenty-four hours a day. This has provided the potential to mount a long-term attack on high costs whilst improving the standard of service (Chorafas, 1988).

Innovative uses of technology will increasingly assist in focusing product marketing on target customer groups and will ensure that products are differentiated from those of competitors. A well-designed computer system, for instance, can provide the necessary lead time for a product to become established and eventually to emerge as a market leader. Similarly, products can be designed that incorporate unique selling opportunities based upon systems that lock customers into products.

Information technology and the branch network should not be regarded as mutually exclusive delivery systems. Technology is typically used to improve the efficiency of the branch and to access target markets, via cash dispensers and so

on. However, in reducing reliance upon the branch network, information technology has enabled banks to introduce key branch banking strategies.

Selected key branches continue to provide the traditional full range of bank
services, while others are designated selective services dependent upon location
and proximity to key branches. This has the potential attraction of reducing
expensive management costs, by avoiding mass replication of management skills,
whilst simultaneously focusing specific products on target customer groups.

The future impact of technology-orientated delivery systems, however, must
not be understated. They will in themselves eventually constitute significant
barriers to entry in the financial services market and will determine the very nature
of future competition. Increasingly, customer perceptions of individual banks'
abilities to manage technology and of which bank has the superior technology will
emerge as crucial factors in determining genuine and sustainable competitive
advantage.

Marketing philosophy

Until relatively recently retail banks adopted a mass marketing approach with
commensurate emphasis placed on full product lines. The principal objective was
to build sales volume for each product line and to have a presence in (rather than to
dominate) most financial markets.

Emphasis is now beginning to be focused increasingly on competitive
positioning. If a bank can position itself favourably within a particular market,
relative to competitors, it can earn high rates of return irrespective of average
profitability within the market. This has introduced the possibility of retail banks
increasingly adopting different and alternative competitive strategies. Some
banks, for instance, will compete by establishing themselves as low-cost producers
of fairly basic and standardized products, the objective being to sell at a price equal
to the market average but to generate higher than average market profits by
maintaining below average market costs. Alternatively, some banks will compete
by selecting a market segment and competing exclusively as a specialist, thereby
gaining competitive advantage over the more broadly based competitors. A competitive strategy based upon differentiation or uniqueness of product is another
emerging strategy which will be greatly facilitated by the existing and potential
developments in technology-driven delivery systems.

Implicit in this change is the adoption of a corporate culture that is
increasingly marketing orientated (Meidan, 1984). Marketing considerations will
permeate into every aspect of the business. There will be a move away from mass
marketing towards a marketing concept increasingly concerned with market
segmentation. Pricing will be increasingly perceived as a marketing tool and based
more on perceived value than on purely cost considerations. In the process, banks
will begin to examine their business portfolios in an endeavour to obtain the
optimum mix of markets and products. This may well result in banks choosing to
reduce their product line and to dominate in a few carefully selected markets.

Management

Traditionally, management in retail banking was essentially conservative and, although risk aversive, was not particularly profit or cost conscious. Emphasis was typically placed upon technical skills associated with lending competence. General management was traditionally based upon divisional lines that reflected broad business markets (for instance, domestic banking and international banking).

The emergence of an increasingly marketing-orientated culture within retail banks will necessitate that management becomes more dynamic. Specifically, emphasis will be placed less on technical skills and commensurately more on selling and marketing abilities. This fundamental change in bank culture is already being reflected in current recruitment and training programmes. Greater attention is now being given to quality recruitment, as reflected in the emphasis on graduates and the use of assessment centres aimed as assessing overall personality, intellect and skill-specific abilities. Training is similarly placing emphasis less on technical aptitude and more on developing specific managerial skills (selling and marketing skills, for example) and attitudinal training (aimed primarily at developing perceptions of oneself, the changing corporate culture and the market environment) (Livy, 1980).

The need to improve cost-efficiency ratios will increasingly necessitate that management becomes more profit and risk conscious. Management by objectives and salary packages linked to individual performance rather than formal grading structures are already beginning to emerge. Cost-efficiency has already been improved by the reorganization of banks along functional lines (rather than broad divisional lines) that reflect business markets and sectors. As it has become increasingly apparent that volume growth is no longer a sufficient source of profit, a matrix style of management has begun to emerge that gives managers responsibility for a specific range of products in a specific target market. This will potentially enable a greater degree of control in managing asset portfolios and changing product mixes.

Emerging issues for the 1990s

The single most important issue facing banks in the 1990s will continue to be declining profitability, as measured by return on assets. Banks have responded by using leverage and have developed substantial off-balance sheet business (particularly in the international sector) to improve the return on equity (Andrews and Sender, 1986). Nevertheless, the capital base of the banking system continues to decline relative to the growth in assets.

Retail banking, however, has already emerged as an important sector in improving the profitability of banks. Continued improvement will be dependent upon combinations of strategies which concentrate primarily on both 'products' and 'costs' in an endeavour to improve market position and the overall cost-effectiveness of the business. These strategies, as summarized in Figure 10.2, will emerge as the major issues facing retail banking in the 1990s, and their ultimate

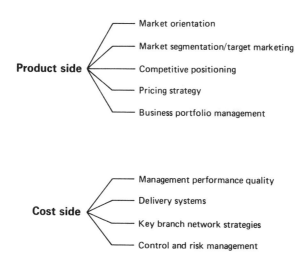

Product side
— Market orientation
— Market segmentation/target marketing
— Competitive positioning
— Pricing strategy
— Business portfolio management

Cost side
— Management performance quality
— Delivery systems
— Key branch network strategies
— Control and risk management

Figure 10.2 Future strategies and issues in retail banking

resolution may well be critical in determining the very survival of some retail banks.

Discussion

In a general sense, UK retail banks in the 1970s tended to perceive competition solely in terms of providing a wide and comprehensive range of products. External considerations such as customer satisfaction and customer need were most definitely not the primary objectives. Consequently, with the advent of competition, particularly from building societies, profit margins came under increasing pressure.

The eventual spate of cost reduction strategies typical of banks in the 1980s was a direct result of this pressure. Experience, however, has clearly indicated the folly of exclusively pursuing such strategies over the long term. The business can very quickly move into a downward spiral, with a consequential reduction in customer base, range of products, market coverage and absolute profitability.

In the foreseeable future the single most important issue facing retail banks in the UK will continue to be the need to maintain and improve profitability against a background of ever-increasing competition. For the reasons already cited this will necessitate the implementation of strategies that essentially focus on both the product side and the cost side of the business.

Competition and profitability factors will mean that retail banks, in terms of their management style, their use of technology, their internal and external infrastructure and their internal and external use of information technology, must be increasingly responsive to market considerations. In essence, they will move from being internally driven organizations towards being externally driven. Customer needs, customer satisfaction, efficiency and quality of service will therefore become of paramount importance in determining the organizational form of retail banks. Indeed, the quality and efficiency of bank customer service will probably become the single most publicized corporate objective.

Logistically, retail banks cannot hope to provide an exceptionally high quality of service throughout a wide range of services or even a universal market. Instead they will increasingly segment the market and will design and price products to meet specific customers' requirements. In universal markets, rather than competing for market dominance, products will be designed and priced to obtain market position. This may well herald the end of the traditional mass production approach to retail bank services and raise major problems for the future in deciding upon which products and in which markets to concentrate.

References

Andrews, S. and Sender, H. (1986) 'Off balance sheet risk: where is it leading banks?', *Institutional Investor*, 20, 75.

Bank for International Settlements (1986) *Recent Innovations in International Banking*. Basle: BIS.

Bank of England (1971) *Competition and Credit Control*. London: Bank of England.

Bank of England (1985) 'Mortage finance and the housing market', *Quarterly Bulletin*, 25, 1, 80–91.

Chorafas, D.N. (1988) *Electronic Funds Transfer*. London: Butterworths.

Hammond, C. (1981) 'Running a profitable branch network, *Bankers Magazine*, July, 11–17.

HMSO (1984) 'Building societies: a new framework', Cmnd 9316. London: HMSO.

Johnson, G. and Scholes, K. (1988) *Exploring Corporate Strategy*, 2nd edn. Englewood Cliffs, NJ: Prentice-Hall.

Livy, B. (ed.) (1980) *Management and People in Banking*. London: The Institute of Bankers.

Llewellyn, D.T. (1985) *The Evolution of the British Financial System*. London: The Institute of Bankers.

Maycock, J. (1986) *Financial Conglomerates: The New Phenomenon*. Aldershot: Gower.

Meidan, A. (1984) *Bank Marketing Management*. London: Macmillan.

Middleton, P. (1987) 'Are non banks winning in retail financial services?', *International Journal of Bank Marketing*, 5, 1, 28–37.

Midland Bank (1981) 'Bank lending in a changing environment', *Midland Bank Review*, Autumn, 17–22.

The Institute of Bankers (1986) *Bank Strategies for the 1990s*. London: The Institute of Bankers.

Chapter 11

A new basis for segmenting the corporate banking market

Julia Schauerman

Overview

The financial services market has, over the past twenty years, become highly competitive owing to the relaxation of certain regulations (leading to a breakdown in the demarcation barriers between financial institutions), the increasing globalization of the market, new competitors entering the market (e.g. large multi-national companies) and decreasing customer loyalty. As a result, marketing has played an increasingly important role in financial institutions. No longer is marketing seen as a mere promotional device; it is now recognized as a means of gaining an understanding of the market (i.e. identifying customer needs, determining how those needs may best be satisfied and developing marketing strategies that achieve the desired market response) and thus is an important determinant of performance in the market.

This chapter is concerned with the market segmentation practices of banks in the corporate banking market. Market segmentation involves the division of the total market (using some basis, e.g. location) into segments. Ideally, the needs, buying behaviour and response to marketing stimuli of the consumers within a particular segment will be homogeneous, whilst members of different segment types will have different needs, buying behaviour, etc. Having identified the different market segments, the company carrying out the exercise can then select certain target segments which it can serve most effectively. Market segmentation should lead to the efficient use of an organization's resources and the satisfaction of customer needs, and make the identification of opportunities easier by focusing on smaller markets rather than the total market.

Over the past twenty years the corporate banking market has become increasingly competitive, whilst at the same time the consumers within the market-place have become more sophisticated and less loyal to their bankers. Thus, if banks are to maintain their position within this market, or indeed improve upon it, they must develop a better understanding of the consumers within it. Traditionally, the corporate banking market has been segmented using location, industry type and/or company size as the basis for segmentation. However, Militello (1984) argues that these traditional bases fail to help banks more fully understand the financial decision-making units within business organisations. Wind (1978), in a general criticism of market segmentation research, has called for the discovery and implementation of new variables as bases for segmentation, believing that the bases already available fail to relate to consumer behaviour and thus fail to be of use to marketing managers.

The chapter proposes that business strategy is a potentially useful method for segmentation. Business-level strategies focus on how a business chooses to compete within a given market. Walker and Ruekert (1987), using theoretical perspectives, normative statements and empirical evidence, argue that different strategy types have different resource requirements (different strategy types require different functional competencies in order to be successfully implemented). It is hypothesized that the strategy type of a business organization will determine the business's financial requirements and influence the financial decision-making unit.

The intention is to show that banks could gain a greater insight into the financial requirements of corporations (and thus develop more effective marketing strategies) using business strategy as a basis for segmenting the corporate banking market, rather than using the traditional bases.

The structure of the chapter is as follows. First, the developments in the market which have led banks to adopt marketing practices are identified, then the importance of bank marketing and in particular market segmentation is explained. Next, the traditional segmentation approaches of banks are critically examined and a new basis for segmentation proposed. Support for this new basis is provided by using the criteria developed by Martin (1986) for judging the appropriateness of segmentation bases. Finally, the research required to make this segmentation basis operational, and to test the suitability of this basis for segmenting the corporate banking market, is described.

It is hoped that the chapter will encourage further research into industrial market segmentation for service industries.

The financial services market

Over the past twenty years the financial services market has become increasingly complex and competitive. This has been the result of certain developments within the market. First, there has been a gradual breakdown of the demarcation boundaries between financial institutions: for example, banks have been diversifying into new business areas traditionally undertaken by non-bank financial institutions. The Government has been instrumental in bringing about such changes through its objective of making the market more competitive, hence the deregulation practices of 1986 which resulted in the 'Big Bang', and the Building Society Act of 1987 which allowed building societies to offer products and services traditionally handled by banks. Secondly, the market itself has become increasingly 'global'. As domestic corporations have begun to operate internationally, their bankers have followed them abroad in an attempt to continue to serve their financial needs. In the UK there has been a growing presence of foreign banks: for example, between 1967 and 1981 the number of foreign banks operating in London rose from 113 to 420. The Second Banking Directive indicates that after 1992 foreign competitors will become even more of a threat, though the creation of one European Market will present UK banks with many opportunities. Thirdly, multinational companies and large retail outlets, having identified the opportunities in this highly lucrative market, have begun to offer financial services and products. Finally, customer loyalty has declined. Due to their increasing sophistication and the breakdown of demarcation barriers, consumers have become more willing to use more than one financial institution to meet their needs and to switch funds for short-term gains.

One of the most dramatic changes in the financial services market has been the changing needs of the corporate customer.

The corporate bank market

'The corporate treasurer is becoming increasingly more demanding on his commercial banker. The demands encompass a wide range of financial services; moreover, these demands are coming at a time when the corporate marketplace is beset with new dimensions of financial service competition, financial disinter-mediation and decreased customer loyalty' (Militello, 1984).

Turnbull (1982a, b) believes that radical changes in the corporate environment (changes in consumer lifestyle, income and spending patterns, liberalization of world trade, growth of domestic and international competition and the impact of rapid technical innovation by corporations) have increased its complexity and 'have led to a widespread use of sophisticated management systems'. This has brought about a breakdown in the traditional relationship between the banker and the corporate treasurer. In the past a relationship would be nurtured between the two parties, and thus most of the corporate treasurer's financial service requirements would be met by one bank. Now 'split banking' has emerged, whereby corporations use a number of financial institutions to satisfy their financial needs. Some corporations are even bypassing financial institutions altogether and placing funds directly into securities (disintermediation).

With competition accelerating in the market, it has become essential for banks to understand the financial needs of corporations and to cater for them. With this level of competition and the wide choice of financial institutions and products and services available to the corporate treasurers, banks are having to expand, to update their products and services, and to upgrade quality levels (through increasing specialization and innovation) in order to hold their market positions. Thus marketing has become the prerequisite for survival and success.

Bank marketing and market segmentation

'The success of a bank depends upon the ability to satisfy customers' financial needs and the effective practice of marketing in the banking environment is becoming recognised as a vital objective' (Meidan, 1983). Until the 1960s bank marketing activities generally amounted to little more than advertising and public relations. Even in the 1970s many banks considered marketing to be mainly concerned with promotion of one form or another. However, owing to the changes that have taken place (legislative, economic and socioeconomic) the market has become highly competitive and consumers of financial services (corporate and retail) now have greater needs accompanied by a more sophisticated approach to purchasing. Thus banks have had to think more about what customers really need and have had to try to meet those needs more effectively than their competitors.

'It is clear that the operations-centred and finance-dominated strategic emphasis of the early 1980s is giving way to a more market driven stance; in particular, compared with five years ago more are centering their activities on their customers' needs and requirements rather than their own products and capabilities' (Hooley and Mann, 1986, referring to the adoption of marketing practices by financial institutions).

In particular, market segmentation has become a very important element in the marketing practices of banks. It enables the user to identify different segments within a given market and, ideally, identifies the needs and buyer behaviour of individuals or organizations belonging to each segment. The bank that can identify those segments which offer it the best opportunities that it is capable of exploiting, thus maximizing its returns, will maintain and possibly improve upon its position within the market.

Market segmentation

The mass marketing approach (the attempt to reach and serve all potential customers within a given market) is recognized today as being unrealistic, and it can lead only to an inefficient use of a company's limited resources. Consumers within a given market are obviously not homogeneous in terms of needs, buying behaviour, demographic characteristics and so on. However, using a given variable, consumers within the market can be divided into segments within which consumers will be more similar to one another than to consumers of another segment type. By focusing its efforts on certain target segments, a company can use its limited resources more efficiently and effectively.

The technique used to identify submarkets within the total market is termed 'market segmentation'. The term and concept have been attributed to W.R. Smith (1956) when he commented, 'Segmentation is based upon developments on the demand side of the market and represents a rational and more precise adjustment of product and marketing effort to consumer and user requirements.'

Wind (1978) described market segmentation as being 'one of the most fundamental and dominant concepts of modern marketing'. This technique divides the total market into relatively homogeneous segments which are identified by some common characteristics. These characteristics should be relevant in explaining and predicting the response of consumers in a given segment to marketing stimuli (i.e. the product and the other marketing mix elements). Having carried out the segmentation exercise, the following questions are asked: 'Do these segments warrant different marketing strategies?' and 'Should we serve all of these segments or focus on a few selected (target) segments?' Assuming that the segments do warrant different marketing strategies and that the user decides to serve only a few 'target' segments, products and services will be adapted or created according to the particular needs of each target segment, supported by a marketing effort to which the segment will be most receptive in terms of such factors as price, promotion and personal selling.

The advantages that market segmentation has over mass marketing are:

- opportunities can be more easily identified and thus more quickly exploited;
- limited resources are used efficiently;
- customer needs, within the target segments, are satisfied.

Segmenting the corporate banking market

For market segmentation to be effective, the segmentation basis used should be related in some way to the purchase decision making of the consumer, in order to identify salient characteristics that indicate the needs and buyer behaviour of consumers in each segment. In this way an appropriate marketing strategy can be designed for each target segment.

Traditionally, the corporate banking market has been segmented using geographic location, industry type and/or size as the bases for segmentation. It is argued here that these bases fail to identify important influences affecting the decision making of the financial decision-making units within corporations, and thus that they only partially explain corporate financial needs and the buyer behaviour of the financial decision-making units within the corporation.

Turnbull (1982c, d) has made some examination of corporate financial service needs and buyer behaviour. This research provides an indication of how such needs and buyer behaviour are influenced by location, industry type and size. Other than Turnbull's studies very little research has been carried out in this area. Turnbull's primary findings were as follows:

- *Location.* European subsidiaries of multinational corporations have little involvement in financial decision making. Most of the decision making is handled at headquarters and it is not apparent that such decision making is influenced by the location of the subsidiary. Research examining the needs of corporations in different parts of the UK was not available.

- *Industry type.* This will indicate the degree of financial service and financial institution usage, and the range of services consumed. Turnbull found that manufacturing companies consumed more financial services of a wider variety and used more financial institutions than service companies. However, this may be due to size: i.e. manufacturing subsidiaries tend to be larger than service subsidiaries. Turnbull did not break industry types down into more specific categories.

- *Size.* The magnitude of the business or division indicates usage levels of services and institutions. As size increases, usage increases.

The traditional bases do provide some indication of financial service and institution usage but, as Militello (1984) points out, they fail to help banks to understand more fully the financial decision-making units within business organizations. Thus purchase motivations are not explained.

'Banks appear to be dissatisfied and frustrated with market segmentation' (Esters and Christenson, 1986/7). This is probably due to the use of unsuitable segmentation bases, which fail to provide the user with the necessary information and thus do not produce the expected benefits. Wind (1978) calls for the discovery and implementation of new variables for use as bases for segmentation, believing that the bases already available, for both consumer and industrial markets, fail to relate to consumer behaviour and thus fail to be of use to marketing managers. This chapter proposes that business strategy is a potentially useful basis for segmenting the corporate banking market.

Business strategy is concerned with how a business chooses to compete within a particular market. This choice determines which skills/competencies the business should possess, making certain functions (e.g. marketing, product research and development, finance) relatively more important than other functions within the business. Thus business strategy type will determine, to some extent, the type and amount of financial resources needed by the business in order to develop and maintain the necessary skills. It is therefore suggested that business strategy, as a basis for segmentation, will identify the financial needs and the related buyer behaviour of the financial decision-making units within businesses.

Criteria for identifying appropriate bases for segmentation

In his research on problem segmentation, Martin (1986) found that there was no procedure for identifying appropriate bases for segmentation, particularly prior to research. Clancy and Roberts (1983) claim, 'there is still no widely accepted and validated paradigm for evaluating modes of segmentation'. The criteria often cited in marketing literature deal with the segments generated rather than the bases themselves. Kotler's criteria, for example, suggest that a segmentation approach is appropriate, and thus of maximum use, if segments exhibit the following characteristics:

- measurability: the size and purchasing power of the segment can be measured (this is dependent on the availability of suitable market research data);
- accessibility: the segment can be reached and served effectively (i.e. a specific marketing effort can be directed at the segment);
- substantiality: the segment is sufficiently large and profitable to be economically viable;
- Actionability: effective programmes for attracting and serving segments can be developed and managed.

These criteria are useful for judging the segments produced after carrying out the segmentation exercise, but they do not guarantee that the basis will have identified the needs and buying behaviour of such segments. Martin, for this reason finding criteria such as these unsuitable for judging the appropriateness of segmentation bases, developed a set of criteria which he believed to be more suitable. For a segmentation basis to be deemed appropriate, Martin argues that it should possess the following qualities:

- determinance: the ability to represent and/or distinguish factors used during the buyers' decision making;
- appropriateness: marketing managers regard the basis as being pragmatically useful;
- predictive power: the basis highlights the causal connection between the characteristics distinguished by the basis and the market behaviour of interest to the marketing manager.

Though the traditional bases for segmentation might be of some use to the marketing manager and might be able to predict usage levels of service and financial institutions, it is suggested that the traditional bases fail fully to satisfy Martin's criteria. However, the proposed basis, business strategy, appears to possess all the necessary qualities.

First, in terms of determinance, implementing a business strategy requires the performance and co-ordination of a variety of tasks and activities across many functional departments (e.g. marketing, finance, production, research and development) within the business unit. Walker and Ruekert (1987) suggest that the relative importance of the different functional departments varies with strategy type. This suggestion is supported by the empirical research findings of Snow and Hrebiniak (1980) and Hambrich (1983). Thus, the strategy type of a business will determine which functional departments are of greatest importance to it: i.e. in order to implement a particular strategy successfully, a business will have to be highly competent in certain areas. This means that business strategy type will determine the financial service needs of a business, both type and amount, and the allocation of financial resources.

For example, a business that adopts an aggressive new product/market position within broadly defined markets, is on the lookout for new opportunities and strives for rapid growth (Miles and Snow (1978) identified this strategy type and named it the 'prospector' strategy) must be particularly competent in marketing, sales, product research and development, and other functions close to the market. On the other hand, a business that takes a more conservative view of new product development and attempts to maintain a secure position in a narrow segment of the market, competing mainly on price and quality (Miles and Snow named this the 'defender' strategy) must be particularly competent in process engineering, production, finance management and control, and other functions which can influence efficiency. The extent to which a company becomes involved with new products and new markets influences which functions are of relatively greater importance and thus will determine needs.

Prospector businesses, keen to become involved with new products and markets, are likely to have insurance, information and advice, and types of finance requirements different from defender businesses which are concerned with efficiency and scale of production. Businesses of different strategy types are likely to respond to the same marketing stimuli (price, promotion, personal selling, etc.)

in different ways: for example, defender businesses will be price sensitive, whilst prospectors will be more concerned with the willingness of financial institutions to finance medium- to high-risk projects.

To implement a business strategy successfully, a business must possess the necessary functional competencies. To develop and maintain these competencies requires resources of a particular type and amount which are then allocated appropriately.

Secondly, concerning appropriateness, marketers can develop packages of financial products and services which meet the needs of businesses pursuing certain business strategies, i.e. enable them to develop and maintain the necessary functional competencies. These packages will be supported by a marketing effort that businesses pursuing certain strategies will be most receptive in terms of price, promotion and so on.

Thirdly, as regards predictive power, the characteristics revealed by this basis should indicate the financial requirements of business organizations pursuing different strategies.

Research implications

This is a conceptual chapter in that a new basis for segmentation purposes has been proposed. However, no empirical work has been carried out to support the hypothesis that this is a more appropriate approach to segmenting the corporate banking market. It is therefore necessary to highlight the type of research that will be required, first to make the basis operational and secondly to test the suitability of the basis.

Making the segmentation basis operational

The segmentation approach proposed in this chapter is the division of the total corporate market into segments, each of which represents a different strategy type. Therefore, to operationalize this basis, it is necessary to produce a list of strategy types which together are collectively exhaustive (every possible strategy type is identified, using one or more variables) and individually are mutually exclusive.

> Strategy describes the fundamental characteristics of the match that an organisation achieves among its skills and resources and the opportunities and threats in its external environment that enables it to achieve its goals and objectives. (Chrisman, Hofer and Boulton, 1988)

This description is based on the Hofer and Schendel definition (1978) which is consistent with the views of most researchers of strategic management. Hofer and Schendel identify and describe three forms of organizational strategy: corporate strategy which concerns the set of businesses with which the complex corporation should be involved; business strategy, which concerns how a business chooses to compete in a particular market; and functional strategy, which mainly concerns the maximization of resource productivity.

This chapter proposes that businesses can be divided up according to their business strategy type and that each group, representing a different strategy, will have unique product and service needs and buyer behaviour. Before businesses can be divided up in this manner, a typology of business strategy types must be developed.

A strategic typology is a group of strategic types, each of which is viewed as having its own distinct pattern of characteristics. The typology should capture the comprehensive and integrative nature of strategy.

For a typology to be of any practical use to researchers the types within it must be:

- mutually exclusive: this enables researchers to differentiate effectively between types; i.e. it is not possible for a member of one type to be assigned membership to any other type at the same time;
- internally homogeneous: members of a type are more similar to each other than they are to the members of other types, so that generalizations about members within a certain type will be valid;
- collectively exhaustive: the types as a whole represent every possible alternative of the variable in question;
- given a relevant name: the name of each type should either embody or be associated with the key distinguishing characteristic(s) used to delineate them, thus making identification easy.

There is no generally accepted typology of business strategy. However, several attempts have been made to derive general types through empirical research, such as that by Miles and Snow (1978). The key characteristic underlying their typology of business strategy is the organization's rate of product/market change. They identified four types:

- defenders: organizations that rarely change their products or markets;
- prospectors: organizations that readily change their products and/or markets;
- analysers: an intermediate category;
- reactors: organizations that are inconsistent in their approach to product/ market changes.

Miles and Snow studied the coalignment of other variables with the key product/ market change variable. For example, defenders tend to compete primarily on price, delivery and quality, they invest a great deal in process engineering, they have relatively mechanistic structures and processes, and they are run primarily under the influence of production and accounting executives. The other types have their own comprehensive profiles.

Empirical research will be carried out to develop a strategic typology suitable for the requirements of this chapter, and use will be made of the theory underlying strategic typologies which have already been developed, such as those of Porter, Miles and Snow, and Walker and Ruekert.

Testing the suitability of the new basis for segmentation

Having developed a strategic typology, the segmentation basis should be tested to see if the financial service needs of businesses can be identified according to their membership of a certain strategic type.

The basis can be tested by taking a sample of businesses and dividing them up according to their strategic type (this requires some measure of strategy), and then a study can be made of the financial service needs and buyer behaviour of businesses within each strategy segment.

Before identifying different measurement approaches, it is important to note that the strategy of a business being observed may be undergoing a change and/or may be an 'intended' rather than a 'realized' strategy.

- *Strategic change.* This amounts to a business reacting to an environmental change in a way that is unfamiliar to its normal way of behaviour. 'A useful view might be that strategic change occurs only when the organisation a) modifies in a major way its alignment with the environment and b) substantially alters its internal features to support a strategy modification' (Snow and Hambrich, 1980). If a business is undergoing strategic change, it is possible that its financial resource requirements will be affected in order to cater for the change. In this transitional state the financial resource requirements may be quite different from those associated with the two strategy types between which it is moving.

However, businesses tend to prefer to apply familiar solutions to new problems, and thus business strategy change appears to be fairly uncommon. Cyert and March (1963), Cohen *et al.* (1972) and Snow and Hambrich (1980) have found a general reluctance amongst business organizations to change their strategy.

This reluctance is probably due to the considerable amount of investment in terms of time, people and money required to develop the distinctive competencies, technologies, structure and management processes needed to pursue a particular strategy. Another important deterrent to changing the strategy type is the fact that 'over time a given strategy type attracts and fosters a set of managerial values and philosophies that are wedded to the strategy' (Snow and Hambrich, 1980).

- *Intended or realized strategy.* The identified strategy type of a business under observation may be the intended rather than the realized strategy. Intended strategy is the way a business wishes to compete within a given market; the realized strategy is the way a business actually competes within a given market.

In general, researchers should have some idea of whether their purposes are best served by observing intended or realized strategies (as will be explained later, the particular measurement approach used will determine whether the strategy type identified is realized or intended).

As far as the research for the segmentation basis is concerned, what is important is the strategy which influences the financial service needs of businesses and the buyer behaviour of the financial decision-making unit within business organizations, whether it be intended or realized.

Measuring strategy types

To test the suitability of this basis for segmentation it is necessary to determine the strategy types of a sample of businesses and to see if there is a relationship between strategy type and financial service requirements and, possibly, the buyer behaviour of the financial decision-making units within business organizations.

The strategy type of a business can be measured in different ways. Snow and Hambrich (1980) list four:

- *Investigator inference*. Using all available information, the researcher identifies the business's strategy type. The researcher is likely to be objective in his/her identification and thus will probably identify the realized strategy. This approach, however, requires a considerable amount of data, thus the sample would have to be small to be manageable. It is probable that the researcher will not have key pieces of information (information that top management believe should be withheld). Snow and Hambrich believe this to be a weak approach.

- *Self-typing*. This approach involves asking managers of the sampled businesses to identify the strategy type of their business organization. This approach enables a large sample of business organizations to be studied. However, managers may have problems identifying their organization's strategy type because their organization seems to be so complex or unique. This is a more subjective approach (i.e. the business's personnel are asked for their opinion), thus intended rather than realized strategies are more likely to be identified.

- *External assessment*. Individuals and organizations external to the business being studied (e.g. competition, industry analysts, consultants) are asked to identify the business's strategy type. Using 'supposed' competitor companies may prove difficult if they operate in different segments of the same market (they may be unable to give any opinion). This approach is fairly objective and thus should identify the realized strategy of the business organization under analysis.

- *Objective indicators*. This approach does not rely on the perceptions of individuals; it relies on any form of data about businesses within the sample that can aid the identification of strategy type (e.g. product/market data and published accounts). However, this type of information is not always available.

In testing the suitablity of the segmentation basis, we are particularly interested in how a business's strategy type influences the financial decision-making unit within it. Thus, the financial decision-making unit's perception of strategy, whether it be realized or intended, is of importance. For this reason the self-typing approach will be used.

Turnbull (1982d) and Militello (1984) identified the financial decision-making unit within business organizations to be generally the finance director and the corporate treasurer. Thus, the strategy type of the businesses in the sample will be measured by asking finance directors and/or corporate treasurers to select from a list of descriptions, each describing a different strategy type, the description that best fits their perception of their organization's strategy. Both Turnbull and Militello have found that the finance function within multi-business corporations has become increasingly centralized, thus the strategy type of any business in the sample that is part of a multi-business corporation will be identified by the finance decision-making unit based at company headquarters.

The financial decision-making units will then be questioned on the financial requirements of their organization and their buyer behaviour.

Current and emerging issues for further research and development

The corporate banking market has, over the past twenty years, become highly competitive. A bank's position within the market is no longer challenged only by other banks but, as a result of the removal of demarcation barriers, by a whole range of financial institutions, both domestic and international. At the same time, corporate customers have become more sophisticated in their buying practices and more demanding, leading to a decline in customer loyalty (fuelled also by the breakdown of demarcation barriers) and the adoption of the split banking philosophy; financial service needs are satisfied by more than one financial institution. The market looks set to continue along the path of increasing competitiveness and complexity, with the European market of 1992 set to throw up a whole host of opportunities and threats.

In a market such as this, an understanding of customer needs and buyer behaviour is essential in the planning of marketing strategies. However, up until now very little research has been carried out in the area of corporate financial service needs and the buyer behaviour of the financial decision-making units within corporations. This explains, to some extent, the failure of marketing academics to develop a segmentation approach which directly relates to such needs and behaviour, hence the continued use of traditional bases – location, industry type and size – which are not wholly satisfactory. In segmentation research in general, methods of segmentation have been developed which fail to provide information that can greatly assist marketers in their marketing strategy plans. Martin (1986) argues that a basis should represent or distinguish factors used by buyers during decision making and be of pragmatic use to marketing managers.

If such a basis is to be developed and applied to the corporate banking market, more research into the financial service needs of corporations and the buyer behaviour of the financial decision-making units within corporations must be carried out.

Business strategy appears to be a potentially useful basis for segmenting the corporate banking market. However, before its worth can be established it must be made operational (the research implications are provided in the main body of the chapter).

Discussion

The corporate banking market is highly heterogeneous and complex, thus an attempt to satisfy the needs of the whole market with one marketing strategy (mass marketing) will almost certainly fail. It makes more sense to divide the market up, using some variable (market segmentation), and to develop a marketing strategy that suits the needs and buyer behaviour of each of the segments that the bank has decided to serve.

The benefits gained from serving certain 'target' segments within the total market are likely to include the efficient use of limited resources, the maximization of returns, the satisfaction of the target consumers' needs, and the ability to identify and exploit opportunities quickly due to focusing on small homogeneous segments rather than on the large and highly heterogeneous total market.

Banks have recognized the importance of market segmentation to the extent that it has become an 'integral and increasingly important element of the banks' marketing orientation' (Lewis, 1984). However, banks appear to be dissatisfied and frustrated with market segmentation (Esters and Christenson, 1986). This is due to the use of inappropriate variables (bases) with which to divide markets.

Martin (1986) argues that market segmentation can be of use to marketers in their planning of marketing strategies only when the basis chosen to segment the market represents or distinguishes factors used during buyer decision making, so that each segment identified will represent unique needs and buyer behaviour. However, the bases that banks have tended to use to segment the corporate banking market (e.g. location, industry type and size), although capable of partially explaining financial service needs and usage levels, fail to explain the buyer behaviour of the financial decision-making units within corporations. Thus, market segmentation practices, using such bases, are likely to prove fruitless.

'The success of a bank depends upon the ability to satisfy customer financial needs' (Meidan, 1983). In this highly competitive market it is essential that banks understand, and then satisfy, the financial service requirements of corporations and the buyer behaviour of the financial decision-making units within these corporations, so that the offer made to the market in terms of product, price and promotion is appropriate and effective. If the traditional bases for segmentation remain those variables most commonly used by banks for dividing the corporate banking market, opportunities will be missed and other financial institutions with more appropriate views of the market will be quick to exploit them.

Conclusion

As the corporate banking market continues to become increasingly competitive, an understanding of consumers within the market is becoming more and more essential. This chapter has identified the importance of market segmentation and has argued that the traditional bases for segmentation (location, industry type and size) fail to provide banks with the necessary understanding of the financial service requirements and buyer behaviour of businesses within the market. Therefore a new basis is proposed, namely business strategy. The way a business chooses to compete within its market, its business strategy, determines which functions are of greatest importance for the successful implementation of the strategy and thus influences product and service needs and resource allocations. The appropriateness of business strategy as a basis for market segmentation was tested using Martin's (1986) criteria.

References

Clancy, K.J. and Roberts, M.L. (1983) 'Towards an optimal target market: a strategy for market segmentation', *Journal of Consumer Marketing*, Summer 1983.

Cohen, M.D., March, J.G. and Olsen, J.P. (1972) 'A garbage can model of organisational choice', *Administrative Science Quarterly*, 17, 1–25.

Cyert, R.M. and March, J.G. (1963) *A Behavioural Theory of the Firm*. Englewood Cliffs, NJ: Prentice–Hall.

Esters, R. and Christenson, D. (1986/7) 'Market segmentation: effective design and use in financial service institutions', *Journal of Retail Banking*, 8, 4, 19–28.

Hambrich, D.C. (1980) 'Operationalizing the concept of business level strategy in research', *Academy of Management Review*, 5, 4, 567–75.

Hambrich, D.C. (1983) 'Some tests of the effectiveness and functional attributes of Miles and Snow's strategic types', *Academy of Management Journal*, 26, 5–26.

Hofer, C.W. and Schendel, D. (1978) *Strategy Formulation: Analytical Concepts*. St Paul, Minn.: West.

Hooley, G.J. and Mann, S.J. (1986) 'The adoption of marketing by financial institutions in the UK', *Services Industries Journal*, 8, 4, 488–500.

Lewis, B.R. (1984) 'Marketing bank services', *Services Industries Journal*, 4, 3, 61–76.

Martin, J. (1986) 'Problem segmentation', *International Journal of Bank Marketing*, 4, 2, 35–57.

Meidan, A. (1983) 'The roles of marketing management in banking', *Quarterly Review of Banking*, Spring, 11–18.

Miles, R.F. and Snow, C.C. (1978) *Organizational Strategy, Structure and Process*. New York: McGraw–Hill.

Militello, F.C. (1984) 'Marketing the corporate treasurer: a financial approach', *Bank Marketing*, October, 31–3.

Snow, C.C. and Hambrich, D.C. (1980) 'Measuring organisational strategies: some theoretical and methodological problems', *Academy of Management Review*, 5, 4, 527–38.

Snow, C. C. and Hrebiniak, L.C. (1980) 'Strategy, distinctive competence and organisational performance', *Administrative Science Quarterly*, 25, 317–55.

Turnbull, P.W. (1982a) 'International aspects of bank marketing', in Turnbull, P.W. and Lewis, B.R. (eds) *The Marketing of Bank Services*. Bradford: MCB Publications.

Turnbull, P.W. (1982b) 'The penetration of the UK corporate market by US banks', in Turnbull, P.W. and Lewis, B.R. (eds) *The Marketing of Bank Services*. Bradford: MCB Publications.

Turnbull, P.W. (1982c) 'The purchasing of international financial services by medium and large-sized UK companies with European subsidiaries', in Turnbull, P.W. and Lewis, B.R. (eds), *The Marketing of Bank Services*. Bradford: MCB Publications.

Turnbull, P.W. (1982d) 'The use of foreign banks by UK companies', in Turnbull, P.W. and Lewis, B.R. (eds) *The Marketing of Bank Services*. Bradford: MCB Publications.

Walker, O.C. and Ruekert, R.W. (1987) 'Marketing's role in the implementation of business strategies: a critical review and conceptual framework', *Journal of Marketing*, 51, July, 15–33.

Wind, Y., (1978) 'Issues and advances in segmentation research', *Journal of Marketing Research*, 15, August, 317–37.

Part 4

Tourism and hospitality management

Introduction

Richard Teare

Tourism and hospitality markets around the world are evolving rapidly. The advent of the internal market in Europe, the deregulation of air travel and the emergence of new tourist destinations in the developing nations are only a few of the important events which are shaping these closely interrelated service industries.

The hospitality industry, encompassing hotel, catering and leisure sectors, is taking a more sophisticated approach to the design of services. Hotels increasingly provide an array of leisure facilities to meet the perceived needs of core and peripheral markets, and branding has become a key feature of advertising campaigns as the national and multinational companies seek to increase market share and exploit niches in the business, leisure and tourism markets. New design- and technology-driven concepts such as the 'budget' hotel and cook-chill food production systems are also making a strong impact on a conservative industry with a traditional view of service, epitomized by skilled, attentive restaurant staff. This concept still has an important role, but the impact of competition, social change and new technology is evident in the diversification of hospitality services which became a feature of the 1980s.

One of the remaining difficulties in tourism and hospitality planning is the problem of obtaining accurate and reliable information. Tourism statistics are notoriously difficult to obtain and verify. Commenting recently on gaps in domestic tourism statistics, one analyst claimed that expenditure in some sectors of the domestic leisure break market can only be estimated because the types of accommodation used by visitors are so diverse. It is therefore appropriate that the whole question of tourism statistics and forecasting should be discussed in the following two chapters.

Hospitality research gathered momentum during the 1980s, and the philosophies, concepts and methodologies which emerged provide some signs and directions for research and development in the 1990s. One of the main challenges for researchers and hospitality managers will be to develop a more comprehensive understanding of the customer experience. Like many other services, production and consumption occur simultaneously, but the duration of consumption and the service delivery environment vary significantly from one sector of the industry to another. These issues are addressed in the final chapter of Part 4.

Chapter 12

Tourism statistics

Stephen Wanhill

Overview

By the end of 1990, world-wide international tourist arrivals per annum are expected to have reached just under 400 million, an increase of more than 100 million since 1980. Current projections indicate that this total will be approaching 600 million in the year 2000 which, together with large volumes of domestic tourist trips, has prompted the view that tourism will be the world's largest industry by the end of the century. Whatever the outcome, it is clear that the tourist industry is now of a size that no country can afford to ignore tourism and the investment opportunities that the industry offers.

Understanding the phenomenon of tourism and formulating policy requires the consistent measurement of tourist flows and knowledge of the structure of the tourist sector. Unfortunately, the growth in tourism has not been matched by the provision of information sources. Whereas most countries have a wealth of data on production industries, tourism and service industries in general are poorly served. Typically, international tourism is measured in terms of the number of visits at frontier points, nights spent in the country at accommodation establishments and expenditure from central bank records of foreign exchange transactions. Domestic tourism, when measured, is usually confined to annual holiday surveys. Supply-side statistics are often limited to recording the number of rooms at places of accommodation and occupancy rates.

The principal disadvantage of current tourism statistics is that in most cases their aggregate nature permits only a limited interpretation and identification of changing demand and supply patterns in the industry. Tour operators and airlines which hold major shares of the market are able to monitor changes from their own internally generated data, but for the myriad of small suppliers and resorts the first indication is often alterations in their bookings with little insight into the factors that may have caused this. The outcome, if any, is usually a series of hasty and unplanned responses which may or may not correct the situation. Part of the problem here is that the economic success of tourism over the past two decades, even in times of quite severe recession, has made it difficult to convince the political system that it should take an active role. Couple this with the fact that during the 1980s governments in general became far keener to let the market system solve their economic worries, and it is easy to appreciate the claim that tourism is a private sector industry which forms no part of the activities of the state. In reality nothing could be further from the truth: the successful development of tourism requires a partnership between the public and private sectors, for many of the goods and services sought by tourists are either publicly provided, such as museums, or are genuine public goods, such as culture and the environment, which are available equally to all and are shared with the host community. As several Mediterranean resorts have found to their cost, the unfettered operation of the market has not led to an integrated tourist development giving a balanced supply of all those things demanded by the tourists, but rather to a crowded and placeless semi-urban building site.

It follows, therefore, that a requirement for successful planning is a statistical programme that starts by defining what is to be measured and can provide information that will throw light on these issues:

* the impact of tourism on the destination;
* the current demand and supply situation facing the tourist industry, by different market segments;
* historic trends leading up to the present position of the industry;
* factors influencing tourist trends;
* the nature of the tourist product and any restrictions on provision;
* market prospects.

Definitions

Webster's Dictionary defines a tour as 'a journey at which one returns to the starting point; a circular trip usually for business, pleasure or education during which various places are visited and for which an itinerary is usually planned'. From this comes the concept of tourism which Burkart and Medlik (1981, 319) defined as 'the temporary, short-term movement of people to destinations outside the places where they normally live and work and their activities during the stay at these destinations'. Mathieson and Wall (1982, 1) use a similar definition but add the rider: 'and the facilities created to cater to their needs'.

The essential interpretation to be placed on tourism from these definitions is that it is about travel to a location away from a person's usual place of residence or workplace, staying there, but only for a temporary period, and carrying out a number of activities which are not solely to do with leisure. Behind this is an economic concept that tourism is about a transfer of purchasing power from one location to another. The popular notion of tourism is somewhat different, as illustrated in Tables 12.1 and 12.2, which are drawn from survey work relating to Londoners' views as to who is a tourist. What is apparent from the tables is that Londoners see tourism as a phenomenon that is more likely to be something to do with foreignness and is very much to do with leisure visitors whether they are staying in the area or are on a day trip. Suppliers of tourist goods and services are also prone to define tourism by the composition of their customers. Thus incoming tour operators are likely to see tourism solely in terms of leisure visitors staying in paid accommodation. However, leisure is not well enough defined to form the sole basis of tourism and would only provide partial coverage of those businesses which are typically associated with tourism: accommodation, transport, restaurants, shopping facilities, attractions and entertainment.

For measurement purposes the World Tourism Organization (WTO) has produced technical definitions which are based on the concept of the visitor (Table

Table 12.1 *Londoners' perceived definition of a tourist, 1978*

	Definitely tourists (%)	Tourists of a sort (%)
Foreign holidaymakers to Britain staying in London	86	8
Foreign holidaymakers on pleasure day trips to London staying elsewhere in Britain	74	18
Foreign businessmen staying in London	12	31
British holidaymakers staying in London	34	27
British people on pleasure day trips to London	25	29
British businessmen staying in London	3	9

Source: NOP.
Note: Base: all respondents = 964.

Table 12.2 *Londoners' perceived definition of a tourist, 1986*

	Tourists (%)
Foreigners on holiday in London staying in hotels	98
Foreigners on holiday in London staying with friends	83
Foreigners in London on business	31
People from elsewhere in UK on holiday staying in hotels	73
People from elsewhere in UK staying with friends/relatives	51
British people on business	15
Londoners visiting attractions in Central London	28
Day visitors from outside London	49

Source: Cleverdon Steer.
Note: Base: all respondents = 1,014.

Table 12.3 *World Tourism Organization definitions*

Visitors:	All persons entering a country other than that of their usual residence for any purpose other than to engage in an occupation remunerated from within that country.
Tourists:	All visitors making at least an overnight stay or a stay of more than 24 hours in the country visited whose journey purpose can be classified as: (a) leisure (recreation, holiday, health, study, religion or sport); (b) business, family, mission, meeting.
Excursionists:	Temporary visitors not making an overnight stay in the country visited (or staying less than 24 hours).

12.3). They are international definitions, but they have also been broadly accepted for measuring domestic tourism. They follow closely the concept of tourism defined by Burkart and Medlik in which the dividing line between who is a tourist and who is an excursionist, or more commonly a day visitor, is the use of accommodation. There is also a convention as to the meaning of the word 'temporary': internationally, a tourist stays no longer than twelve months. Beyond one year a person is deemed to have migrated. On the domestic side, the length of stay varies by country and type of survey. Thus France imposes a maximum stay of four months; after this travellers are considered to be temporary residents. The British Tourism Survey Monthly (BTSM) does not count trips of more than thirty-five nights, while the British Tourism Survey Yearly (BTSY) records trips of up to three months.

As we look forward to the 1990s, it is clear that the current definition of tourism is inadequate. The concentration on accommodation has excluded from the statistics large movements of day tourists which will continue to grow as people have more leisure time and transport becomes easier. Surveys have shown that there are people who take their holidays at home and simply make day excursions. It is sensible to continue to separate stay tourists from day tourists, for it is only the former that consume the totality of the product, but day visits must be included within the phenomenon of tourism. This has the advantage of conforming to popular notions about tourism and is mindful of the future. Thus the definition of tourism I would like to see is: 'the temporary movement of people to destinations outside their normal places of work and residence, and the activities undertaken during the time spent at those destinations'.

Demand measurement

For most countries the starting point for the collection of international tourism statistics has been the International Civil Aviation Organization (ICAO) embarkation/disembarkation (E/D) card for movements, and central bank foreign exchange records for expenditure. The E/D card was designed for immigration control but many countries, particular islands like Singapore, have successfully adapted the card for tourism purposes by asking questions on the country of usual residence, purposes of visit and length of stay. In Australia, both overseas visitors and residents complete E/D cards. However, in Europe, within the EEC bloc the easing of frontier formalities has meant that only the sub-population of passengers from outside the EEC completes E/D cards. Thus, for example, when Greece joined the EEC, the statistical series for the country's main tourist markets was abruptly truncated. Moreover, because of the numerous entry points in Europe, particularly for landlocked countries, it has not always been considered feasible to run frontier checks for tourism purposes and the continental tradition has been, by and large, to collect tourist statistics at the place of accommodation. Thus, Belgium, Denmark, Luxembourg, Sweden and Switzerland do not collect frontier statistics. Those that do collect frontier statistics, for example Germany, often do not make any distinction between travellers and tourists, let alone between stay tourists and day tourists.

The island position of Great Britain limits the number of entry and departure points, thus making easier the collection of frontier statistics. To obtain a United Kingdom perspective, estimates have to be added in from the Isle of Man, the Channel Islands and Northern Ireland. The only difficulty here is cross-border traffic between Northern Ireland and the Irish Republic, where the problems of collecting data are more than just statistical ones. An outline of the principal statistical sources of international tourist movements to and from the United Kingdom is given in Table 12.4. The primary source is the International Passenger Survey (IPS) whose main sponsor is the Department of Employment, the

Table 12.4 *United Kingdom international tourism statistics*

	International Passenger Survey (IPS)	Overseas Visitor Survey (OVS)	Northern Ireland Passenger Survey (NIPS)
Commencement	1961, but with coverage of major ports of exit from/entrance to the UK from 1964. Monthly, quarterly and annual reporting.	1977, with annual reporting. Year runs from October to September.	1959, annually since 1972. Yearly results published.
Coverage	All tourism to/from the UK with the exception of the Irish Republic, the Channel Islands and UK cruises.	All overseas staying tourists to GB of up to 3 months' duration.	All tourism from Northern Ireland.
Design	Systematic random sampling at airports and seaports. Sample size depends on traffic growth but was 175,000 for 1987/88.	Some 4,400 self-completion questionnaires distributed to a quota sample of overseas visitors at sampling points throughout Great Britain.	Systematic random sampling of approximately 10,000 travellers leaving by airports and seaports.

government ministry with chief responsibility for tourism policy. The IPS collects volume and value statistics (country of residence/country visited, purpose of visit, demographics, length of stay, place of stay, expenditure) for all tourism through a random sample stratified by points of entry/leaving. The gaps in the information as indicated in Table 12.4 are filled by returns from other agencies so as to give overall United Kingdom coverage. The IPS does not interview in Northern Ireland, but it does make allowances for tourist flows in the published estimates. The Northern Ireland Tourist Board (NITB) carries out its own passenger survey but, unlike the IPS, interviews only departing passengers. In addition, the NITB also records cross-border flows by tourists to and from the Irish Republic.

The Overseas Visitor Survey (OVS) is a quota sample of non-resident adults who are staying in Britain for a period of three months or less. It is sponsored by the British Tourist Authority/English Tourist Board (BTA/ETB) and is undertaken at sampling points throughout Great Britain according to quota controls set by the IPS results. The OVS is designed to supplement the IPS by seeking information to do with visitor attitudes and behaviour, which is important for overseas marketing.

There are several ways in which statistics on domestic tourism may be obtained.

- destination surveys: contacting tourists during their stay at, for example, a resort;
- site surveys: surveys carried out at attractions, places of entertainment and accommodation establishments;
- traffic surveys: sampling travellers during their journey at traffic cordons or at stopping places;
- household surveys: contacting tourists at their place of residence.

While each of these methods has its own particular advantages, only a household survey offers complete coverage from a known sampling frame which can be used as the basis for grossing up the sample observations to obtain volume and value statistics for the total population. For this reason, all the surveys illustrated in Table 12.5 collect primary data from in-home interviews.

The major source of domestic stay tourist statistics is the BTSM, which is sponsored by the BTA/ETB and the Wales Tourist Board (WTB). The main purpose, and at the same time the principal strength, of the survey is to provide complete coverage of all stay tourist trips (at home and abroad) by the British population. A tourist trip is defined as 'a stay of one or more nights away from home for holidays, visits to friends or relatives, business, conferences or any other purpose except such things as boarding education or semi-permanent employment'. Trips to hospital or convalescent homes for treatment are not included; neither are unaccompanied child trips.

The BTSM sample is selected on a random basis from the Electoral Register. The vehicle for collecting the data is a weekly household omnibus survey undertaken by means of in-home interviews in 180 constituencies. The use of an omnibus survey controls the cost of implementing a nation-wide survey, but it also limits the amount of information collected to the basic volume and value of

Table 12.5 *United Kingdom domestic tourist statistics*

	British Tourism Survey Monthly (BTSM)	British Tourism Survey Yearly (BTSY)	National Survey of Tourism in Scotland (NSTS)	Northern Ireland Holiday Survey (NIHS)
Commenced	1972, as British Home Tourism Survey. Annual and monthly reporting. Became BTSM in 1985. Monthly, annual and trend reports (6 per annum).	1951, as British National Travel Survey. Annual since 1960. Became BTSY in 1985. Annual reporting.	1984, with annual and monthly reporting.	1972, with annual reporting.
Coverage	All staying tourism by GB residents of 1 + nights at home and abroad.	All holidays by GB residents of 4 + nights at home and 1 + nights abroad. GB includes Isle of Man and Channel Islands.	All staying tourism by GB residents of 1 + nights to Scotland.	NI holidays of 1–3 and 4 + nights at home and abroad (outside NI). Trips for other purposes also collected.
Design	2,000 random in-home interviews of adults (16 +) undertaken each month. Trip recall period is the previous 2 months.	3,500 random in-home interviews of adults (16 +) undertaken in November/ December. Boosted by a further 5,280 interviews to raise the sample of abroad holidays to around 2,000. Trip recall period is the past 12 months.	Quota of 2,000 in-home interviews of adults (15 +) drawn each month from randomly selected parliamentary constituencies. The sample is boosted by a further 500 Scottish households. Trip recall period is the previous 3 months.	2,000 quota in-home interviews of adults (16 +) undertaken in November/December. Trip recall period is the past 12 months.

tourism according to purpose, duration, transport, destination, accommodation usage and a few other details.

There is a large area of overlap between the BTSM and the BTSY. However, the BTSY is a particular survey commissioned solely for the purpose of providing annual data on holidays of four or more nights taken by British residents in Britain and one or more nights abroad. It is syndicated to various subscribers by the BTA/ETB and allows for confidential sponsored questions as well as collecting much valuable marketing information, e.g. facilities provided at the destination, brand names of suppliers, booking patterns and methods of payment.

The National Survey of Tourism in Scotland (NSTS) presents a very different case: up until 1983 the Scottish Tourist Board (STB) used the BTSM to provide statistics on the volume and value of tourism to Scotland. As the sample base for the estimates was around 900 adult and child trips, there was concern about the lack of precision. Therefore, the STB decided to commission its own survey, the core of which would be the same as the BTSM. The main survey is run on a quota omnibus, but the additional feature is a separate booster of 500 Scottish households to allow for the fact that some 50 per cent of Scottish tourist trips originate within Scotland. The effect of this sample design, together with the extension of the trip recall period to three months, was to more than treble the sample base for Scotland in the year the NSTS began. Accordingly, this lent greater precision to the grossed-up estimates of tourist trips to Scotland.

The Northern Ireland Holiday Survey (NIHS) is a particular or 'dedicated' household quota survey designed to produce volume and value data on long and short holidays taken by residents of Northern Ireland. In this manner the survey is similar to the BTSY, but the level of detail is not the same: only basic tabular results are presented at a broad level of aggregation. As indicated in Table 12.5, the survey does produce information on tourist trips for purposes other than holiday, but the reliability is such that the estimates are not used for matters other than internal.

The most obvious omission from Table 12.5 is the lack of any coverage on day visitors. Treatment of day tourists has been sporadic, but the Department of Employment has now commissioned a leisure day visit survey for Great Britain as a trailer to the General Household Survey (GHS) which is run by the Office of Population Censuses and Surveys. It is expected that the GHS will deliver an achieved sample of 9,400 households evenly distributed across Britain. The information collected by the trailer will include whether a leisure trip was taken or not, type of trip, number of trips, destination by location and type, origin of trip and various categories of expenditure. Both the NITB and the STB have sponsored their own leisure day visit surveys.

Emerging demand issues for the 1990s

In comparison with other Western European countries, the United Kingdom is well served by tourism demand statistics. At a national level, the IPS produces sampling errors of 1.7 per cent for United Kingdom residents' trips abroad and 2.5 per cent for the number of overseas visitors coming to the United Kingdom. The sampling errors for total expenditure are 2.3 per cent and 2.7 per cent respectively (Griffiths and Elliot, 1988). The BTSM has sampling errors for domestic trips and expenditure within Britain of 5.4 per cent and 6.8 per cent (Domestic Tourism Statistics Review Group, 1988). Undoubtedly, at a national level, the two surveys are able to provide annual and quarterly trends which are meaningful in terms of the overall performance of the tourist industry, but even here, there are difficulties in constructing profile data of current market segments from published cross-tabulations. For example, there is a need to know more about activity and special interest holidays, short breaks in the countryside, in the city and at resorts, and travel by the retired. Furthermore, there is a requirement for uniform coverage of the United Kingdom. In practice, the sampling errors of the different surveys are by far outweighed by the variations resulting from different survey design: thus the results of the NSTS and the BTSM are not comparable in those areas where they are purporting to measure the same population parameters.

However, it is at the regional and local level that major difficulties with the provision of tourism statistics exist. Most tourism projects are necessarily tied to a specific location, but currently it is extremely difficult to assess quantitatively the tourism potential of an area. The tourist boards do collect information on attraction attendances, but destination surveys to build up tourist profiles are relatively infrequent and the national data has to be so severely rounded at the regional and sub-regional level as to make the interpretation of trends, as opposed to broad orders of magnitude, virtually impossible. The latter applies less to the IPS, because of the larger sample size, than to the BTSM. Currently, the BTSM has annual sampling errors for domestic trips to Wales and Scotland of 14.9 per cent and 19.3 per cent. If this is related to quarterly data, the respective errors are 32.8 per cent and 47.8 per cent. A similar situation applies to the tourist regions of England, with annual sampling errors approaching nearly 30 per cent in some cases. If the performance of regional tourism is to be assessed correctly, there is a clear need to improve the level of precision of domestic tourism statistics. For most users the information value of statistics is greatly enhanced if the data are readily available soon after collection. Summary results of the IPS are ready some two months after the interviewing process, while for the BTSM the results appear about $3\frac{1}{2}$ months after the trip has taken place, due to the two-month recall period. The main publications take much longer, but it is possible to anticipate that on-line access to the raw data will be increasingly available as we move into the next decade. This will, however, depend on users' willingness to pay. Generally speaking, demand measurement is not the quickest way to monitor trends: statistical returns from suppliers, such as occupancy rates, attendances and so on, produce a much faster response on market performance.

Statistical Office of the European Communities

With the challenge of creating a single European market by 1992, the pressure to harmonize and standardize the provision of information is increasing and tourism statistics are no exception to this. During 1988 the Statistical Office of the European Communities (SOEC) put forward a draft regulation concerning a

European domestic holiday survey and a draft directive covering a variety of tourism statistics. There is a clear distinction between a directive and a regulation. The former requires specific statistics to be made available for publication, but the methodology to be used for providing the data is the responsibility of the member state. A regulation not only requests specific data, but also insists on the method of collection.

Eleven of the member states of the EC undertake domestic holiday surveys, but the survey designs are such as to make comparisons and aggregation difficult, if not impossible. The regulation demands a holiday survey similar in kind to the BTSY and the NIHS, though the sample design is based on households as opposed to individuals. The essential features of the regulation are:

- a household survey requiring each member of the family to supply relevant data;
- the survey is only for domestic holiday tourism of four or more nights;
- the contents are to cover demographics, holiday characteristics and expenditure.

The possibility of this regulation finding general acceptance is somewhat limited at the moment.

A much better prospect is the SOEC directive. The emphasis is on the supply-side collection of tourism statistics, which is the familiar pattern for many continental countries. The directive requires member states to gather the following statistics on tourism:

- stock of tourist accommodation;
- national and foreign guest flows in accommodation establishments;
- foreign guests in accommodation establishments by country of residence;
- accommodation capacity utilization;
- labour force in accommodation establishments and other tourist activities;
- foreign visitors recorded at the external borders of the European Communities;
- tourist expenditure;
- trends of certain tourist consumer prices.

The implementation of this directive would undoubtedly improve the supply aspects of United Kingdom statistical sources on tourism, which are at present both partial in coverage of the various sectors and incomplete in relation to some of the sampling frames. For example, the 1969 Development of Tourism Act made provision for the statutory registration of accommodation by an Order in Council. This has never been implemented; registration is purely voluntary.

Supply measurement

Tourism is demand led; its influence pervades many sectors of the Standard Industrial Classification (SIC), as is illustrated by Table 12.6. It is therefore not possible conceptually to include tourism within an SIC. This being the case, it is hardly surprising that supply information is often patchy and fragmented.

Within the United Kingdom the principal direct sources concerning the supply side of tourism are accommodation occupancy surveys, employment statistics for tourism-related industries, distributive and service industry inquiries and sight-seeing attendances. Other sources include various transport statistics, local authority financial returns, parts of the retail price index, investment monitors from the tourist boards, and reports by private organizations and associations, such as hotel comparison data and museums data.

Neither the stock of hotels nor the provision of other forms of tourist accommodation (tourist villages, camping pitches, caravans, youth hostels) are known with certainty because there is no statutory basis for collection. All the national tourist boards run monthly hotel occupancy surveys, though with varying sampling frames. The largest of these surveys is the English Hotels Occupancy Survey (EHOS), which has been run since 1971. The design is a panel drawn from ETB records of all known hotels, whereas the other boards draw their panels only from accommodation registered with them. The definition of a hotel is fairly wide because the surveys are designed to cover all types. This is a source of conflict with the large, group-owned hotels, which find that the published averages for room and bed occupancy do not reflect their own results. The solution here is to cross-tabulate the data by hotel classification. At present the EHOS has room and bed occupancy broken down by region and sub-region, by location (small town, large town, seaside, London and the countryside) and by tariff (the minimum single advertised bed-and-breakfast summer rate).

In addition to undertaking hotel occupancy surveys, the WTB and the STB have extended their business monitoring activities to cover self-catering and holiday parks. This has grown out of the lack of precision in the demand statistics and the need to have readily available performance indicators for tactical marketing. Given the SOEC directive, it is likely that the range of accommodation monitored in this manner will be expanded in the next decade.

Employment data are a particular problem. Estimates of the number depen-dent upon tourism in the United Kingdom vary between one and just over two million depending on the methodology used to calculate the figure. The Depart-ment of Employment publishes separate data for Great Britain using the SIC four-

Table 12.6   *United Kingdom 1980 Standard Industrial Classification: tourism-related classes*

Number	Activity
64 and 65	Retail distribution
66	Hotels and catering
71	Railways
72	Other inland transport
74	Sea transport
75	Air transport
76	Transport: supporting services
77	Miscellaneous transport
96	Other services
97	Recreational services
98	Personal services

digit categories shown in Table 12.7. The total number of employees (self-employed are not included) covered by the above categories amounts to about 1.4 million, but it is also clear that a good number of these employees may have nothing to do with tourism, and those in other industries (Table 12.6) who do depend on tourism are not included. Because of this, some researchers (for example, Vaughan, 1986) use spending-based methods for calculating the ultimate amount of employment in tourism. This involves:

- apportioning the number of employees in each SIC class shown in Table 12.6 into tourist and non-tourist activities using tourist expenditure by category;
- adding in the number of self-employed;
- adjusting for seasonal labour;
- counting in the number of persons likely to be employed indirectly and through the induced effects of tourist spending.

The main statistical sources for this kind of exercise in the United Kingdom are the Census of Population (every ten years), the Census of Employment (every three years but supported by a quarterly sample inquiry) and the Labour Force Survey (an annual sample of households). World-wide, the most common way of estimating the ultimate employment in tourism is through input–output tables, which permit the overall economic impact of tourism in terms of output and income to be calculated at the same time.

Distributive and service industry inquiries for the United Kingdom are undertaken by the Business Statistics Office (BSO), principally for the Department of Trade and Industry. They are statutory inquiries whose main purpose is to provide statistics for monitoring output trends in the economy and compiling the national accounts. The relevant inquiry for tourism is that to do with the catering and allied trades listed in Table 12.7. The first major catering inquiry was held in 1950. After 1977 it became an annual investigation, though the information gathered was still confined to turnover, stocks and capital expenditure. From 1985 onwards questions have been included on the number of establishments offering accommodation and the number of letting bedrooms in order to assist in the development of tourism policy.

Unfortunately, the BSO does not delve into recreational services, so all that is available globally on tourist attractions are attendance figures collected annually by the four national tourist boards. These are supplemented by publications on new developments, but comprehensive performance indices of attractions are not, as yet, produced.

Table 12.7 *United Kingdom 1980 Standard Industrial Classification: tourism-related activities*

Number	Activity
6611	Eating places supplying food for consumption in premises
6612	Take-away food shops
6620	Public houses and bars
6630	Night clubs and licensed clubs
6650	Hotel trade
6670	Other transit or short-stay accommodation
9770	Libraries, museums, art galleries, etc.
9791	Sport and other recreational services

Emerging supply issues for the 1990s

Information on the supply side of tourism in the United Kingdom is somewhat limited. It is not possible to obtain national trends, except in certain sectors, let alone to assess the performance of suppliers at a regional level. On the other hand, suppliers themselves are looking for comparative data so as to set their own operating data against a standard. This accounts for the popularity of statistics provided by hotel consultants such as Horwath and Horwath, and Pannell Kerr Forster Associates. It is to be expected that, as the importance of the service sector grows in the economy, so the availability of statistical information will improve. At present, most providers of services find their information base a long way behind what is published for extractive and manufacturing industries, but how far services are likely to catch up begs the question: who is going to provide?

Discussion

Most users of tourism statistics see provision at a national level as a government responsibility. Statistics are part of the social overhead capital of tourism; private organizations provide the raw data and pay for the published results. However, during the 1980s many governments throughout the world rolled back the frontiers of state provision, a policy which is at the heart of the present Conservative administration in the United Kingdom. The danger here is that 'privatization' has become a simple-minded catchword for efficiency, which totally ignores the market failure justification for public goods. The status quo is questioned in the review of the government statistical services by Sir Derek Rayner (HMSO, 1981), where it is argued that there is no more reason for government to act as the universal provider of statistics than in any other field. But Rayner (1979) also found out that the possibility of using trade associations and quasi-public bodies to collect data for national aggregates requires very restrictive conditions, namely:

- associations should cover the vast majority of firms for a particular SIC class;
- there is a reasonably self-contained industrial structure;
- government statisticians should have access to and a say in the processing and collection of the data.

It is certain that the tourist industry does not conform to any of these restrictions.

It is evident that government must shoulder the burden of providing tourism statistics at a national level if they are to be provided at all. The cost of this provision is a fraction of the amounts invested in tourism by both government agencies and developers. It is known that inability to assess the tourism potential of an area to a reasonable degree does deter developers from looking at new locations. This is counterproductive when tourism is being used as an instrument of regional policy.

Revenue can be raised by adding marketing information to the basic volume data collected by the Government. This will enable the raw data to be sold through a distributor for further analysis. Users are prepared to pay more for tourism statistics but the amounts are not large. Large sums are paid for confidential market research only where the user has a major, if not total, say in what data are collected.

As tourism and leisure activities assume a greater role in the economy towards the year 2000, national statistics should enhance their level of precision, coverage and disaggregation. At the local level, national surveys can never provide more than broad aggregates to give a background to any local initiatives on data collection. The prospects for better tourism statistics are good, but there is an area of concern about the political acceptability of further public provision.

To counter this, there is the prospect of European market integration in 1992. There is a genuine desire to rationalize the tourism policies of member states and to harmonize the statistical measurement of tourism. This is particularly important in terms of integrated regional programmes presented to the European Commission for funding, which more and more have tourism projects within the overall package. Member states are likely to be put under increasing pressure to provide additional data on the tourist industry so that their proposals may be properly evaluated and justified.

References

Burkart, A.J. and Medlik, S. (1981) *Tourism: Past, Present and Future*. London: Heinemann.

Domestic Tourism Statistics Review Group (1988) 'Domestic Tourism Statistics within the United Kingdom', Research Report to the National Tourist Boards.

Griffiths, D. and Elliot, D. (1988) *Sampling Errors on the International Passenger Survey*. London: Office of Population Censuses and Surveys.

HMSO (1981) 'Government statistical services', Cmnd 8236. London: HMSO.

Mathieson, A. and Wall, G. (1982) *Tourism: Economic, Physical and Social Impacts*. London: Longman.

Rayner, Sir D. (1979) *The Statistical Services of the Department of Trade and Industry: Synopsis of Findings and Recommendations*. London: Department of Trade and Industry.

Vaughan, D.R. (1986) *Estimating the Level of Tourism-Related Employment: An Assessment of Two Non-Survey Techniques*. London: BTA/ETB, Research Services.

Chapter 13

Skew loss functions and required accuracy levels in probability forecasting for tourism

Luiz Moutinho and *Stephen Witt*

Overview

In science, and even in everyday life, many things are highly predictable. Yet in other circumstances, prediction is often difficult and risky. In making predictions, we are often unsure about the outcome.

Forecasting assists managers to improve decision making. In an organizational design context, forecasting should not be regarded as a self-contained activity, but should be integrated within the planning context of which it is a part. As Peters (1969, 137) points out:

> Forecasting is a prerequisite of planning. It is an approach to economic management which attempts to look ahead to assess whether demands and resources show prospects of being in some sort of balance. Decisions have to be taken now about hotel construction, roads and other public utilities costing many millions of pounds which will not be usable for some years ahead.

The role of forecasts in the planning process is also noted by Gunn (1987, 5):

> Of interest to many tourist businesses is increasing the ability to make forecasts. Decisions on the purchase of new generations of equipment, new sites and new technology may rest on predictions of increased demand for a specific tourism service or product.

It is often stressed that accuracy is the critical characteristic of a forecasting method. For example, Wandner and Van Erden (1980, 381) point out that:

> Since governments and private industry must plan for expected tourism demand and provide tourism investment goods and infrastructure, the availability of *accurate* estimates of international tourism demand has important economic consequences. (italics added)

Archer (1987, 77) also notes the need for accuracy:

> the *accuracy* of the forecasts will affect the quality of the management

> decision . . . In the tourism industry, in common with most other service
> sectors, the need to forecast accurately is especially acute because of the
> perishable nature of the product. (italics added)

Martin and Witt (1988b), in a recent study which reports the views of tourism
academics and practitioners on the desirable characteristics of forecasts, confirm
that forecast accuracy is regarded as the most important property of a forecasting
method.

However, it may not be necessary to obtain *highly* accurate forecasts of
specific values, but only to ascertain whether the probability falls within a particular range of values, in order to support good management decisions. Furthermore, it is usually assumed that there is a cost trade-off when choosing a
forecasting model:

> Generally the less-expensive models yield less-accurate forecasts, and there
> are costs associated with inaccuracies in the forecast . . . Is it worthwhile to
> spend more on an accurate forecasting model than incur the potential costs
> of a less-expensive but poor forecast? (Fitzsimmons and Sullivan, 1982, 118)

Although Martin and Witt (1988a, 1989a, 1989b) have provided some empirical
evidence to the contrary, that more expensive models do not necessarily lead to
more accurate tourism demand forecasts, to the extent that the widely quoted
trade-off stated by Fitzsimmons and Sullivan is true it is important to identify an
acceptable level of forecast accuracy.

A further point of interest in the area of probability forecasting is that when
preparing a forecast the possible difference in the losses resulting from over- versus
under-forecasting should be taken into account wherever possible. As Kunst and
Neusser (1986, 451) point out; 'the true forecaster's loss function . . . may be skew,
with different costs for optimistic and pessimistic mistakes'. Any knowledge
regarding such cost asymmetries should be incorporated in the cost of error or loss
function when evaluating the appropriate management decision.

Decision theory or decision analysis can be used to determine optimal
strategies when a decision maker is faced with several decision alternatives and an
uncertain or risk-filled pattern of future events; that is, states of nature. (Risk is
taken to mean a situation in which various outcomes to a decision are possible, but
where the probabilities of the alternative outcomes are known. Uncertainty
describes a situation in which there is no such probabilistic knowledge or where
the information is fragmentary.)

The opportunity loss of a decision is the difference between the cost or profit
actually realized under that decision and the cost or profit which would have been
realized if the decision had been the best one possible for the event which actually
occurred. When the consequences of various possible courses of action depend on
unpredictable events, a practical way of choosing the 'best' act is to assign values
to consequences and probabilities to events and then to select the act with the
lowest expected opportunity loss.

This chapter examines the precision required for probability forecasts and the
use of skew loss functions as applied to tourism. (For a general discussion of

probability forecasting, the reader is referred to Anderson *et al.* (1984), Green and Tull (1978) and Mao (1969).)

Required accuracy levels

Here we assess how accurate the forecasts of the probabilities associated with the occurrence of alternative states of nature need to be when we are considering problems involving few possible actions and few states of nature.

As an example of this class of problem, suppose that a regional tourist authority is interested in marketing a line of local handicraft products in order to generate additional visitor arrivals and higher spending levels. The product is made by a batch process that through equipment indivisibilities is restricted to the following annual capacities:

A_1: 1 million units
A_2: 2 million units
A_3: 3 million units

The conditional opportunity losses under S_1 (high sales) and S_2 (low sales) are shown in Table 13.1.

Table 13.1   *Conditional opportunity losses: new handicraft product problem (£ million)*

	State of Nature	
	S_1	S_2
Act		
A_1	6	0
A_2	3	3
A_3	0	8

As can be seen from Table 13.1, in this example if S_1 obtains then act A_3 is the best course of action and is accordingly assigned a conditional opportunity loss of zero. If S_2 obtains, however, act A_1 becomes the best course of action. Act A_2 is a kind of 'hedging' act in the sense that the conditional opportunity losses associated with it are not extreme under either S_1 or S_2. The problem facing the tourist product planners is to estimate the probabilities of occurrence of S_1 and S_2 respectively, and in particular they need to know how precise these estimates should be.

Suppose that $P(S_1)$ can vary over the interval 0 to 1. Then $P(S_2)$ is equal to $1 - P(S_1)$. If $P(S_1)$ were equal to 0.1, then the expected opportunity losses (EOLs) of the three acts would be:

$EOL(A_1) = 0.1(6) + 0.9(0) = £0.6$ million
$EOL(A_2) = 0.1(3) + 0.9(3) = £3.0$ million
$EOL(A_3) = 0.1(0) + 0.9(8) = £7.2$ million

Clearly, under these conditions act A_1 (the low-capacity facility) would be preferable to the other courses of action. By assuming various values that $P(S_1)$ could have, we can construct the chart of expected opportunity losses shown in Figure 13.1.

If $P(S_1)$ is less than 0.5, then act A_1 is best, whereas if $P(S_1)$ is between 0.5 and 0.625, act A_2 is best. If $P(S_1)$ exceeds 0.625, then act A_3 is best. If $P(S_1)$ is exactly 0.5 either A_1 or A_2 could be chosen, and if $P(S_1)$ is exactly 0.625 either A_2 or A_3 could be chosen. These 'indifference' points are determined by finding the points on the abscissa where the lines of expected opportunity loss intersect, that is where:

$$EOL(A_1) = EOL(A_2)$$

Letting $P(S_1) = P$, we have:

$$6P + 0(1 - P) = 3$$
$$P = 0.5$$

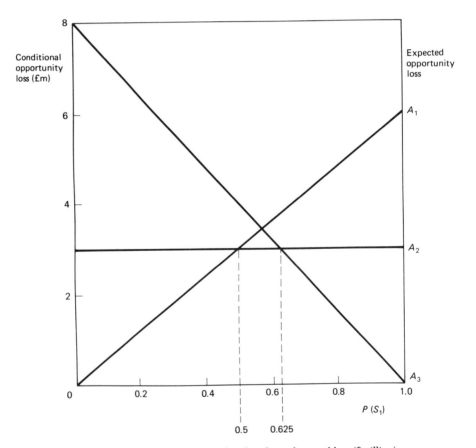

Figure 13.1 Expected opportunity losses: new handicraft product problem (£million)

Similarly:

$$EOL(A_3) = EOL(A_2)$$
$$0P + 8(1 - P) = 3$$
$$P = 0.625$$

The implication of these calculations is that the new tourist product planner does not need to know the precise value of $P(S_1)$, but only that it falls within specific ranges. In terms of the assumptions of this tourism problem, the same act (act A_1) would be chosen if $P(S_1)$ were, say, 0.1, as would be chosen if $P(S_1)$ were, say, 0.4. Although the illustration is simple, it does serve to demonstrate that, in some tourism marketing problems, forecasts do not need to be made with high precision.

Skew loss functions

In more realistic cases a greater number of states of nature and courses of action are possible. For example, in accommodation capacity problems some 'best' level of accommodation may exist for each possible sales level. In tourism demand capacity planning problems, the quantity of beds allocated may vary more or less continuously within a certain range.

Let us now suppose that the same regional tourist authority is interested in determining the 'best' (optimal) number of beds to offer for distribution to tour operators and travel agents. If travel intermediaries' requests for suitable accommodation exceed the quantity available, unfilled requests will result. If the number of beds available in the region exceeds the demand, there will be costs associated with the excess supply of accommodation. For purposes of illustration, suppose that the imputed 'cost' for each unfilled tour operator's/travel agent's request per night is £12.00, and suppose that the cost associated with each bed vacant per night is £3.00. The regional tourist authority is interested in recommending some best level of accommodation capacity that minimizes expected cost under an uncertain tourist demand.

The regional tourism planners should define the probability distribution of the possible tourist demand levels for accommodation in the area. As an example, suppose that the planners are willing to believe that tourist demand for accommodation in the region will exceed 20,000 beds but will be no higher than 80,000 beds. Their 'most probable' estimate of tourist demand is that it will be between 30,000 and 40,000 beds.

The cumulative probability distribution can then be derived from a histogram chart. The smooth curve should be used to approximate cumulative probabilities within the histogram intervals. For example, the estimated probability of tourist demand being less than 35,000 beds can be seen to be approximately 0.45 (Figure 13.2).

To determine the optimal number of beds to be offered to the market, tourism planners would like to find the appropriate balance point where the expected cost of underconstruction just equals the expected cost of overconstruction. Both these costs are proportional to the difference between the amount offered and the

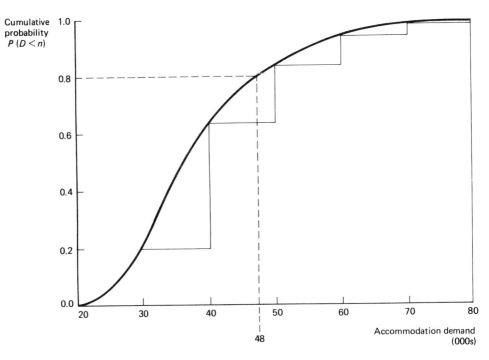

Figure 13.2　Probability distribution: tourist demand for regional accommodation (000 units)

amount requested. Fortunately, however, it is not necessary to construct a payoff table for each possible act and tourist demand level. Instead, the following principle may be adopted: 'Keep increasing the accommodation capacity until the highest level n is reached for which the expected incremental cost of adding the nth unit is still less than the expected incremental cost of not adding the nth unit to the accommodation capacity level.'

If we let D = tourist demand level, C_o = £3.00 = cost per unit per night of over-construction, and C_u = £12.00 = cost per unit per night of underconstruction relative to tourist demand, we have by application of the principle above:

$$C_o P(D < n) < C_u[1 - P(D < n)]$$
$$[P(D < n)](C_o + C_u) < C_u$$
$$P(D < n) < \frac{C_u}{C_o + C_u}$$
$$P(D < n) < \frac{£12.00}{£3.00 + £12.00}$$
$$P(D < n) < 0.80$$

From Figure 13.2, it can be seen that the largest n for which $P(D < n) < 0.80$ is approximately 48,000 beds. This represents the graphical solution to the tourist capacity problem. Had the planners not considered the asymmetry in the costs of over- versus underconstruction, they might have planned for either:

- a capacity level equal to the midpoint of the bar in the histogram with the greatest incremental height (i.e. 35,000 beds) – the modal forecast; or
- a capacity level equal to the median or 0.5 cumulative probability level of the distribution (i.e. 36,000 beds).

In either case, they would have considerably 'underproduced' relative to the solution that takes into account the conditional costs of over-versus underproduction.

Discussion

A manager's skills can be utilized in a variety of ways within the theoretical decision format. These include (1) problem identification, (2) the search for and identification of relevant courses of action, (3) the estimation of alternative consequences of a given course of action and the probabilities associated therewith, and (4) the estimation of the accuracy and cost of alternative investigations.

Forecasts thus play an essential role in the tourism planning process and, although the need for accurate forecasts is often stressed, there are situations in which highly accurate point forecasts are not particularly useful. In particular, in the case of probability forecasting it is often necessary only to know whether or not the probability falls within a particular range of values. Tourism managers can view the selection of forecasting procedures in the same general fashion as any other decision problem under uncertainty and must continually ask: 'What would we do differently if a forecasting procedure yielding greater accuracy could be employed?' Even if increased accuracy can be obtained, it is often not the case that the additional cost entailed is justified.

When knowledge regarding error costs is available, this should be incorporated in the forecast-generating procedure. In particular, cost asymmetries will affect the level of demand to plan for. In this chapter the use of the expected opportunity loss criterion has been illustrated; the optimal forecast is obtained by choosing the tourist accommodation capacity level for which the expected cost of underconstruction is equal to the expected cost of overconstruction.

References

Anderson, D.R., Sweeney, D.J. and Williams, T.A. (1984) *Statistics for Business and Economics*. St Paul, Minn.: West.

Archer, B.H. (1987) 'Demand forecasting and estimation', in Ritchie, J.R.B. and Goeldner, C.R. (eds) *Travel, Tourism and Hospitality Research*. New York: Wiley.

Fitzsimmons, J.A. and Sullivan, R.S. (1982) *Service Operations Management*. New York: McGraw-Hill.

Green, P.E. and Tull, D.S. (1978) *Research for Marketing Decisions*, 4th edn. Englewood Cliffs, NJ: Prentice-Hall.

Gunn, C.A. (1987) 'A perspective on the purpose and nature of tourism research methods', in Ritchie, J.R.B. and Goeldner, C.R. (eds) *Travel, Tourism and Hospitality Research*. New York: Wiley.

Kunst, R. and Neusser, K. (1986) 'A forecasting comparison of some Var techniques', *International Journal of Forecasting*, 2, 4, 447–56.

Mao, C.T. (1969) *Quantitative Analysis of Financial Decisions*. New York: Macmillan.

Martin, C.A. and Witt, S.F. (1988a) 'An empirical analysis of the accuracy of forecasting techniques', *Proceedings of Travel and Tourism Research Association Annual Conference*, 19, 285–98.

Martin, C.A. and Witt, S.F. (1988b) 'Forecasting performance', *Tourism Management*, 9, 4, 326–9.

Martin, C.A. and Witt, S.F. (1989a) 'Forecasting tourism demand: a comparison of the accuracy of several quantitative methods', *International Journal of Forecasting*, 5, 1, 1–13.

Martin, C.A. and Witt, S.F. (1989b) 'Accuracy of econometric forecasts of tourism', *Annals of Tourism Research*, 16, 3, 407–28.

Peters, M. (1969) *International Tourism*. London: Hutchinson.

Wandner, S.A. and Van Erden, J.D. (1980) 'Estimating the demand for international tourism using time series analysis', in Hawkins, D.E., Shafer, E.L. and Rovelstad, J.M. (eds) *Tourism Planning and Development Issues*. Washington, D.C: George Washington University.

Chapter 14

Hospitality research: philosophies and progress

David Litteljohn

> The demand for certainty is one which is natural to man, but is nevertheless an intellectual vice . . . To endure uncertainty is difficult, but so are most other virtues. For the learning of every virtue there is an appropriate discipline. . .
> Bertrand Russell, *Unpopular Essays*, 1950

Overview

The term 'hospitality' is here defined as encompassing those commercial activities which offer customers accommodation, meals and drinks when they are away from home. These three services may be offered singly or in some combination; their nature may also be varied by adjusting the service levels of the constituent parts and, indeed, by augmenting the core by additional services such as recreational facilities or entertainment. It will be a prime objective of suppliers to ensure that the service packages provided are acceptable to their customers and that their own economic targets are met. It is the job of researchers in the field to explore the nature and contexts of hospitality in order to increase the stock of knowledge and interpretations that exist in the field.

Research in the area is reaching a stage of maturity. However, this stage of maturity is more easily exemplified by a greater activity in the field than by any consensus as to its philosophy or direction. Thus research efforts may often be characterized either as debating the best type of approach to use, or as presenting diverse and unfocused topics with little agreed common ground. This is particularly confusing for those in industry who, in the final analysis, should have use for research findings.

The very fact that there is a debate on the appropriate methodologies to use relative to the study of hospitality is, it could be argued, a sign of maturity in itself. In addition, new mechanisms such as international groupings of researchers in the field are being formed to advance the role and function of hospitality research. The growth of activity of this nature can do much to refresh and extend research initiatives.

Maturity, however, must also be developed by agreement as to the best approaches to adopt in further research projects. Any notion that hospitality operations and the environments which surround them are in any way unique is considered simplistic. As organizations which rely on profit for their survival, hospitality enterprises share many characteristics with other commercial (and non-profit-making) organizations. Also, from a demand viewpoint, the fact that customers consume a greater part of the service at the point of production is not a feature that is special to hospitality: it is something which is shared with many service organizations. Thus hospitality providers must be seen within a scenario where they offer a distinctive range of products and services to customers, in perhaps a distinctive set of organizational settings. In both these facets they will have some things in common with other institutions and environments. In other words, they differ in degree rather than in nature.

In this light, three distinct approaches employed in academic hospitality research have emerged. There is that of the natural and physical sciences, which is commonly used to research specific areas in hospitality. This type of work, which can be applied in particular to topics such as food science, has undoubted scientific value. However, its merit in an organizational/hospitality context is far less apparent. This is because the hospitality industry demands analysis which has some practical utility, or at least some perceived practical utility, and there is a significant limit to the extent to which this approach may be applied to issues which require solutions in an organizational setting.

Secondly, there is an approach which addresses itself to the organizational features of hospitality by drawing up boundaries or conditions for hospitality organizations. This hospitality management approach thus aims to filter out extraneous theory and description by providing a strong focus on the charac-teristics of hospitality provision. Model building is seen as an important part of the process of developing knowledge and, in particular, a philosophical base for a hospitality discipline.

Thirdly, there is the hospitality studies approach. Again, like the management approach discussed above, it has as an aim the desire to design solutions to the issues which face hospitality organizations. It suggests that achieving this will largely be an industry-led phenomenon, in the sense that the research issues tackled must not only be analysed within an appropriate organizational framework, but should also be informed by industry preoccupations and results evaluated within an industrial setting. Here the reliance for sound research comes not so much from conforming to a predetermined set of organizational para-meters – which become hurdles rather than barriers – or from a more precise interpretation of management theory. Instead the approach is relaxed in its choice of an appropriate discipline base, being prepared to utilize any area of the social sciences which may provide a useful lever to explore a problem and prise out a solution.

These three approaches have, in addition, been complemented by the specialist areas of tourism, leisure and recreation. With this battery of inter-pretations to choose from, the direction forward may indeed seem unclear.

At a time of potentially great change for hospitality it is suggested that, to be successful in terms of furthering understanding of and application to hospitality operations, wider horizons for hospitality research must not be pursued at the expense of overlooking the special characteristics of the industry.

Aims of hospitality research

Most academic departments in the field have traditionally been driven more by their vocational focus than by a conscious desire to develop a discipline base; although some – a minority – have emphasized a tourism platform, the majority still concentrate around an interdisciplinary approach to providing an appropriate management education. While arguments for the necessity of a research base have been largely accepted, academic communities have real problems of research theory and approach to deal with. In this section the aims of research will be addressed.

Research must be seen as a broad rather than a narrow activity. Defined as 'a broad range of intellectual and scholarly activity including the acquisition, dissemination and application of knowledge, skills and techniques' (Council for National Academic Awards, 1984), it can be considered to embrace postgraduate and other scholarly studies. These latter may lack the equivalence of a post-graduate qualification, due perhaps to the very specific nature or focus of the work. Therefore, research is distinct from routine academic activities – and professional practice; in some way it contributes towards expanding the borders of knowledge in the area.

Within hospitality, academic departments further accept that research should be relevant to industry issues and should underpin the thrusts of the courses operated by them.

Building on the above, four main objectives for hospitality research can be identified:

- to develop insights into areas of hospitality and the discipline of hospitality;
- to underpin the content and direction of academic courses;
- to encourage the development of best practice techniques in industry;
- to stimulate further research by dissemination and experimentation.

These aims are not contentious. They do, however, emphasize the original aspect of research activity which may be contrasted will those of consultancy. Consultancy, whatever its virtues, is essentially a client-led activity and may impose restrictions on the depth of the research effort and the publication of results. While both research and consultancy activities have an important function in updating and enhancing knowledge of industry practices from a teaching perspective, it is through sustained research efforts that comprehension is extended. For instance, a consultant may tackle the how and when questions that an organization may grapple with; researchers will tackle these issues on a somewhat longer time span and will answer the question: why is something done, and why not something else?

A general analysis of quality and quantity of hospitality research

There has been a refreshing increase in the amount of research undertaken by UK academics in hospitality. Some of this springs from the advent of greater provision of degree courses, particularly those at honours level where teaching would be 'greatly impoverished' without it (Council for National Academic Awards, 1984). Some departmental structures have been modified to allow a higher profile to research activities.

A second major factor encouraging the growth in research is the means available for dissemination of information. The British scene has witnessed a significant increase in journals in the field over the past ten years. Whether targeted directly at hospitality, or more broadly at service or tourism fields, they have provided mechanisms for the publication of research issues relevant to hospitality.

This development in output has taken place at a time when academic research initiatives generally within the UK have been subject to economic constraints. A general pruning of academic research budgets has often meant that a discipline base with only a short track record has encountered certain funding difficulties. In addition, academics in the field lack expertise in approaching major national and international funding bodies to gain research project funding. Also there is the view that companies in hospitality have not greatly supported research endeavours. On the other hand, there has been the 'centres of excellence' initiative amongst the English polytechnics, where a limited number of institutions were allowed some extra funding specifically to enhance their research output.

The impact of this research output on industry practices is more questionable. First, the fact that papers are published in academically orientated publications does not necessarily lead to the establishment of research frameworks because the individual pieces of work may lack academic cohesion. Secondly, if written in a manner intended to appeal to the academic community, dissemination of new ideas will stop short of reaching managers in industry. In an applied area such as hospitality, it could be argued that this interaction between academics and industry should be a prime research aim.

In addition to the potential lack of rapport with industry, some research efforts in hospitality may be poor simply because they are not conceptually rigorous and/or are weakly executed. For instance, research samples may be too small or unrepresentative – a particular problem in a large and varied industry. Also, research which centres on quantitative issues of hospitality provision without sufficiently realizing the qualitative variables involved in accommodation, meals and drinks supply runs a high risk of producing flawed interpretations of hospitality.

Thus, while a developing discipline such as hospitality is bound to face a test from more established fields, some feelings of insecurity may not be deemed unusual. Certainly, this need to establish peer acceptability among academics can be seen to cross national boundaries: commenting on the North American hospitality scene, Kent (1988) has observed that 'whatever respect we [i.e. researchers] have earnt there is the nagging thought that it is not enough'. However, the need to achieve this academic respectability must not be seen to dilute the industry orientation of research.

The newly formed International Association of Hospitality Research also addresses this problem of a lack of academic credibility. Four out of its eleven aims refer to the advancement of professional standing.[1] It would therefore appear that problems of research in hospitality revolve around the twin needs of establishing an interaction between the industry which generates the issues and the academics which research them, and the development of the appropriate range of research frameworks and research tools.

To gain a more precise understanding of the quality and direction of research, a survey was undertaken at all institutions offering identifiable hospitality under-graduate degree courses in the UK, as at October 1988.

Survey of UK academic hospitality departments

In all, twenty institutions in the UK were contacted in the autumn of 1988. Excluded from the survey were higher- and further-education institutions which offer hotel and catering courses at sub-degree and postgraduate standard as it was felt that their involvement in supervised academic research would be extremely low. Of the twenty organizations contacted a return of eighteen, or 90 per cent, was obtained. The respondents were four universities and fourteen polytechnics/colleges.

The primary aim of the questionnaire was to gain an overview of the type of research currently carried out at the institutions, the nature of research funding and the extent of staff involvement in consultancy.

The questionnaire asked departments to identify research activity as defined by the number of projects leading to postgraduate research qualifications. In addition, departments were requested to indicate the extent of consultancy work by (1) degree of staff involvement and (2) major externally funded projects not leading to research degrees.

To gain an impression of the direction of research, departments were also asked to classify projects (which led to further degrees) of a natural/physical scientific nature and those employing the methodologies of the social sciences. These categories were not defined – respondents selected as they felt appropriate.

In all, the responding institutions were involved in an impressive 213 projects, 153 of which involved postgraduate work. The results are discussed in greater detail below.

The importance of the social sciences

Table 14.1 shows that, from a total of 91 full-time projects, 54 (59 per cent) were classified as being social scientific. Four respondents had no entry in this category, while two institutions accounted for 34 projects and the highest scoring seven totalled 71 or nearly 80 per cent of projects in these categories. Thus the survey emphasizes the central role of social sciences in exploring hospitality issues, and implies that a research-based strategy is being developed at some institutions. Where the more specialized natural/physical sciences are used, they considerably enhance a department's research profile as judged by research projects pursued: two institutions alone accounted for 23 projects of this type.

Funding of hospitality research

Table 14.1 also indicates the importance of institutional funding of research efforts. Admittedly, the more industry-based consultancy is excluded here. However, from the total of 91 projects leading to research degrees, 69 per cent are funded by academic institutions. It is interesting to compare the ratio of institutionally funded projects to outside funded projects between the two discipline bases identified. Thus the ratio for the social sciences approach is 44 to 10 or 4.4:1 and that for the natural sciences is 19 to 18 or 1.05:1. In other words, although the social sciences account for the bulk of total projects, they account for a lesser number of initiatives funded by outside bodies on an aggregate and relative basis.

This last point may reflect a number of factors peculiar to the two areas; amongst them must be the scarcity of funding sources available to management-based areas of research.

Who is undertaking research?

Turning to part-time research profiles, the survey yielded a total of 62 projects. Academic staff based within the responding departments accounted for 58 per cent of this type of activity (36 projects). The importance of the social scientific approach used in the field was reinforced, with 51 of the programmes (82 per cent) falling under this heading. The remaining 11 fell under the natural/physical sciences heading.

Consultancy

As has been said earlier, consultancy activities have a role in the teaching of hospitality. Sixteen respondents reported a total of 60 major externally funded consultancy projects. As a measure of industry contacts this is a useful pointer, though its utility as an indication of scholarly activity is less satisfactory. The conditions of clients with regard to confidentiality, for instance, may curtail the availability of any direct published work.

The measures of research made above are only a general indicator of the total research activity being carried out in the UK hospitality field. Excluded, for example, are the full range of publications generated, conference papers given and initiatives taken to enhance the delivery of teaching programmes to students. The

Table 14.1 *Full-time research leading to research degrees*

Number of institutions in this category[1]	Institutionally funded			Other			Total		
	Natural sciences	Social sciences	Sub-total	Natural sciences	Social sciences	Sub-total	Natural sciences	Social sciences	Overall total
15	19	44	63	18	10	28	37	54	91

[1] Three institutions did not report any postgraduate work.

measures of research used, however, do highlight the most important developments in the field, and they allow several comments to be made:

- While both the natural/physical science and social science modes of research
  are used, the predominant research methodology employed is that of the
  social sciences, which accounts for 69 per cent of full- and part-time degree
  work.
- Departmental staff involvement in research through part-time degree modes is
  currently high, with 36 from 62 such research projects reported being undertaken by these staff.
- At its current stage of development, it would appear that research in the field,
  though growing, is fragmentary. Based on the survey results above, research
  seems to be driven as much by staff development requirements as by a need to
  explore new areas, develop knowledge, expand revenue opportunities and
  other research imperatives. If it is accepted that research is fragmentary, a
  partial solution could be provided by the development of an appropriate
  framework which would both direct and inform research initiatives.

The development of hospitality frameworks

Nailon (1982) has commented on the need for a theoretical framework, the lack of
which may substitute description for research and may devalue the worth of
individual contributions. His view appears to spring from a genuine desire to
ensure that research in the area derives from a fundamental understanding of the
industry, and a wish to establish a virtuous circle where research aids our understanding of industry issues and encourages further enquiry. The view implies an
apprehension that study through inappropriate disciplines – perhaps the natural
and physical sciences and tourism – could be counterproductive; it is searching for
a discipline for hospitality.

Currently, of course, there is no recognized body of knowledge for the study
of hospitality. Consensus centres on the interdisciplinary nature of management in
the area. However, as exhibited by the course content of hotel and catering degree
programmes in the UK, there is considerable disagreement on appropriate areas of
content.

The diversity of content and theoretical frameworks employed is tempered
by similar vocational aims of courses: they are designed to meet the requirements
of a singular group of activities. Medlik (1980) prefaces his analysis of hotels
(which includes such commonplace management areas as marketing, finance and
staffing/training) by a warning that a *meaningful* treatment requires a real understanding of the special conditions of hotel activity.

There is general, if not universal, agreement about the complexities of hospitality environments. Authors, approaching the subject from different perspectives, may use different phrases and emphases, but on the whole the fact that
hospitality possesses distinct characteristics is not at issue. Nailon lists sixteen
characteristics[2] which serve as a useful summary of current views. These conditions cover a range of perspectives from the nature of consumption to the nature of

interaction between customers, staff and organization, from matters of finance to aspects of information.

These observed differences have their effect on the three main approaches mentioned earlier which are used to research problems in hospitality.

Approach 1: the natural and physical sciences

The natural and physical sciences, with their established discipline base, are used extensively in researching many of the tangible elements of hospitality, such as food science and technical equipment design and testing.

Approach 2: hospitality management

The hospitality management approach focuses on that activity characterized by 'the active co-ordination and balancing of the interrelationship of . . . the external environment, the human resources, the technical infrastructure and the management information system' (Nailon, 1982). By building on conditions which define hospitality situations, the approach encourages the development of a distinctive and discrete hospitality discipline. Models of hospitality provision are hypothesized so that management decisions are formulated within an appropriate context. It is primarily management/resource use maximization driven, and it is interdisciplinary in nature.

Approach 3: hospitality studies

Hospitality studies accepts the a priori characteristics of hospitality, though it considers the activity very much in relation to its wider social and economic environment. In comparison to Approach 2 a greater significance is placed on a potentially wider interpretation of social techniques when analysing a problem or situation, rather than on a more immediate concern with operational issues. Slattery (1983), a proponent of this view, defends this rather relaxed approach to the finding of solutions by making the following provisos:

- research priorities must be firmly based on industry perceptions of what are important issues;
- researchers must not be limited to an ivory tower mentality on completion of their research, but must actively develop mechanisms for the evaluation of their proposed solutions by those working in the industry.

In other words, Slattery places a premium on industry relevance and dissemination/evaluation criteria.

Along with hospitality management, this approach is interdisciplinary in nature, though with its less targeted approach it is likely to be more extrovert and eclectic in the application of social science techniques to hospitality situations. For, like Approach 2, hospitality studies does seek to investigate those areas which will affect the profitability of organizations.

The main features of these three paths are outlined in Table 14.2 and are discussed in greater detail below, emphasis being placed on the differences between rather than the similarities of the approaches. Six variables for the research paths are identified: the concepts used in the research process; the areas researched and their interrelationships with wider aspects; the ways in which practitioners will treat research results; the means of establishing the utility of research; the approach of the researcher; and finally, the general scientific method adopted by the researcher.

Concept of the approach

All three views reject anecdotal, unsystemized approaches and aim to work under tight conceptual bases. However, their methods are different. Approach 1, drawing on the traditions of the natural and physical sciences, possesses a strong and tested set of disciplines. When related to hospitality problems, they are often applied to only a particular area such as technological considerations, equipment or energy efficiency. Areas of investigation are treated as discrete. The application of this approach, which takes no account of the social contexts of hospitality, can do little on its own. For instance, studies of the nutritional balance of meals can have little value to hospitality situations unless tangibles such as customer characteristics and intangible concepts like choice are considered. Ergonomics is an example of an approach which falls under the traditions of the natural sciences, employing as it does anatomical factors together with physiological aspects.

Both the management and studies approaches aim to encompass the social dimensions of hospitality. For instance, Nailon (1982) advances a utility/hedonistic matrix by which to judge types of hospitality provision. However, hospitality studies (Approach 3) is more relaxed in its direction. While maintaining a loyalty to the hospitality industry (which, as previously indicated, may be more loosely defined) similar to that of Approach 2, it allows a broader discipline front to be used in solving problems. Thus an issue concerning customer choice may be researched by a wide variety of means, including psychology, economics and sociology. It is the job of the researcher to choose a discipline appropriate to research methodology and to the means of evaluating proposed solutions. Thus the approach may initially search for models, constructs and concepts in the wider domain of human behaviour rather than in the narrowed hospitality management field. The 'solutions' which the approach may spawn can have validity only when they are tested within the practices of the industry.

Arena of action

By its very nature, the natural science perspective treats the technical areas mentioned in a discrete manner. Cook-chill systems are essentially technical

Table 14.2 *Research paradigms in hospitality*[1]

	Natural/physical sciences (1)	Hospitality management (2)	Hospitality studies (3)
Concept of the approach	Derived from the natural sciences; limited areas of investigation which are treated as independent subsystems	Focused organizational content	Conditions of hospitality accepted; interpretations at the judgement of the researcher
Arena of action	Concentrates on technical aspects	All areas of hospitality management decision seen to breed characteristic organizational types	Hospitality issues seen as part of a broader social world
Types of rationality assumed and types of action	Assumes people rational	Assumes an appropriate model should be designed	Makes no explicit comment
	Maximization of scarce resources through appropriate modelling techniques		Maximization of resources by offering interpretations for selection and evaluation by hospitality managers
Results of action	Tendency to harmony	Tendency towards profit maximization	Value to hospitality managers; evaluative process
Views of the analyst/researcher	Producer of scientific results (objective outsider)	Producer of scientific results and model builder (objective insider)	Producer of scientific results and member of industry; selection, interpretation and monitoring of results of research topic (objective insider)
General scientific method	Predictions and explanations based on abstractions; abstractions utilize natural and physical science tradition	Predictions and explanations based on abstractions which aim to produce hospitality models	Descriptions and explanations of an informed selection of topics based on empirically tested abstractions/theories

[1] I have freely adapted the headings put forward by Swedburg, R. *et al.* in 'The paradigm of economic sociology: premises and promises', *Theory and Society*, 16, 2, 169–213.

solutions to mass feeding requirements. Appraisal and implementation of any such system would require considerable administrative expertise in labour, organization, finance and customer aspects. Integration of these aspects would be a particular strength of hospitality management. By holding out that hospitality organizations would breed some ideal types, the provision of solutions for hospitality problems is considerably enhanced. Against this, the hospitality studies view is less prescriptive. By seeing hospitality issues as part of the broader social world, it may well encourage a more confusing picture for potential researchers. The promise it holds out is one of depth and, through greater exposure to discipline development in other areas, an ability to learn from successes and failures elsewhere and to apply these quickly to hospitality research.

Type of rationality

The natural science approach assumes that research findings will be treated rationally by those who have power and authority. Thus, for example, the provision of better management information should, in itself, lead to better management decisions. Approaches 2 and 3, through utilizing theories of human individuals, groups and organizations, would make no such claim. The hospitality management view would aim to produce models of hospitality organization which would incorporate nature of provision and current wisdom on concepts such as bounded rationality. The hospitality studies approach makes no explicit comments on rationality, but its suggestion that solutions must be evaluated within hospitality contexts implies that it sees rationality amongst customers, staff, etc. as part of an ongoing debate: what advantages derive from assuming that people are rational? are there empirical data to back this up? what measures are appropriate if studies are to be undertaken? and so on.

Types of action

Both the natural science and the management routes would hold that the aim of research is to maximize the use of scarce resources. The former route would ensure this state of affairs through its strong base of scientific methodologies its provision of technical solutions. The management route would deliver through appropriate hospitality modelling techniques, aiming to make management more proactive, and through planning to manipulate the relevant organizational variables to ensure efficiency in resource use. A hospitality studies route would allow these latter notions and others, such as management satisfying behaviour, more play. In an industry which has a large number of bankruptcies and often poor economic performance, which is one where information asymmetries between groups abound, it would seem appropriate that the research net is drawn wide rather than narrow. Again the studies view would lean to this broader interpretation of the use to which findings could be put and the contexts where they may be applied.

Results of action

Once the research of a problem has been completed and a solution proffered, the next stage should lead to the implementation of the technique developed and/or the evaluation of its relevance to hospitality operations. Under a natural scientific approach, the solution arrived at should, on implementation, lead to harmony: it should, given a similar set of technical conditions, apply over a range of situations. However, the volatile states of the hospitality industry are not always conducive to the notion of harmony. Thus the management approach recognizes that the best that can be achieved by implementing a solution is a movement towards profit maximization through a better use of scarce resources. Its worth can then be measured, if need be, in quantitative terms. Hospitality studies recognizes this latter view and further advocates that implementation of research solutions be explored by management and academics working together in industry. In this respect, the studies approach is the most specific of the three frameworks, with its emphasis on evaluation of results. This, together with exhortations for academics to disseminate research results to managers, ensures that industry conditions and trends are most closely understood and hopefully acted upon, and research is seen as an ongoing process rather than an end in itself.

Views of the analyst

The aim of all research is to produce objective situations which will aid those involved in the area. In this respect, the role of the researcher, the extent to which he or she is actively involved in the operational and strategic imperatives of the industry, is all important; distance may add to the objectivity of the research process. Once again, Nailon (1982) points out that there is no such thing as merely collecting facts and proceeding to construct theories; frameworks are necessary to address the researchers' views and preoccupations, otherwise the facts are essentially meaningless and any developed solutions will lack an appropriate context.

It is held here that the abstraction of natural sciences creates objective outsiders; the production of solutions through following rigorous methods of investigation which have then to be carefully applied to the hospitality world. With their greater acceptance of contextural factors, the other two approaches produce researchers who are objective insiders. In the management approach, careful attention is placed on the integrative disciplinary requirement in solving hospitality problems. Approach 3's less defined initial focus requires the researcher to reach wider amongst social science disciplines before a topic is selected and investigated, and solutions evaluated. The informed nature of the research design and testing ensures that the insider profile is present, though the use of social science techniques in a broad sense will require considerable attention to hospitality variables.

The more volatile and evolutionary the industry, the more will the researcher have to be on terms with the forces that shape it. Given the state of hospitality, the arguments for objective insiders are strong.

General scientific method

Approach 1 provides the methodologies of the natural sciences, which possess a high degree of abstraction and tested hypotheses. Approach 2 considers that the development of management approaches is the general way forward and, recognizing both the lack of development of an overall management science base and the particular requirement to provide appropriate solutions for hospitality operations, suggests that a priority of research is the development of a specific hospitality management discipline.

Hospitality studies offers no short cut to employing the whole range of social science methodologies – from economics to organization behaviour and from anthropology to sociology, for example. What is important, in this view, is that topics are chosen which are sensitive to industry perceptions and are researched in such a manner as to relate to relevant factors in the larger social world.

Hospitality frameworks: an initial conclusion

There is no such body of knowledge which can yet be defined as a hospitality discipline. This lack of a discipline base has allowed the evolution of different approaches to fill the theoretical vacuum. These approaches are not necessarily competitive, but they do have strengths and weaknesses. The natural and physical sciences approach is strong at examining discrete areas, but it has been rejected for playing the major role (in terms of projects covered in the survey reported earlier). A weakness appears to lie in its exclusion of the social dimension of hospitality provision.

Both the management and the studies approaches attempt to overcome this weakness by setting their focus on the hospitality organization. Here the problem has been to decide on an appropriate framework. It has been a problem because so much of the previous discussion of the hospitality industry – particularly that generated by the industry itself – tends to be anecdotal and idiosyncratic. The management approach developed from an appreciation of the potential role of the growing stock of knowledge in the management/administration field. However, understanding the limitations of applying general management theory to a particular industry (see Nailon, 1982) it aims to develop a particular approach relevant to hospitality organizations; the conditions of hospitality have been defined and the need for interdisciplinary solutions has been recognized. These conditions (see note 2) act as filters and barriers by which ideas may be tested for their applicability to hospitality situations. In the management approach there is an implicit call for the building of specific hospitality models and the development of a defined hospitality base.

The studies approach agrees in many respects with the sentiments of the management approach. However, it places rather more emphasis on the (outside) environments of hospitality and on the need to draw on a set of social science tools wider than immediate managerial constructs. Bearing in mind its potentially wider interpretation of the term 'hospitality', it treats the conditions of hospitality more as hurdles than as barriers, by which notions are tested for their relevance to managers. It places a great importance on the testing of research results and the dissemination of information. Its lack of a specific call for the development of a hospitality discipline implies that it foresees this arising as a result of rigorous and specific research initiatives rather than being an aim in itself. Before the wider interpretations of hospitality are examined, it is worth considering current trends in the context of the industry.

Some current issues in hospitality and implications for research

In an area of applied research, there is a clear need for research initiatives to respond to major concerns of hospitality – current and future. The analysis below points to some legitimate areas for research and uses the preceding analysis to indicate suitable approaches. It does not set out a research agenda – an action which would be presumptuous and rash.

Nailon (1982) has provided confidence in isolating hospitality management as a specialist area. His identification of specific features of hospitality environments is essentially an explanation of the sociotechnical characteristics involved. As such, it is a focusing of earlier work by authors such as Sasser *et al.* (1978), who examine the creation and management of service delivery systems. The complexities of hospitality operations advanced by Nailon, such as the full management implications of production and consumption intimacy, provide a source of research opportunities in themselves. These are particularly relevant when an industry is relatively stable in terms of structure and types of market opportunity available, for it is then that resource management rather than opportunities for growth, product/service development and so on becomes an organizational priority.

Current developments in the hospitality industry would appear to revolve around internationalization, a transformation in the role of technology and changes in industrial structure. These have fundamental implications on the three contexts of hospitality operations: the customer, the organization and the workforce (Slattery, 1983).

The customer/marketing perspective

Internationalization trends mean that organizations face more complex environments. On the most simple level, it may mean that a small organization deals with a greater proportion of international customers. On the other hand, as an organization spreads its activities outside the boundaries of one country, its operations become more complex (Terpstra, 1985). Cultural and economic differences will have significant effects in terms of the image and use of hotels. Currently, too, developments in information technology are changing established information channels and market distribution systems.

Organization

There are two distinct developments in the management of organizations. First, there is that concerning the changing structure of industry: the growth of organizations in terms of size and range of activities. Trends in the internationalization of hospitality companies have been mentioned already. Commentators disagree only on the extent of these changes, not on their presence (see, for example, International Hotel Association/Horwath and Horwath, 1988; Slattery and Roper, 1987; Litteljohn, 1985).

The growth and diversification of organizations have led to the need to design and operate management systems which are more cost-effective, where planning plays a greater role and where co-ordination is more easily achieved. Organizational development has created both the need and the ability to pursue a search for economies.

The second development refers more to the ways in which organizations perceive themselves. There is currently a heightened view of the service goals of organizations, evidenced within some companies by an increase in the profile given to service variables, and within others in more fundamental shifts from production-based philosophies to consumer-driven service provision – as exemplified in the UK by the attitudes of brewers to their ownership and operation of pubs. Thus more organizations see operations falling under a hospitality banner.

The role of information technology merits special mention. Amongst others, Gamble (1982) has drawn attention to both the role of information within the control/planning aspects phase and its implications for the design of organizational structures themselves.

Workforce

The most important supply-side factors to affect this area are internationalization aspects and new technology.

As companies grow on an international basis, it may be assumed that personnel and industrial relations will become of greater strategic importance. This is caused by the imperatives of provision on an international basis as well as by attitudes held within different host countries.

Operations and decisions affecting the workforce will also be influenced by the opportunities afforded by new technologies. Thus the nature of hospitality sociotechnical systems may be changed and the ratio of labour to capital decreased, while organizations try to achieve an increase in service levels. This type of innovation will require careful management if it is to deliver aims of profitability and customer satisfaction.

The decision-making skills at management level may also require reappraisal if the full impact of information technology is to be felt; essentially managers are changed from operation controllers to opportunity seekers (Gamble 1982).

Implications

Overview

Current issues in hospitality management indicate that many changes in orientation and practices will be driven by factors outside the industry.

If management is to meet the challenges that these wider horizons are to bring to industry practices, it may well be argued that new frameworks with wider interpretations should be employed to research the industry. Thus, for instance, hotel demand may be more fully understood if discussed within a tourism context, and hospitality labour issues may be more usefully considered within the context of trends in service industries. Several candidates are currently on offer: tourism, leisure and recreation on the demand side, and, from the supply perspective, general management, services management and retail management.

A reappraisal of hospitality orientations

There is no simple solution to this complex set of problems, but the debate below will establish a requirement to keep the nature of hospitality in sharp focus. This need stems partly from the relatively specialized nature and conditions of hospitality operations and the variability which exists within hospitality service configurations. These, and the general frameworks which may be used in hospitality research, are shown in Figure 14.1.

As a first step, the figure illustrates the variability of the industry. Variability exists in the sense that it is possible for hospitality organizations to offer any of the three core services exclusively; on the other hand, core services may be offered in some particular combination – a licensed restaurant provides customers with meals and the opportunity to buy alcoholic drinks, while a motorway service hotel combines the offer of meals and accommodation but not (under current UK legislation) alcoholic drinks. Thus concepts which provide hospitality interpretations will have to cover several rather than distinct business and customer orientations. Variety in the industry can become greater if it is accepted that each of the three cores can be offered at different service levels – a fast-food operation obviously meets different service criteria than does a high-spend bistro; as do luxury hotels in comparison to budget lodging.

Variety in hospitality is driven by three further factors: mixed markets within units, multi-location operations and hospitality conglomerates. To illustrate this variety consider a city-centre hotel. It may be dealing with several markets in the course of a week, including short-stay individual business-generated and short-break accommodation markets, and non-residential meal and drink customers. Further, consider a countryside public house with a reputation for its meals. On the one hand it may draw customers for its drink market from the small village where it is situated, while on the other, customers for meals may be prepared to drive considerable distances. The implication here is that management will have to understand how to exploit its resource base carefully in relation to the market opportunities available.

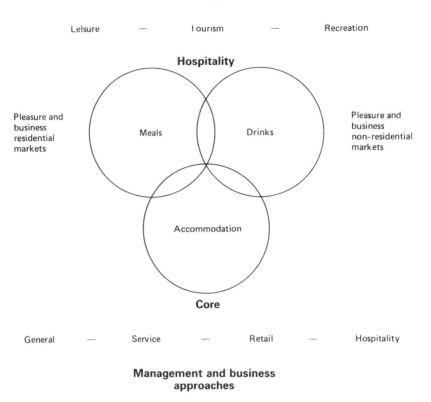

Figure 14.1   Hospitality core and research approaches

This notion of dealing with a variety of customer environments is extended when the notion of an individual unit is expanded to encompass hospitality groups. A hotel group will possess units at different locations; and it is unlikely that hotels, even if their technology base is relatively similar, will face similar market environments. Thus management will have to be flexible in its approach to marketing and operating units. Many hospitality organizations span more than one operation. Increasingly large hospitality organizations cover several specialized areas from luxury hotels to employee feeding, from themed restaurants to budget accommodation. In this respect, research will have to establish the logic of such structures and the validity of general overarching interpretations of hospitality.

Thus characteristics of hospitality operations indicate that they may be operated flexibly and must be responsive to changes in their general and locational environments. With this in mind, it is timely to consider the features of the other approaches on offer.

Wider frameworks

Essentially, the use of wider concepts allows greater depth and integration between the narrower hospitality field and broader areas of knowledge. As Figure 14.1 shows, these may be categorized as either demand- or supply-led frameworks.

The demand-led notions, coming under the heading of consumer and customer approaches, enhance the industry's market orientation by examining the environments of consumers (potential users of hospitality services) and customers (actual users of hospitality services) in depth. To explore fully the difference between the concepts of leisure, tourism and recreation would probably require a volume in itself. Leisure is seen to encompass all those activities which fall within an individual's discretionary time – that time free from work and family duties and not directly aimed at physical maintenance. Clearly, leisure embraces both home-centred activities and those which take place outside the home. Leisure studies may be broad – such as when examining the sociology of leisure and the economics of leisure – or they can be narrow, when for instance they research the provision of 'leisure facilities' in hotels. One approach to leisure would be that it helps to explain the general relationship between work and non-work activities. The more specialized areas of tourism and recreation deal with particular areas of leisure.

Tourism is defined as all short stay travel away from home for a minimum of twenty-four hours (British Tourist Authority/English Tourist Board). It will include in its study not only the motivations of tourists but also the scope and interlinkages of tourism providers – a spectrum of suppliers stretching from travel agents and tour organizers to transport operators, hospitality units and local tourist attractions. In fact, the tourism framework admits a wider interpretation, for the UK definition above allows the further inclusion of business-generated accommodation markets into its area of analysis.

Recreation, on the other hand, is usually related to those activities which are either home based or at least essentially undertaken from home. Essentially, it examines the use of leisure time – the range of activities, participation rates and so on.

All three demand approaches have developed, over time, bodies of knowledge and research tools. These can be applied to the hospitality industry in a number of cases. However, they do not address the whole range of hospitality markets. They particularly neglect non-residential markets which business may generate, such as day conferences, business hospitality and the like. Thus they cannot provide an overarching view of hospitality demand but must be seen as useful tools with which to tackle specific aspects of hospitality.

From the supply side, four approaches are identified: general management, service management, retail management and hospitality management. These frameworks follow a continuum from one which sees management as a universal perspective and studies relevant topics at a high level of generality, through more focused approaches: service management stressing the attributes of the consumer offering; retail management including the service element but extending it into a more particular type of organization, with an implied locational distribution;

hospitality, of course, extending the level of exclusivity, though, as has been mentioned above, there is presently no one agreed thrust.

Porter (1980) has commented on the difficulty of defining industry and concludes that 'it is largely a matter of degree'. Too narrow a view might put a firm or industry in a dangerous position when considering current and future opportunities and threats; on the other hand, too broad a view may create strategic confusion due to the lack of market focus and links between the existing resource base and its future potential.

The main weakness of the wider frameworks, both demand and supply, is that they do not fully cover the range of hospitality situations. They all have strengths and weaknesses but, with the exception of the hospitality approach itself, they see hospitality as peripheral and do not make many connections between the demand and supply sides. Certainly, none of them in any way overarches hospitality and, as developing disciplines themselves, they have their own debates of focus and direction.

The problem for researchers in hospitality is not that the adoption of wider frameworks may encourage too broad a view of hospitality: the review of future development has stressed exactly a requirement to consider developments outside the industry and to research their relationship to hospitality. What is important is that frameworks are applied sensitively to the conditions of hospitality, and that solutions are synthesized which are relevant to industry. The danger of adopting wider frameworks is that too great an emphasis is placed on aspects of slight relevance to hospitality. For successful research there does not seem to be any obvious alternative that omits a strong emphasis on the nature of the hospitality industry.

The future of hospitality research

This penultimate section will examine the discipline/quality aspects of research and its quantity, together with implications for funding and the dissemination of results.

Disciplines of quality

Hospitality is a complex and varied activity involving different service offerings and management orientations. To help research relevant issues, there are a range of approaches. In the first place, stemming from the development of traditional hospitality fields, there are the approaches of natural and physical sciences, hospitality management and hospitality studies. In addition, there are the wider avenues of leisure and management theories.

No doubt, in the hands of an astute researcher, any of the paths could provide results useful to someone in industry. Such a researcher would bring a strong methodology to a problem and an internal rigour to the research process. The danger lies in the possibility that researchers who are not informed in their selection of topics by industry priorities will become involved in peripheral issues.

Further, it has been argued that hospitality is a distinct type of activity, containing sufficient variability to be an area of study in its own right.

The fact that there is currently no established discipline base for hospitality should not inhibit its study. While it would be comfortable to be able to provide an accepted framework on which to build up research work, academic disciplines are things which develop – and indeed change – over long periods. If a hospitality discipline is to emerge, it is difficult to predict how and when, particularly at a time when the industry itself seems to be in a state of flux. Let researchers address themselves to relevant issues – be objective insiders – and problems of a hospitality discipline will, hopefully, become less of an immediate issue.

Quality of research output will be judged by two particular groups: the academics who carry out research, and management in industry. If the research is to make any impact in the latter group it must have not only the face validity implied above, but also reliability and some predictive use: what will be the likely effects of new selection procedures on the operation of hospitality units? how will changing patterns of accommodation demand impact on hotels (where there is an implication on customer, workforce and organization aspects of operation)? This may call for the development of strong interdisciplinary teams which can explore research problems fully and proffer solutions.

At the end of the day, the most important arbiters of quality are those who can provide the resources for more research – and that, directly and indirectly, is industry. While academics can, and must, provide the impetus for research initiatives, they must accept that industry will judge on the quality of research output rather than on promises of sound concepts and methodologies.

Quantity of research

The quantity of published research has earlier been compared favourably with its quality. This, however, is a relative judgement. There needs to be a significant increase in the quantity of scholarly activity if the area is to make the transition into a recognized discipline. To an extent this may be helped by the number of postgraduate courses in the field. However, numbers of these are currently marginal in the UK and development will take some time.

Left to this sort of evolutionary change, the development in the UK of critical mass – crucial to both quantity and quality aspects – may be slow. Hospitality departments are not large. Mechanisms must be developed to achieve proactive research groupings between institutions as well as individual levels, as regards joint projects, information sharing and communication. Bearing in mind global development in hospitality, groups of researchers brought together on an international level may be an added stimulant to relevant research initiatives.

Funding of research

Success in research initiatives is sometimes measured through funds raised. The easiest way to raise money in most areas of hospitality is through consultancy.

This can create a tension between the goal of providing an academic impetus and that of economic justification, for consultancy traditionally means dealing with short-term problems and may therefore lack a solution which advances knowledge in an area. Its confidential basis to a particular client organization may also slow its application to mainstream knowledge.

Bearing in mind current resourcing problems, it is unlikely that institutions will suddenly grant significantly more capital to develop hospitality research initiatives. Yet there is a paradox here. High-cost projects requiring equipment for testing and food preparation are those for which external funding mechanisms and paths exist (e.g. through equipment manufacturers and large-scale meal providers in the public sector of provision). Low-cost projects, such as investigations into personnel and marketing practices in the industry, do not in general attract substantial institutional or external support. Certainly, the tools of the trade in researching social science issues are not excessively expensive. Resources required include time, travelling/subsistence costs and some administrative backup. Any serious attempt to encourage research will have to provide for these resources.

The tension which may exist between research and consultancy will be minimized if two conditions are met. First, consultancy initiatives should spring from solid research initiatives, which implies that researchers in the area should hold to this objective in their research endeavours. The second condition is that research output should be measured in ways other than just monetary value. These conditions are not, of course, watertight in themselves. They may, however, help to provide an appropriate solution. Certainly, investigators must find means of welding research and consultancy initiatives as harmoniously as possible.

Dissemination of information

The issues here relate to communication both between industry and academics, and within each of the sectors.

The best potential means of communication is clearly the printed media. By style and selection of material, the journals currently available allow for communication more within the academic community than between academics and industry. Dissemination can indirectly be aided by involving industry more in the carrying out of research and in its evaluation process, as well as by the development of more appropriate forms of communication between industry and academics. It has been further suggested that this should be complemented by institutional/departmental co-operation within the UK. This could circumvent problems of isolation experienced by certain specialist staff and further form the basis of strong interdisciplinary teams able to mount complex research and consultancy projects and to respond better to the needs of industry.

These are essentially strategies for academics to become more systemized in their approach to the industry. However, there is a further need to increase the flow of communication about research projects between academics and hospitality managers. Publications must be developed which pursue this aim with determination.

Conclusion

While much has been achieved over the past ten years in hospitality research, significant challenges still lie ahead in establishing the role and contribution of research and industry.

Hospitality is a complex acitivity. It is also a fast-moving area. At this stage of development, it must not be confined to a search for educational certainty – if such exists. Research must see an exciting priority as increasing the stock of relevant knowledge and interpretations on offer to hospitality managers.

This increase in knowledge may be achieved by the range of disciplines outlined, applied in a manner sensitive to the characteristics of hospitality. It is suggested that this will require research which is interdisciplinary in nature and which involves industry in the selection and evaluation process of topics and solutions. An approach such as hospitality studies would appear to capitalize on industry specifics and wider frameworks, and it may provide an appropriate vehicle for considering research design into many social aspects of hospitality. Social science methodology must also be applied in a manner which allows a predictive value to research results.

Finally, academic departments must be prepared to manage their research activities more comprehensively if they are truly to relate to industry in a meaningful way, and they must create mechanisms for contact and feedback to ensure that research becomes mutually beneficial.

Notes

1. The International Academy of Hospitality Research was founded at Virginia Polytechnic Institute and State University, USA in April 1988. In addition to US hospitality university departments there were representatives from Australia, Canada and the UK. The mission of the academy is to advance research in the hospitality field by strengthening the role and function of all research-related aspects at national and international levels.
2. Nailon's Characteristics of Hospitality Environments (paraphrased) are as follows. Activities are concerned with satisfying basic physiological needs (1) and associated psychological ones (2); customers' satisfactions are individual in nature (3), transient (4) and require immediate attention (5). Owing to customer presence they become part of the product (6) and inject an uncontrollable element into the production process (7), even if only for a short time (8). Staff–customer relationships have an unsupervised, personal facet (9) and may introduce problems in organizational authority (10). Business factors include rapid cashflow (11), perishability of the product in terms of unstockability (12) and inability of replication (13). The industry meets different market needs (14), suffers from demand instability (15) and monitoring business activity requires high-speed feedback (16). (Nailon, 1982.)

References

British Tourist Authority/English Tourist Board (published annually) *British Tourism Survey*. London: BTA/ETB.
Council for National Academic Awards (1984) *Handbook 1985*. London: CNAA.

Gamble, P.R. (1982) 'Some implications of computers for hospitality managers', *International Journal of Hospitality Management*, 1, 1, 3–10.

International Hotel Association/Horwath and Horwath (1988) *Hotels of the Future/ Strategies and Action Plan*. London: Horwath and Horwath.

Kent, A.W.E. (1988) 'Hospitality research: in search of self', Paper presented to the first meeting of the International Academy of Hospitality Research, Virginia Polytechnic and State University, Blacksburg, Va., April.

Litteljohn, D. (1985) 'Towards an economic analysis of trans-/multinational companies', *International Journal of Hospitality Management*, 4, 4.

Medlik, S. (1980) *The Business of Hotels*. London: Heinemann.

Nailon, P. (1982) 'Theory in hospitality management', *International Journal of Hospitality Management*, 1, 3, 135–43.

Porter, M. (1980) *Competitive Strategy*. New York: Macmillan/Free Press.

Sasser, W.E., Olsen, P.P. and Wycoff, D.D. (1988) *Management of Service Operations*. Boston: Allyn and Bacon.

Slattery, P. (1983) 'Social scientific methodology and hospitality management', *International Journal of Hospitality Management*, 2, 1, 9–14.

Slattery, P. and Roper, A. (1987) *UK Hotel Groups Directory 1986/87*. London: Cassell.

Terpstra, V. (1985) 'The changing environment of international marketing', *International Marketing Review*, Autumn.

Chapter 15

An exploration of the consumer decision process for hospitality services

Richard Teare

Introduction

Understanding how consumers decide, purchase and evaluate hospitality services is important for the design and management of service delivery, and also for the development of consumer theory in the service sector. This chapter examines the characteristics of hospitality services, and considers how they influence the extent and duration of the decision process used by consumers to evaluate the hotel leisure product. Two main themes are developed: the role of prior experience and the extent of consumer involvement in the decision process. In conclusion, a matrix showing the interaction between prior experience and product involvement is presented, together with a discussion of the managerial implications.

An overview of the consumer decision process: a paradigm in transition

Anderson (1983) and Peter and Olson (1983) have advocated the need for a theoretical framework or paradigm (Kuhn, 1970) in consumer research to help interpret empirical observations. This viewpoint is strengthened by the findings of Bagozzi (1984), Foxall (1980a, 1980b) and Jacoby (1978), who have commented on the limited success of attempts to construct and test theory in isolation from existing theory. Hunt (1983) has also argued that any given theory has meaning and significance only within the paradigm from which it is derived.

The dominant tradition in consumer research is the cognitive paradigm. The most well-known models of consumer behaviour assume that consumers have considerable capacity for receiving and handling quantities of information and for undertaking pre-purchase search and evaluation of alternatives. The consumer is also assumed to process information in a rational way, and by so doing becomes progressively convinced of the need to purchase the focal brand. The central component of these models is an extended consumer decision sequence in which information is received and classified by the individual (McGuire, 1976).

Reviewing consumer choice models, Hansen (1976) identified a common characteristic which is an ego-involving sequence of cognitive, affective and conative change. A typical pattern, in situations where choice is preceded by the evaluation of alternatives, may include experiences of uncertainty and anxiety.

This produces a sense of inner conflict as the possible outcomes are considered. Olshavsky and Granbois (1979) have suggested that the purpose of cognitive activity during decision making is to reduce anxiety and conflict by gradually resolving sources of uncertainty. The assumes that the consumer can formulate and apply evaluative criteria to predict the possible outcomes of each purchase option. The procedure is aided by the use of decision rules, which are developed from information received, processed and stored in memory. The role of decision rules is to provide stability and consistency during decision making, enabling the consumer to undertake a standardized form of comparative assessment and evaluation.

Cognitive theories and models of decision making presuppose that the consumer is motivated to find the optimum solution for complex purchase decisions. However, as the number of purchase options increases, it becomes more difficult for the consumer to decide. If, for instance, product knowledge is limited, the consumer may aim more realistically to make a satisfactory rather than an optimal decision (Fletcher, 1986, 1987).

Although the cognitive paradigm remains influential, there have been a number of sustained criticisms. These can be summarized as follows:

- comprehensive models of consumer decision making are often too complex and/or too generalized to test empirically (Bagozzi, 1984; Jacoby, 1978), indicating that an alternative approach, located much closer to observable consumer behaviour, is needed;
- empirical research has often revealed low correlational consistency between decision process components (Ajzen and Fishbein, 1977; Foxall, 1983, 1984);
- consumers are thought to use less information than the cognitive paradigm generally assumes (Jacoby *et al.*, 1977; Olshavsky and Granbois, 1979), and too much information may actually impede rational decision making (Jacoby *et al.*, 1974);
- sequences other than cognition–affect–conation have been shown to describe more accurately the consumer choice process: for example, the low involvement hierarchy, and alternative views of the learning of brand preferences in response to advertising, have been proposed (Krugman, 1965; Ray, 1973; Robertson, 1976).

Foxall (1986) has argued that the success of the cognitive paradigm is actually impeding various forms of theoretical progress which run contrary to the fundamental assumptions of the paradigm. He suggests that this is because there are so many 'ready made' explanations which can be inferred for any observed behaviour. This problem is less acute in service industries than in manufacturing, because the consumer decision process is shaped by the nature of the service activity and the perceived benefits of purchase. For example, Moutinho (1982, 1984) found that the tourist product purchase is rarely spontaneous, and is often preceded by planning and saving over a long time period. This pattern is indicative of an important decision with clearly recognizable risks. For instance, return on investment is finite because it is restricted to the actual holiday experience, and the purchase outcome is intangible, as the consumer returns home with nothing more than an emotional feeling about the relative success or otherwise of the holiday.

To identify how the nature of hospitality services might influence the consumer decision process, it is helpful to consider the operational characteristics from the different perspectives of the consumer and the producer.

The concept and characteristics of hospitality services

The origin of the word 'hospitality' can be traced to the Latin noun *hospice* meaning a 'place of entertainment or of shelter'. Usage of the generic term 'hospitality industry' to describe what is traditionally known as the 'hotel and catering industry' is a comparatively recent development in the UK, following wider acceptance in the USA and mainland Europe (Burgess, 1982).

Hospitality services are associated with the commercial provision of catering, accommodation and leisure facilities, and can be classified as profit centred (e.g. hotels and restaurants) or cost centred (e.g. employee and institutional catering). The service offering consists of both tangible and intangible components, which are designed and managed by the producer with the aim of satisfying the needs of the consumer. The interrelationships between the producer and the consumer are depicted in Figure 15.1.

Promotional activities such as advertising and direct mail to consumers may stimulate initial contact, typically by telephone or written enquiry. The main consumer–producer interaction occurs at the point of service delivery, where satisfaction with the consumption experience will be determined by product design features and the behaviour of service staff.

Referring to the environment in which hospitality managers work, Nailon (1981) observed that many operational problems occur because the consequences of service interactions are not fully understood. Cassee (1983) agrees, identifying the need for empirical research focusing on the behaviour of consumers and producers of hospitality services in different contexts. As the period of consumption can extend over several days in the case of the hotel leisure product, consumer–producer interactions are necessarily varied and complex.

Hospitality services and the consumer perspective

Hospitality services have both functional and expressive roles to fulfil. The consumer is primarily concerned with the desire to satisfy basic physiological needs such as hunger and thirst. These are accompanied by more complex psychological needs such as identity, status and security.

Psychological needs may be determined by expectations derived from the consumer's lifestyle and prior experience. They may also be motivated by aspirations to experience surroundings beyond current lifestyle expectations.

Consumer needs require an immediate response from the producer. If they are not satisfied, complaint behaviour may be triggered by physiological discomfort or psychological ego-defensive mechanisms. The consistency and quality of

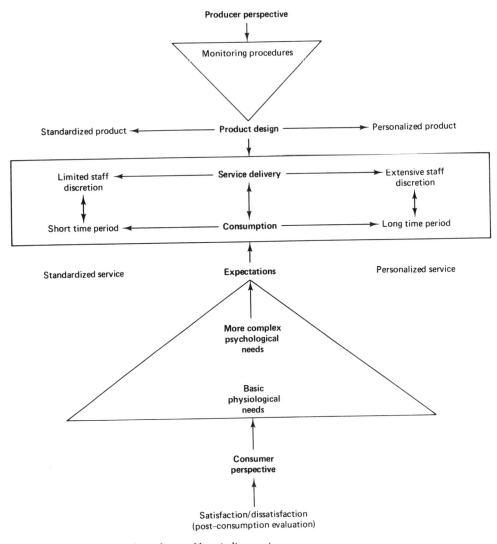

Figure 15.1   The interdependency of hospitality services

service delivery is important because the consumer has little or no control over the environment in which consumption takes place. For instance, service efficiency is vulnerable because of the demand fluctuations which occur in hospitality operations throughout the day, week, month and year.

Hospitality service interactions are typically short and variable in nature, with the degree of formality influenced by the situation and personalities of the participants. Every consumer has a unique set of expectations about the role of staff during service delivery. If these expectations are not met, the consumer may feel dissatisfied, although the feeling may be internalized if it is not strong enough to cause complaint behaviour. For example, non-verbal communication by staff relating to the expected payment of gratuities may cause the consumer to feel irritated or embarrassed. This source of dissatisfaction is unlikely to be reported to management.

Consumer satisfaction is derived from different kinds of service experience and interaction which are unique to the occasion and situation. For example, the time period for using hospitality services can vary from several minutes (a fast-food restaurant) to a week or more (staying in a hotel). Consumption over a longer time period will require a more sophisticated form of consumer evaluation. This is because satisfaction with service delivery is linked to the accumulation of many impressions from successive and usually transient experiences and interactions. The evaluative procedure must be able to cope with this complexity, and provide the consumer with an overall post-consumption measure of satisfaction.

Hospitality services and the producer perspective

As hospitality services are usually consumed at the point of production, the consumer becomes involved in the production process. The consumer arrives with a set of needs and expectations about the product and the environment in which the service will be delivered. The producer's ability to control and regulate service delivery depends on the use of sensitive monitoring procedures and corrective measures. When service delivery occurs over a long time period, as in a hotel, continuous performance monitoring must be used to minimize service variability.

Hospitality managers need to understand the service interaction dynamics for their type of operation, and the important implications for staff recruitment, selection and training. This is because the highly personalized form of interaction during service delivery can exacerbate the problem of service variability. For example, if the consumer arrives tired and tense after travelling a long distance, the receptionist must be able to recognize and respond appropriately to his or her psychological state. This is because the initial interaction is likely to have a critical role in the formation of first impressions.

Hospitality services with an accommodation component usually have high fixed costs and sensitive profit ratios. The pattern of business is often irregular and subject to short-term sales instability (Kotas, 1975, 1977). To minimize these effects, reduced cost options such as leisure breaks are increasingly used to penetrate specialist market segments and improve operational efficiency and profitability.

Hospitality services cannot be stored like manufactured products; the revenue from unsold meals or bedrooms over a given time period cannot be recouped. Similarly, product experiences cannot be precisely replicated. For instance, the atmosphere in a restaurant will be affected by the number of customers who are being served at any given moment in time. Too few or too many customers can create an undesirable impression. If the restaurant is too busy and complaints occur, the manager can only offer to compensate the dissatisfied customer, he or she cannot erase the recollection of an unsatisfactory product experience.

Service and manufacturing industries also have different consumer–producer interface characteristics. The different orientation of service delivery means that management theories and methods developed in manufacturing industries have limited application to service product management problems. As many as 90 per cent of the staff in service organizations have direct contact with the consumer, compared with only 10 per cent in manufacturing (Irons, 1983). The natural focus for consumer research in hospitality services therefore occurs at the place where service interactions are concentrated, during simultaneous production and consumption.

The consumer decision process for hospitality services

The decision process for a leisure product is likely to be taken after joint consultation with family members and with greater caution than might be expected for non-leisure hotel use or non-residential hospitality services. This is because of the comparatively high personal investment of time and money, and the need to assess carefully the associated costs and benefits involved. Derived from the two different perspectives, Figure 15.2 shows the changing emphasis between consumer- and producer-dominant assessment, with the changes corresponding to the three main stages of the decision process: pre-purchase, consumption and post-consumption.

Stage 1: pre-purchase

When joint or family decision making occurs in the course of reaching agreement on a purchase decision, role specialization is commonplace. Role adoption will be determined by personal, consumer-related factors such as self-confidence and assertiveness, and by the product-related factor of prior experience. Stage 1 assumes that consumer-related factors are the dominant influence on the purchase decision, because the subjective interpretation of product information and product recommendations feature prominently in pre-purchase activity.

If family members have limited prior experience, the perceived risk is likely to be higher, requiring greater personal involvement in the decision process to resolve sources of concern. Conversely, consumers with extensive prior experience will be able to make a purchase decision more easily and with greater confidence. In this situation, consumer-related factors are less dominant because product knowledge provides a stabilizing influence. Therefore, the relationship between prior experience and product involvement is important because it is likely to determine the amount of time, the extent of information search and the overall level of involvement required to assess the purchase options and reach a decision.

Stage 2: consumption

The hotel leisure product provides the consumer with personalized service over a long time period of between two and four days. As the needs of consumers cannot be fully anticipated during consumption, hotel staff must be able to exercise

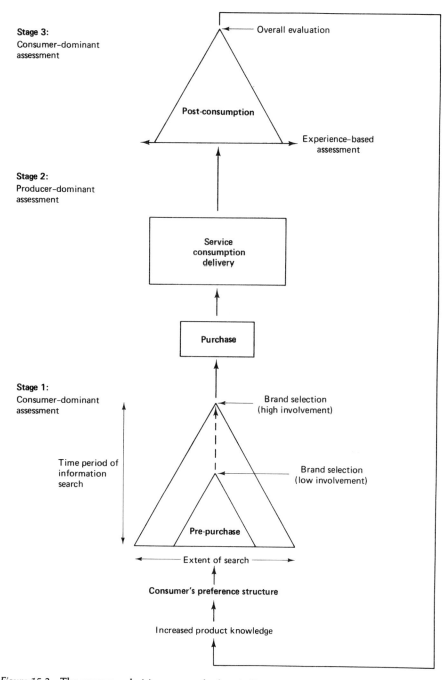

Figure 15.2 The consumer decision process for hospitality services

discretion during service delivery in order to respond effectively. Stage 2 therefore assumes that product-related factors such as service interactions and subjective impressions of product experience will have a greater impact on satisfaction that internalized consumer-related factors such as prior expectations. This is because the consumer becomes part of the product during consumption, helping to create atmosphere in restaurants and bars and simultaneously assessing the many tangible and intangible impressions and interactions which occur. The consumer must integrate all of these individual assessments to evaluate post-consumption satisfaction.

Stage 3: post-consumption

The overall feeling of satisfaction formulated during post-consumption is an enduring, cumulative measure derived from the many assessments made during consumption. Although the consumer may need to recall sensory product-related impressions such as visually appealing guest room design features, the final evaluation is more likely to be influenced by consumer-related factors. These are principally 'end-state' feelings of a psychological nature, such as feeling relaxed and refreshed. If the outcome of Stage 2 is a negative psychological state, such as increased tension, then the consumer is likely to experience an overall feeling of dissatisfaction during post-consumption evaluation, and this in turn will influence brand attitudes and future purchase intentions.

Understanding consumer behaviour: two emerging themes

The descriptive framework in the previous section raises a number of questions about the extent to which product experience affects the level of consumer involvement in the decision process. Ultimately, the strategy adopted by the consumer will depend on how difficult the task is perceived to be, and on how much effort and attention is required to make an acceptable choice between purchase alternatives. This relationship is considered in the following two sections, using examples from consumer interviews relating to the hotel leisure product decision process.

The role of product experience in the decision process

Alba and Hutchinson (1987) suggest that consumer knowledge has two major components: familiarity and expertise. They define familiarity as the number of product-related experiences that have been accumulated by the consumer, and expertise as the ability to perform product-related tasks successfully. They propose that increased product familiarity results in increased consumer expertise.

The extent of pre-purchase search is likely to depend on the consumer's familiarity with the product category (Howard and Sheth, 1969; Bettman, 1979;

Punj and Staelin, 1983). Search behaviour generally begins with the recollection of information held in memory, as the consumer tries to determine whether choice can be based on prior experience. Insufficient information or experience will activate external information search: '[On hotel selection] I like to make sure I've done my groundwork . . . I don't like to get there and have problems . . . if things are wrong at the initial stage it can spoil everything . . . you start picking fault then.' As the decision process continues beyond information search, use of internal and external sources of information may alternate (Bettman, 1979).

Product familiarity can lead to increased learning during subsequent purchase decisions (Johnson and Russo, 1980). This enables the experienced consumer to feel confident about searching less information, to be more selective and to use decision rules instead of repeating preliminary explorations of external information on subsequent purchase occasions.

The latitude of product acceptance is likely to narrow as new experiences are assimilated. For example, a consumer with extensive prior experience is able to equate acceptance or rejection with a wider experience-based understanding of hotel standards: 'We've developed a knowledge of hotel standards . . . it has been a learning experience . . . as you stay in hotels which are above or below a certain standard, you begin to understand the differences.' A reference standard is commonly used by consumers for making attribute-based comparisons. They are usually described in terms of experiences which fall above or below the reference point experience: '[On comparison with other recent hotel experiences] So far there hasn't been anything that's below the standard of other hotels we've stayed at'; 'I think if anybody came here first, they would come back again . . . we've compared everything with this hotel.'

LaTour and Peat (1979a, 1979b) suggest that prior experience and product satisfaction are linked by comparison levels for important product attributes. They found that comparison levels were determined by prior experience and the experiences of other consumers. Situationally induced expectations were not encountered in their study, suggesting that consumers attribute greater priority to the other two sources of product information. They also found that consumers with limited prior experience of the test product derived more satisfaction from the product than those with extensive prior experience. This is probably because experienced consumers have developed more sophisticated comparison levels. For example, there is often a direct relationship between product experience and increased expectations: 'On the whole I think we have been spoilt . . . when other people say it's "superb" we've often thought "How on earth did they think this is good?" . . . once you've experienced something that is good, your standard is set.' Experienced consumers are also more likely to recognize the importance of consumer–producer interdependence: 'You could come into contact with fifteen or twenty staff on a weekend like this . . . just one who was off-hand could tip the balance, especially if it occurs when you register at reception.'

The influence of product knowledge on the consumer decision process can be summarized as follows:

- consumer groups with a moderate level of product knowledge and prior experience are inclined to rely more heavily on currently available information than on product knowledge (Bettman and Park, 1980);

- brand-based information processing is more likely to occur among consumers who are familiar with the product category, and attribute-based processing among consumers who are less familiar (Russo and Johnson, 1979; Bettman and Park, 1980; Beattie, 1981);
- consumers tend to start with product attribute-based evaluations and comparisons, turning to brand processing in the later stages. This suggests that attribute-based comparisons are more easily undertaken. Experienced consumers also tend to make comparisons against established standards in order to evaluate alternatives and make trade-off decisions (Bettman and Park, 1980; Beattie, 1981).

These findings suggest that experienced consumers are able to construct a prototype for the product class within an internal knowledge structure, and to process information schematically. This enables the consumer to make the fullest use of similarity and difference information.

The role of product involvement in the decision process

Involvement is considered to be a causal, individual difference variable which affects purchase behaviour. It has been defined as: 'an unobservable state reflecting the amount of interest, arousal or emotional attachment evoked by the product in a particular individual' (Bloch, 1981).

The degree of consumer involvement in a product category is recognized as an important variable in the context of advertising strategy, which may lead to different patterns of consumer decision making (Krugman, 1967; Vaughn, 1980). Characteristic differences include the number of product attributes used to compare brands, and the duration of the selection process. The degree of product involvement in pre-purchase decision making is linked to antecedents such as perceptions of product importance, risk, symbolic or sign value and hedonic or emotional value (Laurent and Kapferer, 1985).

Bloch and Richins (1983) have argued that product importance has been inadequately defined and understood. In their view product importance has three dimensions:

- perceived product importance: the extent to which a consumer links a product to salient enduring or situation-specific goals;
- instrumental or situational importance: a temporary perception of product importance based on the consumer's desire to obtain particular extrinsic goals that may derive from the purchase and/or usage of the product;
- enduring importance: a long-term perception of product importance based on the strength of the product's relationship to central needs and values.

The correlation between product importance and high involvement is most usually associated with limited prior experience or, in the case of experienced consumers, with an important purchase motive: 'We haven't actually managed to get away this year . . . so we thought we'd pick a very good hotel rather than one which would just be reasonably good.' Perceived risk has been identified as an outcome of uncertainty about the product. The sense of risk is commonly associated with the place and mode of purchase, and with the financial and psychosocial consequences of product purchase (Stem, Lamb and Maclachlan, 1977). Consumers with limited prior experience are likely to feel uncertain during brand selection. In the case of hotel selection, the desire to reduce the level of perceived risk may lead to increased involvement at the pre-purchase stage as the consumer tries to assess acceptability: 'I would have phoned anyway to try and find out what the hotel was like . . . I like to think the weekend's going to be right, I don't like to get there and wish I'd phoned and found out . . . if you don't phone and make contact, you've no comeback.'

Most empirical work on product symbolism has paid relatively little attention to how products are used by consumers in social situations. Solomon (1983) suggested that the subjective experience of product usage contributes to the consumers' structuring of social reality, self-concept and behaviour. He argued that the symbolism embedded in many products may in fact be the primary reason for purchase and use. The hedonic appeal of the hotel environment and surroundings is an important determinant of product involvement. For example, the appeal may relate closely to lifestyle aspirations: '[The appeal is] the nice feeling you get whenever you walk through the place, the walnut panelling on the walls . . . it gives me a nice secure feeling . . . it's the sort of hotel that you would stay in if you had unlimited money.'

In the following section, a product experience–involvement matrix is presented which relates limited and extensive prior experience to high, moderate and low involvement strategies. The matrix can be used to identify differences between consumer groups in the decision process for hospitality services.

A product experience–involvement matrix for hospitality services

The traditional marketing response to the task of consumer classification and product positioning is to segment the market-place using socioeconomic or demographic variables. Table 15.1 highlights the potential of a non-standard approach based on prior experience of the product category and product involvement in the decision process for hospitality services. The two product experience categories represent consumers with little or no prior experience of hotels, and those with substantial experience of using hotels in different contexts. The three product involvement categories represent high, moderate and low involvement strategies, and their selection depends on factors like the importance of the product purchase, the level of perceived risk and how confident the consumer feels about the purchase decision task. The six components of the matrix and the implications for managing and marketing hospitality services are explained below.

Table 15.1   *Product experience–involvement matrix for hospitality services*

	Prior experience	
	Extensive	Limited
Product involvement High	High product importance; clearly defined expectations and selection criteria; well-focused research.	High perceived risk; uncertain expectations; diffuse research, using many information sources.
Product design	Provide clear promotional information on performance parameters, both core and peripheral services.	Ensure that decision support is given with sensitivity, both written and verbal enquiries.
Moderate	Increased involvement associated with new or problematic situations; systematic search using established information channels.	Perceived risk moderated by pre-knowledge or recommendations of product suitability; limited information search to confirm brand selection.
Product design	Anticipate the spectrum of usage situations and design for maximum flexibility of use.	Concentrate decision support on promoting key product attributes to increase brand-based confidence.
Low	Rapid purchase decision based on high personal confidence; little or no information search and pre-purchase discussion.	Typically a repurchase situation, from which confidence and purchase assurance is derived.
Product design	Convey quality standards directly and concisely; concentrate on brand-based benefits.	Aim to broaden the product appeal by generating additional brand purchase options and opportunities.

Extensive experience and high involvement

Consumers with extensive prior experience develop the ability to categorize and differentiate between hotels and leisure break brands because they have clearly defined expectations and selection criteria. The duration of pre-purchase activity also depends on the degree of confidence with which they are able to use established procedures for risk reduction and the narrowing of choice options. If the primary motive for purchase is especially important to the consumer, this will complicate the decision process and lead to the use of a high-involvement strategy. The most effective support can be given to consumers in this sub-group by providing promotional material which focuses on important selection criteria and thereby facilitates rapid assessment and evaluation.

Limited experience and high involvement

There are several reasons why consumers with limited prior experience commonly use high-involvement strategies. First, there is a need to rely more heavily on external sources of information for risk reduction and assurance. These sources typically include travel intermediaries, telephone discussions with central reservations and hotel staff, and recommendations from experienced others. Secondly, uncertainty about price–quality relationships relating to standards, services and facilities available in the various grades of hotel accommodation necessitates a more cautious approach. In this respect, the degree of perceived risk closely relates to the perceived importance of the occasion and the level of financial investment it represents. The degree of uncertainty associated with the purchase decision indicates that the sensitivity and responsiveness of the producer in dealing with questions, and in establishing a rapport with the consumer, will be particularly important.

Extensive experience and moderate involvement

Prior knowledge and familiarity with different usage situations and requirements generally increases personal confidence in decision-making ability and reduces the level of involvement necessary to make a purchase decision. In resolving problems or dealing with new situations, consumers with extensive prior experience tend to use moderate involvement strategies. The shift from low to moderate involvement typically occurs during brand switching or if the consumer is conscious of vicarious responsibility arising from reservations made on behalf of, or in conjunction with, others. As the consumer is likely to be looking for solutions to new or evolving problems or attempting to improve on prior experiences, the producer can assist by emphasizing brand flexibility, ease of booking, access and other factors in the promotional literature.

Limited experience and moderate involvement

Although inexperienced hotel users normally employ high-involvement strategies, there are two common sources of moderation. These are pre-knowledge of hotel suitability, and acceptance of recommendations made by more experienced others. If these factors are influential during pre-purchase, they have the effect of reducing the inherent level of perceived risk, which under normal circumstances would require more extensive search and more detailed consideration. An appropriate response from the producer is to develop brand-based confidence by identifying and dealing with perceived risk factors which may intervene and cause the consumer to use a high- rather than moderate-involvement strategy.

Extensive experience and low involvement

The relative ease with which experienced hotel users are able to make purchase decisions is closely associated with product knowledge and familiarity, personal confidence and family decision-making roles. Product familiarity, derived from experience-based knowledge and the categorization of hotel types, styles and designs according to personal preferences and needs, will increase the consumer's ability to make consistent and confident decisions. Low-involvement strategies are also associated with repeat purchase situations, especially when there are multiple reference sources confirming the appropriateness of the purchase decision. The producer can provide support by focusing the consumer's attention on quality standards which emphasize brand benefits.

Limited experience and low involvement

There are exceptional circumstances which help to explain why inexperienced hotel users might use a low-involvement strategy. This may typically occur when the consumer's prior experience is concentrated within one hotel group or at one hotel, so that pre-knowledge overrides uncertainty. As with moderate involvement, there are also circumstances which require an immediate response, such as the need to find a house prior to job relocation. Other types of leisure break experience such as self-catering may have been associated with specific sources of dissatisfaction in the past like poor weather. If the intention is to take a family break, then a hotel with indoor leisure facilities, though more expensive, may be perceived as a safer investment. The producer should therefore concentrate on extending the brand appeal by concentrating on the repeat purchase opportunities in different locations, situations and circumstances.

Implications for managing and marketing hospitality services

As can be seen, in marketing to consumers with different profiles of experience and involvement in the decision process, it is important to identify patterns of behaviour and the appropriate responses.

For consumers with limited experience of specialized hospitality services, the need for decision support right across the organization will be greater. For instance, sensitive handling of telephone enquiries by reception staff will reinforce interest and reduce perceived risk. Conversely, failure to understand the assessment and information gathering roles of this kind of preliminary contact may affect the chances of the enquiry being converted to a purchase decision. Typically, the decision process is longer, involves more information sources and informal contacts, and therefore requires a well-coordinated organizational response.

In contrast, the greater product knowledge of experienced consumers will tend to mediate the level of involvement in the decision process. Decision making is typically a more rapid and confident process, which requires a different marketing emphasis. Promotional information should be designed to support a shorter, more incisive decision period by emphasizing well-understood concepts such as quality and individuality, as they provide the criteria on which decision rules are based. Although the decision process is likely to be shorter, consumer expectations will be clearer, with service quality comparisons occurring naturally during consumption.

In responding to the challenges of the 1990s hospitality managers must carefully monitor operational procedures and service interactions. In this way, they will become more responsive to changing consumer expectations and the consumption experience. By focusing more closely on the consumer perspective, managers will also be able to recognize more easily the differences in the assessment criteria and procedures used by consumers. In this respect, a deeper understanding of the interactions between prior experience and product involvement will be critical to their success.

References

Ajzen, I. and Fishbein, M. (1977) 'Attitude–behaviour relations: a theoretical analysis and review of empirical research', *Psychological Bulletin*, 84, 888–918.

Alba, J.W. and Hutchinson, J.W. (1987) 'Dimensions of consumer expertise' *Journal of Consumer Research*, 13, March, 411–54.

Anderson, P.F. (1983) 'Marketing, scientific progress, and scientific method', *Journal of Marketing*, 47, Fall, 18–31.

Bagozzi, R.P. (1984) 'A prospectus for theory construction in marketing', *Journal of Marketing*, 48, Summer, 11–29.

Beattie, A.E. (1981) 'Effects of product knowledge on comparison, memory, evaluation, and choice: a model of expertise in consumer decision-making', *Advances in Consumer Research*, 9, 336–40.

Bettman, J.R. (1979) *An Information Processing Theory of Consumer Choice*. Reading, Mass.: Addison-Wesley.

Bettman, J.R. and Park, C.W. (1980) 'Effects of prior knowledge and experience and phase of the choice process on consumer decision processes: a protocol analysis' *Journal of Consumer Research*, 7, December, 234–48.

Bloch, P.H. (1981) 'Involvement beyond the purchase process: conceptual issues and empirical investigation' *Advances in Consumer Research*, 9, 413–17.

Bloch, P.H. and Richins, M.L. (1983) 'A theoretical model for the study of product importance perceptions', *Journal of Marketing*, 47, Summer, 69–81.

Burgess, J. (1982) 'Perspectives on gift exchange and hospitable behaviour', *International Journal of Hospitality Management*, 1, 1, 49–57.

Cassee, E. (1983) 'The management of hospitality', in Cassee, E. and Reuland, R. (eds) *The Management of Hospitality*. Oxford: Pergamon.

Fletcher, K. (1986) 'Search behaviour: an analysis of information collection and usage during the decision process', unpublished PhD thesis, University of Strathclyde.

Fletcher, K. (1987) 'Evaluation and choice as a satisfying process', *Journal of Marketing Management*, 3, 1, 13–23.

Foxall, G.R. (1980a) 'Academic consumer research: problems and potential', *European Research*, 8, 20–3.

Foxall, G.R. (1980b) 'Marketing models of buyer behaviour: A critical review', *European Research*, 8, 195–206.

Foxall, G.R. (1983) 'Marketing's response to consumer behaviour: time to promote a change?' *Quarterly Review of Marketing*, 8, 4, 11–14.

Foxall, G.R. (1984) 'Consumers' intentions and behaviour', *Journal of the Market Research Society*, 26, 231–41.

Foxall, G.R. (1986) 'Consumer theory: some contributions of a behavioural analysis of choice' *Management Bibliographies and Reviews*, 12, 2, 27–51.

Hansen, F. (1976) 'Psychological theories of consumer choice', *Journal of Consumer Research*, 3, December, 117–42.

Howard, J.A. and Sheth, J.N. (1969) *The Theory of Buyer Behaviour*. New York: John Wiley.

Hunt, S.D. (1983) 'General theories and the fundamental explananda of marketing' *Journal of Marketing*, 47, Fall, 9–17.

Irons, K. (1983) 'How to manage services', *Management Today*, November, 90–168.

Jacoby, J. (1978) 'Consumer research: a state-of-the-art review', *Journal of Marketing*, 42, Winter, 87–96.

Jacoby, J., Chestnut J.W. and Silberman, W.S. (1977) 'Consumer use and comprehension of nutrition information', *Journal of Consumer Research*, 4, September, 119–28.

Jacoby, J. Speller, D.E. and Kohn, C.A. (1974) 'Brand choice behaviour as a function of information load', *Journal of Consumer Research*, 1, February, 63–9.

Johnson, E.J. and Russo, J.E. (1980) 'Product familiarity and learning new information', *Advances in Consumer Research*, 8, 151–5.

Kotas, R. (1975) *Market Orientation in the Hotel and Catering Industry*. Leighton Buzzard: Surrey University Press.

Kotas, R. (1977) *Management Accounting for Hotels and Restaurants*. Leighton Buzzard: Surrey University Press.

Krugman, H.E. (1965) 'The impact of television advertising: learning without involvement' *Public Opinion Quarterly*, 29, Fall, 349–56.

Krugman, H.E. (1967) 'The measurement of advertising involvement', *Public Opinion Quarterly*, 30, Winter, 586–96.

Kuhn, T.S. (1970) *The Structure of Scientific Revolutions*. Chicago, Ill.: Chicago University Press.

LaTour, S.A. and Peat, N.C. (1979a) 'Conceptual and methodological issues in consumer satisfaction research', *Advances in Consumer Research*, 6, 431–40.

LaTour, S.A. and Peat, N.C. (1979b) 'The role of situationally produced expectations, others' experiences and prior experience in determining consumer satisfaction', *Advances in Consumer Research*, 7, 588–92.

Laurent, G. and Kapferer, J.N. (1985) 'Measuring consumer involvement profiles', *Journal of Marketing Research*, 12, February, 41–53.

McGuire, W.J. (1976) 'Some internal psychological factors influencing consumer choice', *Journal of Consumer Research*, 2, March 302–19.

Moutinho, L. (1982) 'An investigation of vacation tourist behaviour', unpublished PhD thesis, University of Sheffield.

Moutinho, L. (1984) 'Vacation tourist decision process', *Quarterly Review of Marketing*, 9, 3, 8–17.

Nailon, P.W. (1981) 'Theory and art in hospitality management', Inaugural Lecture, University of Surrey.

Olshavsky, R.W. and Granbois, D.H. (1979) 'Consumer decision making: fact or fiction?' *Journal of Consumer Research*, 6, September, 93–100.

Peter, J.P. and Olson, J.C. (1983) 'Is science marketing?', *Journal of Marketing*, 47, 111–25.

Punj, G.N. and Staelin, R. (1983) 'A model of consumer information search behaviour for new automobiles', *Journal of Consumer Research*, 9, March, 366–80.

Ray, M.L. (1973) 'Marketing communication and the hierarchy of effects', In Clarke, P. (ed.) *New Models for Mass Communication Research*. Beverly Hills: Sage.

Robertson, T.S., (1976) 'Low commitment consumer behaviour', *Journal of Advertising Research*, 16, 19–24.

Russo, J.E. and Johnson, E.J. (1979) 'What do consumers know about familiar products?' *Advances in Consumer Research*, 7, 417–23.

Solomon, M.R. (1983) 'The role of products as social stimuli: a symbolic interactionism perspective', *Journal of Consumer Research*, 10, December, 319–29.

Stem, D.E., Lamb, C.W. and Maclachlan, D.L. (1977) 'Product performance and consumer satisfaction: a new concept', *European Journal of Marketing*, 11, 4, 312–19.

Vaughn, R. (1980) 'How advertising works: a planning model', *Journal of Advertising Research*, 20, October, 27–33.

Summary: managing and marketing services–emerging themes for the 1990s

Richard Teare, Luiz Moutinho and *Neil Morgan*

Throughout the book many of the challenges and opportunities which are likely to influence the development of services in the next decade have been discussed. In order to summarize and comment on the strategic implications, a number of general themes are identified. These are concerned with the role of services, their design and delivery, the creation of the single European market in 1992 and the global development of services.

Changing perspectives on the role of services

In terms of output and employment, the service sector became increasingly dominant in Western economies during the 1980s and is now beginning to influence world-wide economic development. For this reason much of the strategic thinking and planning of international corporations is concerned with managing and marketing services. Identifying trends and detecting market opportunities and threats are fundamental tasks in proactive management, and it is essential that decision makers have access to reliable and accurate information in order to analyse the market-place effectively.

Of particular importance is the nature of the relationship between the firm, its employees and the customer. Each interaction represents a moment of truth during which the responsiveness of the organization is exposed and tested. More attention and concern for customer care at the point of service delivery will be necessary to succeed in the competitive markets of the 1990s. This has already become an important focus for research and development.

The idea that goods and services can be positioned and compared using a continuum approach has been gaining support, particularly in the marketing literature. A variety of measures have been adopted, with goods typically clustered at one end of the continuum and services at the other. This approach can, however, be misleading because it does not fully recognize the interrelatedness of the production and distribution functions. Goods must be surrounded by support services, and services are often wrongly classified as non-production-based activities. In this context, a more integrated view is necessary.

Improving quality in the design of services

The relatively short history and rapid growth of the service sector has occurred without the benefit of a theoretical framework grounded in practice. Consequently, awareness is growing of the gap between received theories, philosophies, tools and techniques of management and the needs of service organizations. This has resulted in research focused on important issues such as the definition and management of service quality.

The pre-eminence of the quality issue in the manufacturing sector is exemplified by the success of Japanese industry in the 1980s. This is likely to become a critical factor in the service sector during the 1990s, with a number of implications for the role of marketing within organizations.

One of the most important issues will be the management of service quality. The criteria used by service firms to develop their quality assurance programmes are often different from those used by their customers to assess the service experience. The task of research will be to explore the gap between the two perspectives and to identify how the customer experience can be more fully integrated into the design of services. Once the customer perspective is more fully understood, it will enable a more flexible and effective response to the internal marketing potential that exists within most service firms.

The value of a service experience to the customer is closely related to the derived benefits. As customer choice increases in the 1990s, the market for customized services is likely to expand. This is also an area in which research will have an important role.

Improving the quality of service delivery also meets another organizational objective, which is to enhance the value added component of the service package. There are two advantages which stem from a systematic approach to improving service quality. First, competitive advantage is gained if service quality is clearly perceived by customers. Secondly, the drive to improve standards and achieve consistency becomes embedded within the organizational culture.

In the pursuit of total quality control, many service firms are extending their operational base by building their own supply and distribution networks. This trend is likely to continue as service firms expand and prepare to compete in the single European market and new international markets in the developing nations of the world.

Implementing change in the delivery of services

As changes occur in the market-place, service firms will have to develop new strategies to maintain market share. Technological developments in material and information processing and the availability of skilled personnel are likely to have a major impact on policy, planning and strategic direction. Service firms will need to respond to these challenges with appropriate programmes for recruitment, personal development and training at all organizational levels, from operative to executive.

Social and demographic change will also require a strategic response. Service firms that fail to identify and interpret market trends will lose market share to alert competitors. Effective action will require gathering more information about customers, defining market segments with greater precision and giving higher priority to brand differentiation.

1992 and the European arena for services

A source of economic and political tension during the 1980s was Europe's inability to compete effectively against non-European rivals in the manufacturing sector. The Single European Act of 1987, enabling the completion of an internal market within the European Economic Community by 1992, will provide new opportunities, particularly for service firms.

In preparing an internal market without trade restrictions, a wide range of fiscal, economic and technical regulations need to be harmonized. As a result of this, expansion by merger or acquisition and associated activities such as obtaining finance and establishing distribution channels will become easier.

To realize fully the opportunities which will arise, service firms will need to assess the marketing opportunities, the cost of sales implications and the difficulties associated with achieving operating standards in the culturally and economically diverse sectors of the internal market.

Secondly, service firms will need to acquire more detailed knowledge of the market sectors and to establish representation in member countries. This may require a multinational management team, and the development of linguistic skills within the organization. Gaining competitive advantage will also involve planning in order to maximize the benefits of reduced transportation and communication costs and to assess the possible savings which might be made on resource costs.

The global development of services

Major service firms are increasingly looking to international markets in the search for future profitability. As the European Economic Community prepares for 1992, globalization as a strategy for service firms is becoming even more important, especially where domestic markets have reached a mature stage of development. To compete effectively it will be necessary to create an organizational structure that sees its mission, markets and requirements as global, and invests and develops its personnel with due regard to the different cultures of the countries in which it operates. Globalization is likely to assist the process of diffusing new service developments across national boundaries and, as the interest in globalization intensifies, service firms will need to ensure that their international networks and brands are well established and maintained.

Both European and global markets are already subject to competitive pressures, and the next decade is likely to be a very demanding period for the service sector. If service firms desire to expand, they will need to identify now the many opportunities and challenges that the 1990s are likely to bring.

Index